BOLLINGEN SERIES XXVIII

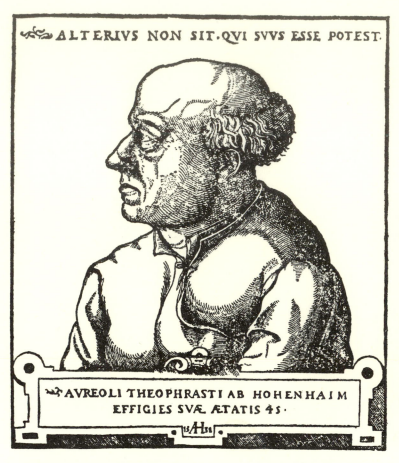

ALTERIVS NON SIT·QVI SVVS ESSE POTEST·

AVREOLI THEOPHRASTI AB HOHENHAIM
EFFIGIES SVÆ ÆTATIS 45·

AV. PH. TH. PARACELSI, NATI AN. 1493. MORTVI. AN. 1451.
ÆT. SVÆ 47. EFF.

PARACELSUS

SELECTED WRITINGS

EDITED WITH AN INTRODUCTION BY
JOLANDE JACOBI
TRANSLATED BY NORBERT GUTERMAN

BOLLINGEN SERIES XXVIII

PRINCETON UNIVERSITY PRESS

Originally published in German as
Theophrastus Paracelsus: Lebendiges
Erbe, by Rascher Verlag, Zurich, 1942.

Library of Congress catalogue card no. 58-8987
SBN 691-09810-7
Manufactured in the United States of America

CONTENTS

CONTENTS

CONTENTS

LIST OF ILLUSTRATIONS

FOREWORD TO THE ENGLISH EDITION

THE AUTHOR *has asked me for some introductory words to the English edition of her book on Paracelsus. I am more than willing to comply with this request, for Paracelsus, an almost legendary figure in our time, was a preoccupation of mine when I was trying to understand alchemy, especially its connection with natural philosophy. In the sixteenth century, alchemical speculation received a strong impetus from this master, notably from his singular doctrine of "long life"—a theme ever dear to the alchemist's heart.*

In her book, Dr. Jacobi emphasizes the moral aspect of Paracelsus. She wisely lets the master speak for himself on crucial points, so that the reader can gain first-hand information about this strange Renaissance personality, so amply endowed with genius. The generous use of original texts, with their vivid, imaginative language, helps to develop a striking picture of the man who exerted a powerful influence not only on his own time but also on succeeding centuries. A contradictory and controversial figure, Paracelsus cannot be brought into line with any stereotype—as Sudhoff, for instance, sought to do when, arbitrarily and without a shadow of evidence, he declared that certain aberrant texts were spurious. Paracelsus remains a paradox, like his contemporary, Agrippa von Nettesheim. He is a true mirror of his century, which even at this late date presents many unsolved mysteries.

An excellent feature of Dr. Jacobi's book is her glossary of Paracelsus' concepts, each furnished with a succinct definition. To follow the language of this physician, this natural philosopher and mystic—a language freighted with technical terms and neologisms—is not easy for readers unfamiliar with alchemical writings.

The book abounds in pictorial material which, coming for the most part from Paracelsus' time and from the places where he lived, rounds out and sharpens the presentation.

C. G. JUNG

Fig. 1. A Tribute to Paracelsus—Apparently a Kind of Broadside

PREFACE

An anthology is always a hazardous enterprise—not only because the compiler, however much he may aim at objectivity, is always influenced by the tastes of his time and his own intellectual leanings, but above all because he undertakes to convey the idea of an integrated whole through an arrangement of its separate parts. But just as the cosmos dissolves into a thousand contradictions when we focus our attention on its individual manifestations, so a great personality will break down into seemingly irreconcilable and irreducible contradictions as soon as one attempts to define it by successively describing its different facets. And the greater the man's scope, the more complex and dramatic his career, the truer this becomes.

Paracelsus, who lived at a time of revolutionary changes, is one of the most enigmatic figures in history. This self-willed genius was charged with all the dynamism of an impetuous and turbulent age. Thus any attempt to encompass him in his totality and uniqueness by a selection from his work seems to offer little prospect of success. For this reason, we have deliberately refrained from seeking special texts with which to document each of the widely ramified domains of Paracelsus' thought and activity. We have instead concentrated on the essential and permanently relevant features of this solitary genius. If we discard those elements of his work which have only a secondary or historical significance, we begin to discern that luminous inner unity, in whose revealing light his illogical method of exposition, his lack of conceptual clarity, all the seeming incongruities of his psychology and thought, appear as tributaries to a broad, powerful stream.

If we follow this method, we obtain a certain number of

texts in which the Paracelsian conception of the world is summed up. This conception is centred around his basic concern with man's relation to God, which permeates and illumines every sphere of his thought. Paracelsus' entire contribution can be described as a development of this single theme in ever new variations, reminding one sometimes of the mysteriously interlaced and often surcharged late-Gothic ornaments, and sometimes of the clear, noble lines of a Bach fugue. His basic motif is man as the beginning and the centre of all creation. In man all life culminates. He is the centre of the world; everything is seen in terms of man. "In him God and nature meet" (Sartorius von Waltershausen). As image of God, he holds the highest rank in the cosmos. Through the principle of a hierarchical order of creation, ascending from matter to God, Paracelsus unites all the antinomies of a paganizing mysticism of nature and a pious Christian faith. How asceticism and enjoyment of the world, Christian love and sober experimental knowledge, the spirit of scientific observation and the hope for redemption, keen observation and emotional exuberance, critical reason and volcanic temperament, could be fused in the unity of his personality remains today, to us who are torn asunder, both a mystery and an object of nostalgia. In whatever form he sought apt expression for his great insights into man, God, and the world—whether in the media of medicine, magic, alchemy, astronomy or in the other aspects of the life and thought of his time—his real striving was always to speak of man, his relations to the Creator and creation, his dignity and his way, his duties and his tasks.

Only a few men before him and hardly any after him have conceived an anthropocentric system so lofty and at the same time so rational. In it everything follows logically from one source; it is a system that elevates profession to vocation, trade to art, and science to wisdom. As against this great line, everything else about Paracelsus strikes one as a mass of rank vegetation, withered or in bloom, but never genuinely relevant to the understanding of his work. Adhering faithfully to our main line, we have avoided specifically medical material, whether of a diagnostic or of a therapeutic nature. We have kept the texts free from the paraphernalia of superstition, which for so long obscured the true image of Paracelsus. Accordingly, we have omitted the aspects, too often emphasized, of astrologer, soothsayer, sorcerer, visionary, alchemist, and maker of amulets and magic seals. Since modern thought has lost touch with the profound truth of which these activities were the vehicle, we are in no position to do them full justice; today we must inevitably misunderstand them. We have become too far removed from those great relationships, which were still very much alive for Paracelsus. But since all the elements of Paracelsus' work are organically interlinked, the main features of the fields we have neglected will be apparent from the material presented here to the more penetrating reader.

For the same reasons we have also omitted all polemical texts, all eccentric and overly subjective passages in the works. Whether these peculiarities can be psychologically interpreted as manifestations of resentment, of over-compensation, or of a volcanic psyche in which the seething contradictions of the age were concentrated, or whether they are characteristic of the coarse language of that time, they have little bearing on the essence of Paracelsus' personality and will. Behind them and untouched by them, there rises the authentic Paracelsus, the dauntless, never-weary seeker of God, the humble mortal. This aspect of Paracelsus reflects those values which are and will always be indispensable to our Christian civilization. They constitute the "living heritage," which has at times been ignored, but which today, with the emergence of new intellectual currents, moves into ever brighter light and exerts ever stronger influence. We shall, however, be able to recapture its profound ultimate meaning only when this world, which has so many times been despoiled of its gods, once again rediscovers the path to its true God and His complex cosmic order.

As late as 1921, Hans Kayser, in the preface to his Paracelsus anthology (quite an excellent work of its kind), stated that the world of Paracelsus is "quite alien to our time, and only rarely comes into contact with it." But today, Paracelsus has a greater message for us than he had for our fathers. This does not seem to be accidental; and if there is today increasing understanding of him, there are more cogent reasons for this than the four-hundredth anniversary of his death, in 1941. Like him, we are living in a time of great transition; we, too, are bridges across an impetuous stream, connecting a sinking shore with a shore that is barely beginning to emerge. His predicament is similar to ours, and we can share in his longing. For this reason, the ideas of Paracelsus should not, as was formerly the case, be reserved for the physician, natural scientist, philosopher, or mystic, but should also be made accessible to the constantly growing number of interested laymen of all strata. May this selection from his works impart a glimpse of his immense vision to those who once again have opened their minds to praise of creature and Creator, to those who are on the way to a new reality.

In order to make Paracelsus accessible to the educated layman, the style has been adjusted to present linguistic usage. Paracelsus' German is often opaque, arbitrary in structure and phrasing, and sometimes deliberately obscure. To transpose it into modern idiom has of course been more than a mere work of "translation," and has inevitably required interpretation. This seemingly bold approach will appear justified upon closer examination.* Paracelsus spoke and wrote the High German of his time; however, his own language was extremely personal in character. He himself coined innumerable words based on

* [Accordingly, the present English version is based on Dr. Jacobi's modern German texts. The original texts, however, have been consulted throughout.—TRANS.]

garbled Latin or on Swiss dialects. Apparently in order to give sharper and more effective expression to his thought, he never tires of piling term upon term, figure upon figure, and he constantly repeats himself. This verbosity greatly hampers the understanding of his writings. Because he had a new and original vision of the world, he was forced to create his own language, dynamic, racy, and colourful, which suited his purpose better than the abstract, conceptual German or the Latin of his scientific contemporaries. His writings are woven through with passionate outbursts, rhetorical phrases, and queer comparisons, with indistinct ideas, which to him seemed to reflect the actual course of life better than rigid traditional concepts and words. Despite the power that emanates from his works, they often strike one as an impetuous first draft, in which he attempted to clarify and preserve the stream of his thoughts without first reducing them to the essentials—and this may be one of the reasons why his writings have so often been misunderstood.

We have only a few original manuscripts of Paracelsus; our main sources are the editions of Huser, Bodenstein, and others, published long after his death, and this circumstance no doubt accounts for the numerous obscurities that remain in the texts despite the critical work accomplished by such scholars as Sudhoff. For although these editions are based on the original manuscripts, they surely contain many errors and distortions that came about because the handwriting is difficult to decipher. Moreover, Paracelsus almost always dictated his writings, and this so rapidly "you'd think it was the devil speaking in him," as his pupil, Oporinus, maintained; they were also written down by his pupils from memory, and some were even translated extempore into Latin. That is why almost every one of his works has a different linguistic character, and the reader must attune himself to each one. We cannot, by any stretch of the imagination, call Paracelsus a polished writer. And since we are here interested only in the general and timeless elements of his thoughts, our chief concern has been to capture the meaning of the texts in a language familiar to all. Literal accuracy has often been sacrificed in behalf of a clearer presentation of Paracelsus' ideas and intentions. Our selection makes no scientific claims; our aim has been above all to present a readable introductory survey. In the case of Paracelsus, a free presentation is less subject to misinterpretation by the layman than the original text.*

It was inevitable that in such a "translation" some of the medieval flavour of language and content should have been lost, although we have always respected Paracelsus' figures of speech, and although the cuts we have made have been solely at the expense of the weeds and rough edges, and do not mar the original rhythm of thought. Throughout the book we have attempted to preserve the sharpness and vigour of the Paracelsian language, and have eschewed offensive modernisms.

It is hoped that the numerous illustrations included in this volume will contribute to an understanding of the spirit of Paracelsus' time and will cast further light upon the subject matter of the selections. All the illustrations are contemporary; Paracelsus himself was probably acquainted with a number of them. They eloquently testify to the vitality, depth, and creative originality of the art that developed everywhere soon after the invention of printing. Many books of that period are illustrated with excellent woodcuts and engravings. Some of them are mystical or symbolical, others represent scenes from everyday life; in their ensemble they provide a cross-section of the ideas and customs of the late Middle Ages. The pictures in this book are in large part the work of the leading illustrators of that epoch, among them several great contemporaries of Paracelsus, such as Dürer, Leonardo da Vinci, Holbein,

---

* [A sample of Paracelsus' original language was contained in the German edition of this work. Dr. Jacobi described it as offering "a picture of Paracelsus in his subjective and perhaps most original aspect, where emotion predominates over ideas." In the present edition it has been translated into English as the "Credo," pp. 3ff. Figure 4, p. xlix, reproduces a page of an original edition of one of Paracelsus' works.—Trans.]

Burgkmair, Amman, and Weiditz. They will, we hope, not only serve to revive the atmosphere of that time, but also appeal to the reader's artistic sense, and help to orient him in the subject-matter.

The texts were selected from the Sudhoff and Matthiessen edition of Paracelsus' complete works.° For the linguistic adaptation of the texts and the glossary we have consulted the original Huser editions, the editions of Adam von Bodenstein and Steyner, the anthology of Hans Kayser, and a number of other works, which are listed in the bibliography. The biographical sketch preceding the selections is not intended to supply complete data on the life of Paracelsus or even to give a full evaluation of his personality. We hope rather that it will encourage the reader to immerse himself in the numerous available descriptive and interpretative biographies. Some of the more important titles are included in the bibliography. Among the older biographies, those by Strunz and Netzhammer, and among the most recent, those by Betschart and Sticker, are deserving of particular mention; readers interested in religious problems are referred to the work of Sartorius von Waltershausen.

Illustrations, bibliography, and especially the glossary are intended to serve as guides for the student. The language of Paracelsus does not yield to the usual exegetic treatment. The best way to grasp its latent content—and this latent content is always the most essential in Paracelsus—is to submit freely to the dynamic vigour of its images. Accordingly, our glossary has been stripped of technical content and serves only to clarify unfamiliar Paracelsian terms.

It is hoped that the arrangement of the material around a central idea, the modernized language, and the illustrations will commend the present anthology to the reader. In an index to the Paracelsus literature appended to *Acta*

° [See the key to sources for explanation of the reference numbers following each paragraph. The sources of the pictures are given in the list of illustrations.—TRANS.]

Paracelsica, i–v (1930–32), Karl Sudhoff has listed 1089 items, covering the extraordinarily extensive literature on Paracelsus up until 1930. Publications since then are listed in *Nova Acta Paracelsica:* Jahrbuch der Schweizerischen Paracelsus-Gesellschaft, vols. I–V (1944–48), and in George Rosen, "Some Recent European Publications Dealing with Paracelsus," *Journal of the History of Medicine and Allied Sciences,* vol. II, no. 4 (autumn, 1947), pp. 537–48. Despite the copious literature on Paracelsus, we hope that the present anthology will prove valuable—particularly in English-speaking countries, where the unique figure of Paracelsus has remained almost unknown to the general reader. One reason for this may be that his difficult, eccentric phrasing and frequently abstruse style make the translation of much of his work nearly impossible.

The only purpose of this anthology is, through the words of Paracelsus, to give modern man in his predicament that strength and faith which radiate from all creative natures and their works—to help the reader to gain new courage from the contemplation of the Paracelsian *compositio humana,* the nobility and dignity with which he endowed the concept of man.

I wish once again to express my sincerest thanks to Dr. C. G. Jung for his assistance in the preparation of the glossary, to him and Mr. Oskar Schlag for permission to use valuable pictorial and literary materials, and above all to Professor Horst von Tscharner, who was helpful to me in the philological clarification of the text. I am grateful also to the book antiquaries Art Ancien S. A., Zurich, who have put at my disposal a number of the illustrations published in this book.

Zurich, Fall, 1941
Summer, 1950
                                JOLANDE JACOBI

NOTE FOR SECOND EDITION

Since the first edition of this book, the figure of Paracelsus has continued to command the interest of scholars. The great philosopher-physician has been the subject of a number of new studies, no more successful than earlier efforts in deciphering his secret. In the cultural turning-point at which we find ourselves today, this unique man, with his paradoxical personality, remains a precursor of the split and scattered yet so many-sided and creative nature of contemporary man, the antinomies of which modern depth psychology is striving so hard to reconcile.

In this new edition, some thirty of the woodcuts have been replaced by better and sharper prints; for one or two more, new and superior representations have been substituted. The glossary has been reworked; the list of illustrations and the bibliography have been corrected and brought up to date. For this work I am grateful to Mr. J. Schroeter, of Zurich, who has given it close attention. It is hoped that this book will continue to contribute to the deeper understanding of this still-fascinating figure of the early sixteenth century.

J. J.

Autumn, 1957

NOTE ON THE SECTION ORNAMENTS

The ornamental devices set between the chapter-sections of this anthology are medieval alchemical symbols for gold in its various stages and forms.

Goldmaking—symbol of transforming man and nature, of leading the world to its fulfilment, of purifying the soul that it may partake of the highest stage of wisdom—was a most important problem to Paracelsus, as to the medieval alchemists with their hermetic philosophy. The goals symbolized by goldmaking formed the mainspring of Paracelsus' work. What was in question was not ordinary gold; to quote an alchemistic saying, *aurum nostrum non est aurum vulgi* ("our gold is not the gold of the common herd").

The meanings of the devices used in this work are as follows:*

Chapter I		*materia prima,* the primary substance from which gold is derived.
Chapter II		*aurum foliatum,* leaf gold, gold in its dissolved and already purified original stage.
Chapter III		*calcinatio auri,* the sign for the reduction of gold to powder through heat, an important stage in the process.
Chapter III		*aurum potabile,* potable gold, gold as mystical, rejuvenating medicine and elixir of life.
Chapter IV		*aurum musicum,* wire or thread gold, used for the stringing of musical instruments.

* According to G. W. Gessmann, *Die Geheimsymbole,* Berlin, 1922.

NOTE ON THE SECTION ORNAMENTS

Chapter V

aurum, gold as symbol of the sun, suggesting a rotary movement, a symbol for the cyclical nature of the process.

Chapter VI

aqua regis, royal water, nitromuriatic acid, in which gold is dissolved.

Chapter VII

⊙

simplest, most ancient symbol for gold and the sun as the supreme light.

Alterius non sit qui suus esse potest

Fig. 2. Paracelsus

PARACELSUS: HIS LIFE AND HIS WORK

> Let no one who can be his
> own belong to another.

WE know the life of Paracelsus only in its bare outline. His works, which suggest an almost superhuman achievement, and a few scanty data concerning his sojourn on earth are all the concrete material we have about him. The rest lies enveloped in an imposing aura of myth, which only lends brilliance to the supratemporal aspect of this enigmatic figure. A rather slightly built man, with sensitive, nervous hands, a relatively large, bald skull framed in unruly hair, blazing eyes, deep-set and mysterious; a man of an easily irritable temper—such is the outward picture that has been preserved. Quaint alchemic kitchens in which he is said to have worked are still to be found at various places; with their strange crucibles, retorts, and other vessels, they are awesomely shown to the curious traveller, who is also told strange tales about the ancient miracle-working doctor. The stations on the path of hardships and struggles which Paracelsus walked from his birth to his death bear witness—in so far as we know them—to an unsettled, tormented career. There are wide gaps in the existing records, and later generations have amply filled them with fact and fancy. And then, towering above everything else, there are his works, the innumerable writings that he left behind; they are evidence of a titanic energy, a creative urge and intellectual force that break open new horizons and stream irresistibly through the ages. These writings are more than a record of ideas; they are by their very nature an image of those spiritual depths in which words and life lie, still undifferentiated, in the woof of myth. As such, they combine legend and statement in a living configuration, which is justified only by itself, which can never be measured by the yardstick of comparison or logic, and even less judged on the basis of analytical dismemberment.

The essence of a man whose mind reaches down to the primordial depths can never be apprehended in the recorded documents of his biography. A man's true personality is always more than his biographical development. For to be a personality means always to possess a mysterious something which cannot adequately be described in words and can be apprehended only intuitively. The essence of a personality is its living core, which draws its sustenance from the fertile womb of the soul's depths; in these primordial depths of the soul there lies hidden the treasure of the eternal images which are the fountainhead of everything creative. And the more a man penetrates into these depths and by reviving them becomes suffused with their mysteries,

the more compelling will be his influence and the stronger
the fascination that he gives out. But when this essential
kernel of personality is so overpowering that its radiant
energy breaks open its solid individual shell and so to speak
dissolves it by piercing it a thousand times, analytical
descriptions and explanations become inoperative, and the
realm of legend and myth asserts its rights. In this realm
mediation is no longer necessary, for its language is a
language common to all men, and everyone can find access
to it in his own soul's depths. In this language, everything
individual has room only as a symbol, and in the myth it
becomes integrated with the universal. In the myth, the
individual destiny is exalted to the domain of the timeless
and becomes a symbol valid for all time. Only a man who,
looking into the mirror of the symbol, has gained a profound
vision of his unique individuality as a part of the perennial
human universality can truly entrust himself to the great
common life-stream that flows through mankind. Only then
can he free himself from his isolation and become aware of
his wholeness—which encompasses both worlds, the individual and the collective. Therefore, the periods of spiritual
and intellectual stress, when man no longer finds his proper
place because he has largely lost the inner connexion with
these timeless primordial depths, are also the periods of the
birth and flowering of myths. In such periods, life comes
forth enhanced from the symbol-pregnant images of myth,
and men become particularly receptive to the truths that
lie hidden in them. And each time these images are summoned forth, they release an echo of joyful rediscovery,
bringing solace and freedom to the solitary soul. Therein,
ultimately, lies the mystery of the influence of an individual
destiny conceived as a symbol.

In our view this is true of the life and work of Paracelsus.

Philippus Aureolus Theophrastus Bombastus von Hohenheim, called Paracelsus, was born in Einsiedeln, the venerable Swiss place of pilgrimage, in 1493. He was the only

child of Wilhelm von Hohenheim, a Swabian nobleman of the house of the Bombasts, and Els Ochsner, a bondswoman of the Benedictine abbey of Einsiedeln. It is said that Wilhelm was born out of wedlock in an impoverished family of knights, and that throughout his life the circumstances of his birth were a source of unhappiness to him. On a beautiful wooden panel which can be seen today in Salzburg, he appears as a dignified and thoughtful man, with an intelligent, somewhat melancholy expression; in his right hand he holds a carnation, the customary sign of betrothal. Els Ochsner, descendant of a family of peasants living on grounds belonging to the abbey, was, as stated in a contemporary document, "under the authority of the abbot." (According to feudal law, inheritance was determined by the so-called left or weaker hand; that is why the feudal lord, in this case, the Benedictine abbot, had a claim on Paracelsus' estate.) Thus we find at the cradle of Paracelsus medieval chivalrous virtue and aspiration to higher culture on the side of his father, healthy earthiness and deep piety on the side of his mother. This widely divergent heritage no doubt explains to some extent how it came about that his rather weak and fragile body harboured such a profusion of tensions.

The landscape from which the child received his first impressions may have influenced him in the same direction. Surrounded by austere, towering mountains, the little village of Einsiedeln lay as though in a soft, motherly shell, rigidly separated from the surrounding world yet humbly spread open to the sky. Situated in the midst of dark pine forests and green meadows, cut through by the foaming torrent of the Sihl, it was, with its great church, annually visited by thousands of pious pilgrims, a faithful image of the life in which eternity and transience meet in a daily-renewed struggle. Past the Devil's Bridge, near which, according to an old tradition, stood the house in which Paracelsus was born, the pilgrims' path led to the shrine of the Mother of God—of extraordinary symbolic significance for Paracelsus himself. The bridge itself is symbolic, as linked with his birthplace. For Paracelsus was a true man of the declining fifteenth century, with its deep contradictions, which brought forth such powerful creative personalities as Luther, Michelangelo, Leonardo da Vinci, Kepler, Copernicus, Erasmus of Rotterdam, Dürer, Holbein, and other geniuses.

Fig. 3. Einsiedeln in 1577

This is not the place to outline this epoch and the rôle Paracelsus played in it; such a task may be reserved to more extensive biographies. But without penetrating into the spiritual structure of that critical age, whose revolutionary significance in European history is parallelled perhaps only by our own, and in whose formation Paracelsus himself played such a crucial part, we cannot begin to do justice to the personality of Paracelsus.

Even against the background of his own time, Paracelsus

remains a unique phenomenon, uninfluenced by ephemeral ideas. To classify him under any label is well-nigh impossible. And if his biographers characterize him sometimes as a man of the Renaissance and sometimes as a figure of the Gothic era, this only goes to show that his personality was all-inclusive, and that this very inclusiveness, which integrated all antitheses into a creative whole, constituted his essential nature.

The harmonious marriage of his parents ("In the home of my parents it was quiet and peaceful"), the striving for unity that characterized Switzerland at that time, and the country's eternal religious spirit must have served to counterbalance the great contrasts to which he was exposed by his heredity, his natural milieu, and the critical time in which he lived. They formed the counterweight with the help of which he succeeded in transcending all the contradictions of blood and environment, of intellectual and spiritual, inner and outer limitations, in a higher synthesis.

Paracelsus was only nine years old when he entered upon his great wanderings. After the untimely death of his mother he moved with his father to Villach in Carinthia, "my second fatherland, next to the country of my birth," as he calls it. This father, a physician himself, wanted his son to take up his calling, and christened him Theophrastus in honour of Tyrtamus Theophrastus of Eresus on Lesbos, a follower of Aristotle. Later he gave the blond boy the pet name of Aureolus. From his earliest childhood, Paracelsus saw his father giving medical comfort and aid to visiting pilgrims, and he desired to emulate him. It was his father who first initiated Paracelsus into the wonders of nature, who gave him herbs and stones, water and metals, as friends, and who taught him the rudiments of medicine. But soon the boy was drawn to travel farther in the world, from village to village, from town to town, from country to country, in order to satisfy his unquenchable thirst for learning. There remains almost no historical trace of the road that Paracelsus travelled in his passionate urge for experience and knowledge; we learn something about it only from scattered indications in his writings. From these we also know that at an early date he acquired knowledge of metallurgy and chemistry and an acquaintance with alchemy; however, it was only later that he was fully initiated into its mysteries by Sigmund Füger of Schwaz in the Tyrol.

In addition to the University of Vienna, he probably attended a number of universities in Italy, where he acquired a thorough professional training in all the contemporary branches of natural and medical science and studied the doctrines of the Greek philosophers as well as the great physicians Hippocrates, Aretaeus, and Galen. In 1515, he won his doctor's hat in Ferrara. At about the same time, animated by a desire to excel in his profession, he adopted the surname of Paracelsus in conformity with humanistic usage. This gesture as well as his noble patronymic of Bombastus (derived from *Baumast*)—which later generations erroneously considered a mocking nickname, because of his extravagant manner of speech—contributed a great deal to his reputation for pride and conceit.

Although he was now doctor of medicine and learned in all branches of science, and could have settled down and practised his profession, he still desired to see more and add to his learning and experience. As though hunted by the Furies he travelled from land to land, and there is hardly a country in Europe that he did not visit. On his path he found war and peace, villages and cities, seas and mountains, poverty and riches. No one was so insignificant or so important in his eyes that he refused to learn from him. "Learn and learn, ask and ask, do not be ashamed," is a call that constantly rang in his ears. Bath attendants and magicians, herb-women and gypsies, monks and peasants, were just as welcome to him for this purpose as learned physicians, pious abbots, knights, princes, and even kings. To learn and to help—in these aims the restless wanderer spent himself. According to his own statements, he must have travelled from Spain, Portugal, France, England, across all of Germany, as far as Sweden and Moscow, and thence again through Poland, Austria, Hungary, Croatia, and Italy, down to Sicily, Rhodes, Crete, Constantinople, and Alexandria. In 1522 he took part in the wars of Venetia, and later served as army surgeon in the Netherlands and Denmark. The universities of Paris, Oxford, Cologne, Vienna, Padua, Bologna, were stations in his quest for knowledge. One is amazed at his haste; it is difficult to conceive how he could have travelled so far in only a few years' time, considering the state of communications in the sixteenth century—although it was the custom of scholars and scientists at that time to visit distant cities. This feat alone smacks of legend.

Though Paracelsus' life knew no anchor, though it was a constant journeying, all his creative activities are deeply rooted in an immovable philosophical foundation. He was like a mighty oak tree: his unshakable faith in the divine order and its meaningful articulation was the root from which grew the stalwart tree of his work. This work deployed itself in a broad crown of which only the most outward branches and leaves represent his historical life. Paracelsus was a fanatic of experience. In his view, books and universities could impart only a paper knowledge, which inevitably failed when confronted with the realities of life. In his eyes, only what is based on personal experience, on direct vision, has value; that alone is truly trustworthy and is far above all speculation and invention. What treasures of such "experienced knowledge" must have been gathered by this most receptive of men in the course of his endless travels!

Nature and man revealed their most mysterious depths to him. Their harsh cruelty, but also their gentle helpfulness, were daily brought before his eyes. He became more and more keenly aware of the tragedy of human existence, but also of its nobility, and he became more than ever determined to help reduce this discrepancy by an activity that integrates theory and practice, word and deed, into a single synthesis. For this reason, the practice of medicine was in his eyes a sacred task, a kind of priestly mediation between God and patient, both a duty and a high privilege.

Such a view implies a sacred obligation on the part of the physician to strive for his own perfection. Only if he bears continuously in mind that he is but an instrument of God and that the patient is also God's creature, participating in God through his immortal soul, can the physician undertake a cure. For a materialistic century like the nineteenth, which came close to defining the soul as merely "an effect of hormones," this view was hard to accept; but now that the human person as a whole has again moved into the focus of medical practice, now that we are faced more inescapably than ever with the precariousness of our existence, the Paracelsian conception has taken on new life. For Paracelsus, morality, honesty, disinterestedness, and self-knowledge were basic elements of medical ethics. Cure can come only from the words of the heart, they alone can work miracles. To be a physician means to receive a mission from God and to carry out His orders—or to fail without recourse.

Paracelsus did not yet sense the rift that later opened between science and religion. It is possible that in the depth of his soul he was not unaffected by the schismatic current of his time; but what we know of his philosophy and his activities reveals a grandiose singleness of purpose. In his conception, to explore the wonders of nature is not desecration, to harness its energies is not mechanization, and to describe man's nature as determined by his three "bodies"— the elemental, emotional, and spiritual—is no reduction of man to matter. For in the great integrated totality in which all created things are interrelated, nothing has a life that is absolutely its own: man, the earth, and the cosmos are only meaningful parts of an organic whole, which down to its last particles is ruled by God and His order. Treatment of the plague, of wounds, of syphilis, gout, epilepsy, or any other disease, is a "mission," and so is the preparation of herb juices, the smelting of metals, or the analysis of mineral waters; for God has created all of these to serve man, the highest of creatures, the most beloved by God. But they can serve him only if he works toward this aim in the right way, that is, in a way pleasing to God. For creation and everything belonging to it were released by God while they were still in an imperfect state. The created world has been given over to man in order that he may fulfil it. More than that: man's original and specific mission is to lead it to perfection; he has been placed in the world solely for this purpose.

The world is enveloped "in a darkness that strives for light" (Strunz)—this idea is of fundamental importance for the whole world-view of Paracelsus. It permeates every field of Paracelsus' activity down to the last details, and only in the light of it does his activity appear wholly consistent. Those aspects that have been decried as superstition, magic, soothsaying, quackery, appear in this light as small mosaic stones of a single great theme—the understanding and fulfilment of the world by man who has been charged with this mission by the Creator. Philosophy conceived as the theory of natural science, and astronomy conceived as the science of interaction between man and the cosmos, are the indispensable prerequisites for the carrying out of this mission. But the very essence of the process of fulfilment is prefigured in alchemy. Without alchemy, everything remains meaningless; to study it, to be versed in it, to practise it, is to rise from the blindness of unconscious life to highest consciousness, is to become seeing. The medieval hermetic alchemy, for which the transmutation of metals was not merely a concrete chemical, material process, but also a psychic and spiritual process symbolically associated with the transformation of matter, is the vehicle of this fundamental Paracelsian idea. The liberation of gold from its dross—i.e., the alchemistic process of the gradual transformation of *materia prima*, the unfinished, nonpurified primal matter, into *materia ultima*, the purest and most accomplished form of matter—represents a symbolic pattern that is followed by everything that is created. The developmental path of the soul, conceived as the maturation of the personality; the conquest of natural forces by magic; the "preparation" of poisonous herbs for the purpose of extracting their mysterious, healing essences; the treatment of the human body in order to free it from the "impurity" of disease—all these are mere symbols for the same striving.

Paracelsus is today celebrated as the first modern medical scientist, as the precursor of microchemistry, antisepsis, modern wound surgery, homeopathy, and a number of other ultramodern achievements. He is considered a revolutionary figure in medicine, and not without reason was he called *Lutherus medicorum*, the Luther of the physicians, even in his lifetime. A countless wealth of intuitions coupled with insights won in tireless experiments makes the works of Paracelsus a very treasure trove and bears witness to his incomparable creative power. But the principles that Paracelsus applied, whether it be the doctrine of concordance, or correspondence, between the outward and inward, or the principle of the complementary pairs of opposites ("The physician and the remedy belong together like man and wife"), supply the scaffolding of his theoretical edifice. Upon the principles of analogy, identity, and compensation are based chiromancy, physiognomics, his whole doctrine of signatures, and the most various "magic arts," on the one hand, and his astronomical, medical, and psychological insights, on the other. Today, after four centuries, they strike us as curiously familiar, even though their full significance for Paracelsus could only be understood through a religiously grounded total conception of the world.

For although the basic idea of alchemy—the purification of gold from its dross, i.e., the manufacture of gold from a base metal—permeates this whole theoretical edifice like the conscious design of an architect, it is erected on the foundation of a Christian belief in revealed religion; without this foundation, it would collapse like a house of cards. The gathering of experience is a mission and a prerequisite; the world has been created to be known and used. In this sense, self-knowledge is also knowledge of the world, and vice versa. God can dwell in him who has known both; such a man can consider himself an "initiate" and pursue the highest goals. But to be initiated, to be knowing, is a gift of God. And the charisma falls only to him who strives, only to the man of faith.

Differing opinions have been expressed concerning Paracelsus' attitude toward Christianity. But most authorities agree that deep religiosity is an essential part of his life and work. There was no doubt a large element of paganism in the mysticism of nature that was then becoming widespread, and that powerfully affected him too; Paracelsus himself admits this. But in his view this kind of mysticism is no more and no less pagan than everything that is natural, everything that is steeped in transient materiality. And we remain pagan as long as we absolutize all this, conceive of it as independent, as severed from the Creator, and deal with it as such. But if it is considered in a meaningful relation to the divine world order, it leads to knowledge of the miraculous works of God.

The fascinating and profound concept of the "light of nature" which the world gives forth as its inner radiation and which is manifested in man as self-revelation of nature, as the gift of consciousness, of the natural faculty of understanding, is only of secondary importance for Paracelsus. Just as human consciousness is sustained by the spiritual spark of divine knowledge, of the immortal light in us, so the light of nature is "kindled" by the light of the Holy Ghost. The light of nature shines to the end that man may "know" in its reflexion, and thus prepare himself to "be absorbed into grace" (Strunz). Goethe's Faust concurs: *Wenn Natur dich unterweist, dann geht die Seelenkraft dir auf* ("If nature is your teacher, your soul will awaken"). Paracelsus' animation of nature ("the forces of nature

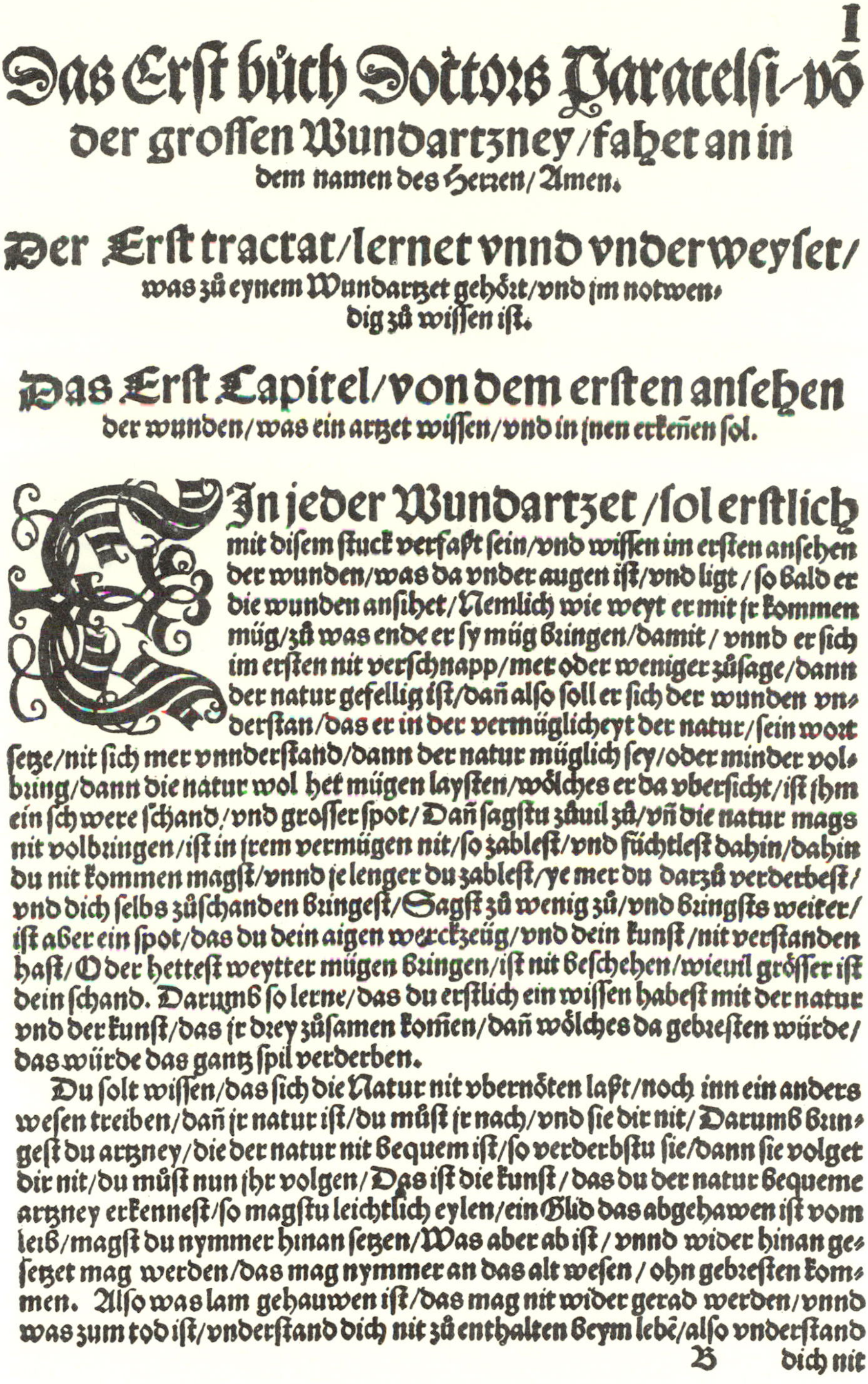

Das Erst buͦch Doctors Paracelsi, voͦ
der grossen Wundartzney / fahet an in
dem namen des Herren / Amen.

Der Erst tractat / lernet vnnd vnderweyset /
was zuͦ eynem Wundartzet gehoͤrt / vnd im notwen∗
dig zuͦ wissen ist.

Das Erst Capitel / von dem ersten ansehen
der wunden / was ein artzet wissen / vnd in jnen erkeñen sol.

In jeder Wundartzet / sol erstlich
mit disem stuck verfaßt sein / vnd wissen im ersten ansehen
der wunden / was da vnder augen ist / vnd ligt / so bald er
die wunden ansihet / Nemlich wie weyt er mit jr kommen
muͤg / zuͦ was ende er sy muͤg bringen / damit / vnnd er sich
im ersten nit verschnapp / met oder weniger zuͦsage / dann
der natur gefellig ist / dañ also soll er sich der wunden vn∗
derstan / das er in der vermuͤglicheyt der natur / sein wort
setze / nit sich mer vnnderstand / dann der natur muͤglich sey / oder minder vol∗
bring / dann die natur wol het muͤgen laysten / woͤlches er da vbersicht / ist jhm
ein schwere schand / vnd grosser spot / Dañ sagstu zuͦuil zuͦ / vñ die natur mags
nit volbringen / ist in jrem vermuͤgen nit / so zableßt / vnd fuͤchtleßt dahin / dahin
du nit kommen magst / vnnd je lenger du zableßt / ye mer du darzuͦ verderbeßt /
vnd dich selbs zuͦschanden bringeßt / Sagst zuͦ wenig zuͦ / vnd bringsts weiter /
ist aber ein spot / das du dein aigen werckzeüg / vnd dein kunst / nit verstanden
haßt / Oder hetteßt weytter muͤgen bringen / ist nit beschehen / wieuil groͤsser ist
dein schand. Darumb so lerne / das du erstlich ein wissen habeßt mit der natur
vnd der kunst / das jr drey zuͦsamen koñen / dañ woͤlches da gebreßten würde /
das würde das gantz spil verderben.

Du solt wissen / das sich die Natur nit vbernoͤten laßt / noch inn ein anders
wesen treiben / dañ jr natur ist / du muͤst jr nach / vnd sie dir nit / Darumb Brin∗
geßt du artzney / die der natur nit Bequem ist / so verderbstu sie / dann sie volget
dir nit / du muͤst nun jhr volgen / Das ist die kunst / das du der natur bequeme
artzney erkenneßt / so magstu leichtlich eylen / ein Glid das abgehawen ist vom
leib / magst du nymmer hinan setzen / Was aber ab ist / vnnd wider hinan ge∗
setzet mag werden / das mag nymmer an das alt wesen / ohn gebreßten kom∗
men. Also was lam gehauwen ist / das mag nit wider gerad werden / vnnd
was zum tod ist / vnderstand dich nit zuͦ enthalten beym lebē / also vnderstand
B   dich nit

Fig. 4. First page of *Der grossen Wundartzney . . .*,
Augsburg: Heynrich Steyner, 1536

around me reveal themselves with a mysterious urge") is not animism, and his spiritualization of nature is not pantheism. For the authentic Christian principle of Paracelsus' philosophy is that God's spirit breathes in all created things but indirectly, through the light of nature; only in man does it also live directly, outside the natural light, in the immortal body, which is the very centre of his soul. If we thus bear in mind the whole of this Paracelsian conception and take cognizance of its full scope, we shall be deeply impressed by its greatness and logical consistency from a Christian point of view. We may in the strictest sense call it "catholic," i.e., all-embracing, universal.

True, in matters of dogma, as in everything else, Paracelsus was self-willed, independent, and often even rebellious. In all his relations with authority and tradition he was a "protester." But it was perhaps this very peculiarity of his character that prevented him from becoming a follower of Luther, as many others did at that time. His rebellious nature led a number of eminent Protestants to hope that he would fight on their side. It seems that they even vied with one another for his adherence. But Paracelsus avoided all purely denominational concerns. He was interested only in what lies deeper, in the pure roots of religion. And this, he thought, could never be found within the formalism of earthly institutions. He yearned for a renewal of the church, for a spiritualization and internalization of Christianity. He was forever lashing out, with characteristic impetuosity, against the church's emphasis on ritual, against its alleged rigidity and narrow-mindedness. He stormed against the conceit, the pomp, and the worldly preoccupations not only of his professional colleagues but also of the church dignitaries, and he never wearied of propagating his own conception of the "original gospel," which knows only love, charity, poverty, and humility. He believed in a Christianity of good works, whose communicants would give themselves entirely to the simple stream of faith that flows in every humble heart, and would let all their actions

1

spring from this source. "Faith without works is dead," he repeated time and again. God does not rejoice in ceremonies, he insisted, but in pure hearts. The sincerity of this conviction is demonstrated by Paracelsus' own life. Although he was poor, harried, and tormented throughout his career, no one ever asked his help in vain. No labour seemed to him excessive when his fellow man was in need of him. In his testament he provided that his few belongings be given to the poor. One is strangely moved in reading a list of the objects he left behind—a few gulden, a few pieces of clothing, some trinkets, a Bible concordance, a copy of the Holy Scriptures with the commentaries of St. Jerome, an edition of the New Testament, a pharmaceutical compendium, and a *Collectanea Theologica*. They form a truly impressive contrast with the tremendous richness of his works.

Equipped with an exploring mind, an unprecedented power of integrating vision, an ardent soul full of faith and helpfulness, and animated by a fanatical consciousness of his calling, Paracelsus began to practise his profession when he was barely thirty years old. He was eager to harness his energies, to carry out in practice the ideas that he had found to be correct and good, and to make a place for himself among men. Is it surprising that he encountered great difficulties? That he reaped mistrust, enmity, and slander? That he remained all his life solitary and self-sufficient, a rolling stone? His fellow men saw only the superficial, disturbing aspect of him; and because the unusual has at all times aroused irritation and resistance, Paracelsus, like countless other great men, was misunderstood and persecuted. But, as he says prophetically, as though referring to himself: "Only he who has known defeat can achieve victory. He who remains alive cannot be victorious, because he has never been smitten. Only he who has been smitten, carries off the victory. He alone has stood his ground." And he also says: "When I am dead, my teachings will live."

His first attempt, in 1525, to gain a foothold as a physician in Salzburg, the old and venerable city of princes, ended in failure; perhaps not without justification he was suspected of having made common cause with the ringleaders in the Peasant War, and was compelled to leave in haste. In 1526, after a number of brief visits to Ingolstadt, Munich, Neuburg, Tübingen, Rottweil, Freiburg, Baden-Baden, and other towns, he settled in Strassburg, this time, as he thought, for good. He was inscribed in the city register as a surgeon, and in accordance with the regulations in force at the time, became a member of the guild of grain merchants and millers. But it was not his fate to lead an orderly burgher's life. Less than a year later, following a call from Basel, he was again on the move. Now at last the upward path seemed open to him. But again it was only a pipe dream. Basel was indeed to be the scene of his greatest tragedy. Here his outward career suffered the grave and abrupt setback from which he never recovered. Only for a short time did he enjoy the worldly fame that his academic position brought him. The treatment by which he succeeded in curing the famous Basel printer Johannes Froben, who had suffered an apoplectic stroke, covered his name with glory. Paracelsus, who was fundamentally asocial, who had wandered from place to place on the highways, who had grown up in a peasant milieu ("By nature I am not subtly spun, nor is it the custom of my native land to accomplish anything by spinning silk"), now suddenly found himself surrounded by an ardent and refined intellectual life. In the home of the artistic printer he met the best minds of the city, among them the brothers Basilius and Bonifatius Amerbach; Oecolampadius, the city pastor and leading Lutheran; Holbein, the greater painter; and Erasmus of Rotterdam, who wrote in a letter of thanks for his medical advice: "I recognize the deep truth of your mysterious words not by any knowledge of medicine, which I have never studied, but by my simple feeling . . ."—quite a flattering admission from the mouth of one of Europe's most eminent humanists.

In 1526, the municipal council of Basel appointed Paracelsus city *physicus*, and this carried with it the post of *ordinarius*, or professor at the university. He was relieved from urgent daily cares, and every opportunity seemed open to him—he had as many patients as he could desire and no end of ambitious students to whom he could transmit his knowledge.

In the announcement of his lectures he wrote: "My proofs derive from experience and my own reasoning, and not from reference to authorities." And in another passage: "It seems imperative to bring medicine back to its original laudable state, and, aside from striving to cleanse it of the dregs left by the barbarians, to purify it of the most serious errors. Not according to the rules of the ancients, but solely according to those which we have found proved by the nature of things through practice and experience. . . . It is not title and eloquence, nor the knowledge of languages, nor the reading of many books, however ornamental, that are the requirements of a physician, but the deepest knowledge of things themselves and of nature's secrets, and this knowledge outweighs all else. . . . The physician's business is to know the different kinds of disease, to understand their causes and symptoms, furthermore to prescribe remedies with discernment and perseverance, and according to the special circumstances to help everyone as much as possible. . . . By way of introducing the students to my own methods, I shall now be able, thanks to the generous appointment of the Basel authorities, to explain for two hours daily the manuals of practical and theoretical therapeutics, and of internal medicine and surgery, of which I myself am the author, with the highest diligence and to the great benefit of my listeners" (quoted by Betschart). Among the subjects of lectures that he announced for the summer term of 1527 were the following: "(1) Propositions on internal diseases and their remedies—stomach and bowel troubles, worms, epilepsy, consumption, rashes, gout, asthma, fevers, headaches, disorders of the womb, toothache, ailments of the eyes and ears. . . . (2) Lessons on general pharmaceutics and prescription of remedies. General introduction into special pathology and therapy. (3) On the treatment of external wounds, injuries, furoncles, ulcers, swellings, growths. (4) During the vacations, particularly the dog days, special lectures on diagnosis by pulse and urine, on purges and blood-letting, an interpretation of Hippocrates' aphorisms and commentaries on Macer's *Herbal*" (quoted by Sticker). There is no doubt that this document reveals tireless intellectual effort and much new, independent, and often revolutionary thinking.

Not only in his content, but also in his form Paracelsus overthrows all traditional ideas. His purpose is to prevent the pruning of all spontaneous growth, "the mutilation of young trees," as he calls it, and to make room for new shoots. In defiance of all tradition, he lectured in German instead of Latin, thus arousing scandal and opposition. True, he was not an orator, and he himself maintained that "I cannot boast of any rhetoric or subtleties, but I must speak in the language of my native country, for I was born in Einsiedeln, a Swiss by nationality." But the ardour of his inner conviction lent him magical power. His assault against established customs, his seeming conceit, his exuberant and self-assured manner of speech—it was in Basel that he seems to have coined his proud motto, *alterius non sit qui suus esse potest*—made him unpopular. But the opposition he encountered only increased his will to assert himself. He was suspected of not having a genuine doctor's title, of being a charlatan; but this made him even more aggressive and violent. He became the butt of all manner of attacks. A lampoon ridiculed him as "Cacophrastus." He retorted with greater passion and fury, answering every word of abuse by sharper abuse. Deeply wounded as a scientist and man of honour, he could no longer control his irritation. He stormed against every consecrated custom, ridiculed the solemn official dress, the vanity, the "obsolete theorizing and speculations," the sophistry, of his colleagues. He lashed out against all past and present venerable teachers of medicine, called them chatterers, bunglers, fakers, liars, cheats, quacks, and even murderers and thieves. He publicly cast Avicenna's classical book on medicine into the bonfire which the students made in the marketplace on St. John's Day, "so that all this misery may go in the air with the smoke." Nor did he find a single redeeming quality in the apothecaries, whom he regarded as cheats and profiteers. Angered because he had allegedly been swindled out of his fee by the Canon of Basel, and rebuked by the court, he thundered threats in a lampoon against the judiciary, and what was even more unpardonable, he went so far as to attack the town fathers, his own superiors, excoriating them for their bias and pride. A certain bluntness was not at all unusual in the polemics of the day; but Paracelsus exceeded all permissible limits. His mood is made clear in the famous passage from his preface to *Paragranum*: "Avicenna, Galen, Rasis, Montagnana, Mesue, and others, after me, and not I after you! Ye of Paris, ye of Montpellier, ye of Swabia, ye of Meissen, ye of Cologne, ye of Vienna, and those who dwell on the Danube and the Rhine, ye islands on the sea, thou Italy, thou Dalmatia, thou Sarmatia, thou Athens, ye Greeks, ye Arabs, ye Israelites, after me, and not I after you! Even in the remotest corner there will be none of you on whom the dogs will not piss. But I shall be monarch and mine will be the monarchy, and I shall lead the monarchy; gird your loins! . . ."

After less than a year of public teaching—he held his chair from March 16, 1527, to February 15, 1528—he had only enemies in Basel. The whole town surged against him in one great wave of hatred, which washed him away. The authorities issued a warrant for the arrest of the unruly professor; but he had vanished under cover of night. Once again he sought a home on the highway, his truest companion.

His respectable existence and his academic career were ended for good. A new period of wandering began. But it no longer led him to outward brilliance; only his inner light grew more intense with each new disappointment. Paracelsus became more and more "homeless." No place could hold him longer than a few months, and in most towns he stopped for only a matter of days.

Fleeing from Basel he sought refuge in Colmar. His friend Laurentius Fries received him hospitably. But host and guest diverged in their scientific views, and soon parted company. In 1529, Paracelsus, after countless other stations, was in Nuremberg, where his dammed-up energies found release in a large number of writings. In 1530, however, he was on the move again. This time he travelled southwards. In Beretzhausen he gave himself a short respite, which proved significant for his work; for it was here that he wrote his *Paragranum*. Then he journeyed on to Regensburg, and in 1531 to St. Gallen, where he stayed with Johann von Watt, called Vadianus, mayor and city physician, to whom he dedicated *Paramirum*, another of his fundamental works. Here, and during his extensive wanderings in the canton of Appenzell, which led him to his native village of Einsiedeln, Paracelsus seems to have undergone his deepest spiritual experience. It was here that the way of the hermit took possession of him to the depth of his being, never again to relinquish him. With this period are associated the more than a hundred religious treatises, filled with yearning for God, in which he approached the ultimate metaphysical problems. In his youth Paracelsus, led by curiosity and thirst for knowledge, had turned his eyes earthward, but now, at the age of thirty-eight, he deliberately turned his gaze to the transcendent realm. The stone church of Einsiedeln, which in a sense had presided over his birth, had assumed greater transparency and luminosity of outline, and had developed into a world shrine. But in the same period, Paracelsus turned away from the world and came to look upon his earthly existence as a brief stopping place, a time of proof and trial. He felt less and less at home in his earthly life, less and less able to cope with it. In vain were all his efforts to prove the gentleness and charity of his soul to men, in vain were all his knowledge and his cures that often bordered on the miraculous. His fame spread to every land; but Paracelsus himself, the man, the weary, struggling wanderer on earth, met with hostile rebuffs, ingratitude and slander, wherever he went. Dissension and struggle, poverty and care, were his constant companions.

His life grew increasingly unsettled. He bitterly complains that he is "again despised," "for the pack that attacks me is large, but their understanding and art are small." Carried away by his own passion, pursued by the passions of his enemies, he was compelled to flee the mountains of his native canton—this time for ever. From Switzerland he went again to Austria, first to Innsbruck, then to Hall and Schwaz in the Tyrol, and then, in 1534, to Sterzing on the Brenner and Meran, which was being ravaged by the plague. He lived like a beggar or a tramp, seldom sleeping two nights in the same bed, as he states in one of his writings. In 1535 he journeyed from valley to mountain, and then back to the valley, up and down, back and forth, in a constant struggle with poverty and inner unrest. He went to the spa of Pfäffers, and proceeded by way of the Vintschgau and Veltlin to the Upper Engadine. In 1536 he was in Bavaria, in Augsburg and Ulm, where he arranged with Steyner and Varnier, two great printers, for publication of his work; in the same year his *Greater Surgery* was printed. But in 1537 he was again on his way eastward. His stations were Eferding near Linz, Chromau in Moravia, and Vienna, the imperial capital. He longed for rest and a permanent residence. He hoped for aid from Emperor Ferdinand I, to whom he dedicated some of his writings and who seemed well disposed toward him, even receiving him twice in audience and promising him one hundred gulden to hasten the printing of his works. But again Paracelsus was disappointed. Instead of the expected material and moral aid, he received only a new addition to his bitter treasure of experience with the powerful and wealthy of this world.

Was it worth while to continue the struggle? How often did Paracelsus ask himself this question? And how deep must have been his sense of duty to his mission and his work to enable him always to conquer the "slowly strangulating failure" of his career by ever renewed surges of creation! When his continued sojourn in Vienna was made impossible by the machinations of his enemies, he went again to Carinthia. In 1538, while in Villach, he was informed of his father's death—"Wilhelm von Hohenheim, my father, who has never forsaken me," had "died and been buried" four years earlier. Now he too was lost, and Paracelsus' last earthly tie was broken. Had forebodings of his own death already cast their shadow on his heart?

He was now forty-five years of age, and he devoted himself to his work with extreme intensity. From St. Veit an der Glan, whither he had moved from Villach, he went on pilgrimages throughout Carinthia, through the mountains, vales, and lakes that he had loved in his youth. It was a kind of farewell. He felt that he had to expound his creed, to render his accounts, to defend himself; that he must again explain his beliefs and aims. Thus he composed his famous *Defensiones*, his seven pleas in his own defence, which also sum up the bitter and painful experience of a man who reaches the summit only to start on the downward path. To serve as a frontispiece for the *Defensiones*, he had his portrait made by Augustin Hirschvogel, an itinerant draftsman from Nuremberg, first in 1538 in profile, and a second time in 1540. These portraits would seem to disclose his true state of mind at this time. His readiness to help his fellow man was still unabated—he never left unheeded the call of those in need, and often spent hours and days on horseback, hastening to the bedsides of his patients. His writings of this period, ardent in tone and rich in ideas, suggest no weakening of his vitality. The portraits, especially the later one, are more revealing. The carriage of the head is intended to express undaunted pride and seriousness of purpose, but the eyes are weary, lightless, and as though turned inward. Dark shadows surround them, and his sunken cheeks are seamed with suffering. The tense energy with which his hand clutches the pommel of the sword seems to express convulsive will rather than firm grasp. The millstones of life have worn down the radiance of triumphant vitality. It is only noon, but already the mists of night are descending.

Hardly a trace has been preserved of the last three years of his life. The great silence into which he was soon to enter spread slowly around him. A trip to the Salzburg region via Breslau and Vienna, a written consultation, a visit to the Wolfgangsee—these are all that is known. He was gravely ill. Would he otherwise have declined to visit a patient in Pettau, "because of his weak body," as he wrote in his letter to Baron Sonneck? Had he not always shown his readiness to serve the sick? It seemed as though fate were fastening the last shackles on this "wayfarer," as he called himself. From August, 1540, following a summons of Archbishop Prince Ernst of Bavaria, he was again in Salzburg, the beautiful old episcopal see on the Salzach. As he dwelt in the corner house on the "Platzl," where a tablet today honours his memory, the River Salzach flowed beneath his window like the stream of life; as he gazed heavenward, his eyes met the towering fortress of Hohensalzburg. Here in Salzburg he may not have found it difficult to gather his thoughts and to prepare for the great last journey.

The harvest was ready for reaping. On September 21,

1541, at noon, he suffered the last stroke. Opinions differ as to whether it resulted from a cancer of the liver or from atrophy of the kidneys. His sickness must have come upon him suddenly, for he suffered the stroke at the Inn of the White Horse, which he was never again able to leave by his own strength. There, in "the little room," sitting on a "cot," on St. Matthew's Day, "the twenty-first of the month of September"—that is, three days before his death— in the presence of Master Kalbsohr, the sworn imperial public notary, and several witnesses, he dictated his testament, "sound in reason, mind and spirit." The man who had always rebelled against tradition and order made a formal will, in order that each should be given what belonged to him. For now he was about to appear before the eternal judge, the supreme physician, and at this point self-made laws were no longer applicable. At this point, the cycle must be completed, and the tragic earthly struggle of perishable human nature with the eternity of divine nature must be renounced.

Paracelsus' will is a moving document of his true humility and humaneness. The five points that it comprises are permeated by the genuine Franciscan spirit. He begins by committing "his life, and death, and his poor soul to the shield and protection of Almighty God, in the steadfast hope that the eternal mercy of God will not allow the bitter sufferings, the martyrdom, and death of our Saviour, Hallowed Lord Jesus Christ, to be fruitless and of no avail to him, a miserable man." He goes on to provide for his burial place and the services to be held for the salvation of his soul, and finally he distributes his poor belongings, bequeathing a few gulden to each his friends and relatives in Einsiedeln. But as his universal legatee he appoints "the poor, the wretched, and the needy people who have no stipend or other provision made for them."

On September 24, 1541, when he was barely forty-eight years old, the light of nature was extinguished in his soul. The path of knowledge came to its end. But the eternal light which burned in this soul returned to God—as Paracelsus hoped unshakably on his deathbed—to its true dwelling place, to shine more brightly, and "experience joy upon joy, eternity upon eternity."

Paracelsus the man, who began his career interpreting God's commandments independently, but who in his innermost heart turned more and more to the laws of Christ, ended as a faithful son of the church and on his deathbed humbly asked for the sacraments, in order to be worthy of salvation. *Vitam cum morte mutavit*—"He exchanged death for life"—states the inscription engraved on his tomb in the cemetery of St. Sebastian in Salzburg, where he found his last resting place among the poor of the almshouse.

About the intimate life of Paracelsus we know even less than about the external vicissitudes of his existence. He himself tells us nothing of his personal affairs. Of simple, human or all-too-human matters, of his parents, friends, and his relations with women, or of himself as a private individual, nothing or next to nothing is said in all his copious writings. His friends are also silent on this score. The few extant references to his way of living, his excessive love for wine, the fears which allegedly made him keep his sword at his side even at night, his aversion to the other sex, are probably the malicious inventions of pupils or colleagues who for one reason or another became hostile to him. He could hardly have had much time for worldly pleasures, and as a rule he had insufficient money. Always on the way, always giving comfort and aid to those in need, driven to his experiments by his urge for knowledge, or absorbed in colloquy with his God, he may well have expended all his strength in pursuit of his mission. His life, his will, his internal driving force, were devoted only to his work. In his writings he often expresses the belief that not every man should have wife and children. For after his prophets and apostles, Christ also appointed his disciples

or stewards—these are, first and foremost, the physicians—
and it is their most sacred duty to follow their mission.

Paracelsus' work reveals not only a titanic energy, but
also a deep sense of duty to his calling. This work exhausted
Paracelsus the man, prematurely consumed his vital energies.
Having burst open the prison of his body, his work stands
before us with all its contradictions and its marvellous diversity, as an independent, self-sufficient world. Aside from
the enormous purely technical and intellectual achievement
that it represents, it is also unique in its creative plenitude
and passionate ardour. It pours out of him like glowing
lava from a fire-spitting volcano, first flooding and burning
all old traditional values, and then turning into fertile soil
for even richer growth. The volumes thus far published of
the Sudhoff-Matthiessen edition comprise more than 8,200
pages.* A number of other works have been lost, and several
others are still in manuscript awaiting publication. Paracelsus' written works treat of every domain of life and
knowledge. To attempt even briefly to discuss them as they
deserve would be to go far beyond the framework of this
biographical note. Here we shall merely attempt to cast
some light on a few points. The following attempt to arrange
his work in articulated segments is undertaken for the sake
of greater clarity; it also corresponds to the chronological
order.

Until 1525, Paracelsus was chiefly preoccupied with
medical and therapeutic problems. Before that year, he
wrote his eleven treatises on various diseases, such as dropsy,
consumption, colic, apoplexy, worms; a number of works
devoted to gout and the tartaric, or stone, afflictions; as well
as the *Herbarius* and other treatises on *materia medica* and
mineral springs. To the same early period, however, belong
"On the birth of perceptible things in reason," *De genera-
tione hominis* ("On the origin of man"), and *De morbis*

* A list of the contents of this edition will be found in the Key to
Sources, pp. 235ff.

amentium ("On the diseases that deprive man of reason").
Though these works embody his first anthropological and
philosophical insights, they still suggest the earthliness
characteristic of his youthful mind.

In the following years, from 1526 to 1528, which include
the period of Paracelsus' academic activities in Basel, the
medical element is still predominant. The range of the
medical subjects treated is astoundingly wide, comprising
surgery, internal and external diseases of all kinds, and the
preparation of the most complicated drugs, often involving
the art of transforming metals and minerals. Within the
same period falls his most important early work, the *Nine
Books of Archidoxus,* a manual of the secret remedies, their
virtues and forces. This work contains in germ all the
mature knowledge of the most deeply hidden causalities
of nature, which Paracelsus would later reveal. At about
the same time he wrote *De renovatione et restauratione*
and *De vita longa.* Both of these are "books of initiation"
into the secret knowledge of death and rebirth and are
already permeated with the symbolism of hermetic alchemy.
With them, Paracelsus, then barely thirty years of age,
enters the multiform realm of the Mothers. And in *De vita
longa* he states the creed that gave substance to his life in
the words: "The striving for wisdom is the second paradise
of the world."

Feverish activity filled the next years, in which Paracelsus
strove to effect a complete transformation of medical theory
and practice. Disappointed by what he had seen of contemporary medical knowledge, Paracelsus rejected all tradition lock, stock, and barrel; relentlessly he attacked the old
"humoural medicine" and lashed out against his colleagues
who clung to anatomy, "the dead carcass," instead of considering the living body as a whole. He now wrote his
treatises on open wounds, on smallpox, paralysis, tumours,
cavities, etc., the *Three Bertheonei Books* ("The Little
Surgery"), and his basic contributions, written in Nuremberg, to the study of syphilis. But the "purified monarchy"

of medicine, as he calls it, did not seem to welcome his drastic methods, for only a negligible part of these writings found a publisher. Through the intervention of the university authorities, the printing of his book *On the Origin and Derivation of "the French Disease,"* and of others of his works, was forbidden. The world refused to listen to new ideas; officials and dignitaries were just what they have always been. "Whoever stands up against you and tells the truth must die," Paracelsus observes in bitter disillusionment. But such bitterness is not his only or even his predominant attitude. The childlike enthusiasm and piety of his German romantic soul inspire yet another answer, which can be found in his preface to the *Book of Hospitals,* dating from 1528/29. "The supreme reason for medicine is love," he writes. And: "The main substance of the art lies in experience and also love, which is embodied in all the high arts. For we receive them from the love of God and we should give them with the same love."

From 1530 to 1534, Paracelsus was at the height of his creative activities. Although all of his previous writings have a philosophical and metaphysical substratum, the two great books dating from this period, the *Paragranum* and the *Paramirum,* display for the first time the full brilliance of his powerful philosophical vision. In their completeness, they are among the best and most characteristic Paracelsian writings; they are also his best known works. Following his disappointments in Basel and Nuremberg, he intended *Paragranum*—this is shown by its whole tenor—as a settlement of accounts and at the same time as a solemn statement of principles. After several sketchy attempts, Paracelsus in this book formulates "the principles of true medicine" in a grandiose and sharply articulated system. "But because I am alone," he pleads, "because I am new, because I am a German, do not scorn my writings, do not let yourself be drawn away from them." And driven by his anger, but also lifted by his self-assurance, he adds: "That you may henceforth understand me rightly, how I establish the foundations of medicine on which I rest and will rest, namely in philosophy, namely in astronomy, namely in alchemy, namely in virtue! But just as I myself take these pillars, so you must take them, and you must follow me, not I you!"

Thus the four main pillars upon which he founds his medicine are: philosophy, the science of the material and elemental aspect of creation; astronomy, the science of the sidereal aspect of creation (these two disciplines in their interrelations and their essence are the prerequisites for penetrating the structure of man, who is a microcosm exactly corresponding to the macrocosm, or the whole of creation); alchemy, the science of these natural phenomena and of their inner meaning; virtue (*proprietas*), the fourth pillar, which gives the physicians the support without which the other three could never be solid. In line with his earlier *Opus Paramirum,* in which he describes the five *entia,* i.e., disease-causing active principles—*ens veneni, ens naturale, ens astrale, ens spirituale,* and *ens deale*—Paracelsus now wrote *Volumen Paramirum,* giving a fundamental anthropological analysis of man's structure. Here he expands his thesis on the four basic elements of man and cosmos (water, earth, fire, air) and the three basic substances (sulphur, mercury, and salt); he unfolds all the aspects of his doctrine on the nature of the Matrix, the Womb (here he discusses all the problems of man and woman, sexuality, and related diseases); and he delves into a number of psychic phenomena and diseases.

He often approaches the most recent insights of the modern psychology of the unconscious, and just as his pharmaceutics makes him a precursor of modern chemotherapy, he may well be regarded also as a pioneer of modern psychotherapy. His faith in the "healing word," in the radiating efficacy of the physician's personality, is part of the modern psychologist's indispensable stock-in-trade. But since in Paracelsus each insight is ultimately rooted in ethics and religion, all these questions lead him back to God and the primordial problems of good and evil—he sees each disease as a conflict between good and evil. In his view the material-elemental body cannot sin, but only the sidereal body, i.e., the soul. Accordingly, only the soul, or its immortal spiritual part, is subject to the last "judgment" and thus has a hope of resurrection. Good and evil are powers created by God, realities, which man must take into account, and which therefore the physician must know thoroughly. Good fortune and good health reside in the just measure and in a harmony that accords with the law of creation: the destruction of this harmony and proportion brings degeneration and disease in its train. Thus Paracelsus' views lead back to the Platonic conception that harmony, beauty, the Good, and the True are identical. Besides these two important books, the writings of this period include treatises on hysteria (*Von den hinfallenden Siechtagen der Mutter*), on falling sickness (*Von den hinfallenden Siechtagen*), on the comets, on the plague, on the mineral springs of Pfäffers, and numerous other minor works. Though they contain many pearls, they seem little more than ornaments surrounding his crowning work.

Paragranum and *Paramirum* are a complete exposition of ideas that had matured for a long time; thus they conclude a period in Paracelsus' development. At the same time, they point ahead to his increasing concern with the problems of the absolute. To this field of knowledge Paracelsus devoted himself wholeheartedly, as is shown by the above-mentioned theological writings, numbering 123, which constitute more than half of all his works. These date from the years around 1533 and reflect a crucial turning-point in his life. Most of them have not yet been published; a small number were included in the first volume of the second part of the Sudhoff-Matthiessen edition, which, it is planned, will have approximately ten more volumes. Of these we shall mention the treatises *De religione perpetua*, *De summo bono et aeterno bono*, *De felici liberalitate*, and *De resurrectione et corporum glorificatione*, which all exist in German, and especially *Vita beata* ("Book of the beatific life"), which is among the most moving professions of a pure soul. In these works Paracelsus displays an extraordinary knowledge of the Scriptures and of Catholic liturgy. The preface to his *Libell über die Pest* ("Pamphlet on the plague") bears the proud signature "Theophrastus von Hohenheim, professor of Holy Writ, doctor of the two medicines." The treatises on the Last Communion, on the Holy Mother of God, on the Gospel of St. Matthew, on the dogma of the Trinity, etc., demonstrate a truly fanatical preoccupation with the material. With typical Paracelsian self-wilfulness, they attack the official doctrine of the church, but in the depth of the sentiment that speaks from them, and the earnestness that inspires them, they are nevertheless documents of a marvellous religious ardour which will leave no reader indifferent. The spirit of the miracle of the Pentecost breathes in every line of them.

Having talked at length with his God and apparently recovered some peace of soul, he again turned to medical fields. The problems previously treated in his *Three Bertheonei Books* regained his attention, and the studies he now undertook resulted in the *Books of the Greater Surgery,* published in two successive editions in 1536 and 1537. Designed on a grandiose scale, the *Greater Surgery* covers this whole important field, and even today is a treasure trove for the surgeon. This was the only great publishing success of his life. His contemporaries, who otherwise showed so little understanding of his work, now listened with approval. Apart from this one, his only works to meet with no opposition were his numerous "prognostications." Such "forecasts" were in great vogue at that time, and presumably Paracelsus composed them to earn some money, but also in part no doubt because he found in them an appropriate vehicle for his admonitions and tirades, as we can see from his interpretation of the *Papstbilder* and the *Figuren des J. Lichtenberger.* In any event it would be erroneous to consider them as predictions of the future in the usual sense, even though Paracelsus, thanks to his mantic and intuitive gifts, might have been able to forecast or surmise some aspects of the future. These prognostications, as well as his so-called *Practica,* which were circulated with calendars, bear little relation to the main body of his works, although they include many profound thoughts.

But Paracelsus no longer sought security on earth or the approval of men. And even medicine was now for him only a stage on the path to the supernatural. Soon he left its tangible domains and returned to the realm of the incomprehensible. Words at best can give only a veiled notion of the adventure upon which he now embarked. He attempted to order and record what his inner eye had seen and experienced in the many years of his struggle against the world and the super-world. The accumulated material was elaborated in 1537 and 1539; today it forms a volume of more than five hundred closely printed pages. He called this work *Astronomia magna, or the Whole Sagacious Philosophy of the Great and Small World.* Any attempt to sum up the content of this unique book in a short sketch would expose it to incomprehension and misunderstanding. Only the deepest absorption in it can help one to understand it. It is a most mysterious work and presents the most mature and the ultimate of Paracelsus' cosmological and anthropological insights. Soaring on the wings of a magical and artistic spirit, it evokes and formulates the subtlest essential problems of being. The cosmosophic philosophy herein embodied is conceived as a guide to the supreme initiation into the mysteries of God and nature.

To give a glimpse of the immense range of this work, we shall briefly quote the titles and topics of some of its sections, in which, as he observes in his preface, he describes the "action of the internal heaven" with help "of the spirit that emanated from the Father." The "nine members" into which he divides his "sagacious philosophy" are: *Magica* (on will power); *Astrologia* (on the spiritual influences and their reactions); *Signatum* (on the knowledge of the inner essence as obtained through outward signs); *Nigro-*

mantia (on apparitions); *Necromantia* (on second sight); *Artes incertae* (on the arts of the imagination and inspiration); *Medicina adepta* (on the occult science of supernatural cures); *Philosophia adepta* (on the wisdom of alchemistic skill and contemplation based on the science of the supernatural); *Mathematica adepta* (on the science of occult relations, geometry, cosmography, measures, weights, numbers).* This is the first of the four books; the others encompass even more out-of-the-way domains under similar headings, and offer the ultimate, most occult knowledge of diabolical and divine things. He who possesses this knowledge has discarded the fetters of materiality while he is still here on earth.

With *Philosophia sagax*, Paracelsus reached the pinnacle of his work. His *Occulta philosophia* and *Archidoxis magica* attack the same themes and elaborate them in a still more sibylline manner; they are hermetic writings to which we have lost the key. After this final survey from the heights, which he made at the age of forty-five, and after which he began his descent into the valley of the beyond, he produced several minor but only two major works—the *Defensiones,* his passionate apologia, and the *Labyrinthus medicorum,* a last admonition and warning. Then he lost himself in the pathless realm of mysteries which can no longer be expounded in writing.

It is impossible to draw an exact picture of the doctrines that inspired Paracelsus; without doubt he was to some extent influenced by the Neoplatonists and the early Gnostics. Numerous alchemists, philosophers, and physicians, among them Agrippa von Nettesheim and the famous Abbot of Sponheim, as well as the surgeons Hieronymus Brunschwig and Hans von Gersdorff, are often named as his teachers. Paracelsus himself deeply influenced the intellectual development of the following centuries. German mystics and romantics, from Gerhardus Dorn and Jacob Böhme to Novalis, were moved by his profoundly mystical

* Titles as quoted by Sticker.

writings. Separate works of Paracelsus were published shortly after his death by Adam von Bodenstein and Johannes Huser, but the first complete collection appeared only fifty years after his death. Since then they have on countless occasions been violently attacked and passionately defended, and subjected to arbitrary interpretations. But in the spiritual life of mankind, it has always been a small group that has held up the torch of the spirit. It is this group that carries it through centuries, from generation to generation. To this small group Paracelsus belongs.

A restless wanderer for whom the earth was but a place of sorrow—such is the figure of Paracelsus as he is known to us. Compressed within a short span, station follows station, place follows place, and the breath-taking journey never ends. Beset by inner and outer tribulations, this man stands before us in all the precariousness of his earthly existence, and his struggle becomes the symbol of the struggle between darkness and light. Paracelsus has repeatedly, and rightly, been described as a true example of the Faustian man. A genuine European in his unquenchable urge for knowledge, torn asunder and yet magnificently whole, he might have said with Faust:

> *Und was der ganzen Menschheit zugeteilt ist,*
> *Will ich in meinem innern Selbst geniessen,*
> *Mit meinem Geist das Höchst' und Tiefste greifen,*
> *Ihr Wohl und Weh auf meinen Busen häufen,*
> *Und so mein eigen Selbst zu ihrem Selbst erweitern,*
> *Und, wie sie selbst, am End' auch ich zerscheitern.**

History reveals many curious coincidences, and it is perhaps something more than accident that made Georg

* [. . . all that's dealt
The heart of man, all, all that men have felt,
Shall throb through my heart with an equal throe.
I'll grapple the great deeps, the heights above;
Upon my head be all men's joys and griefs;
So to their stature my sole self shall grow
And splinter with them on the roaring reefs.

—Trans. by G. M. Cookson.]

Sabelicus, on whose life the Faust legend was based, a contemporary of Paracelsus. In the place where myths are born, Paracelsus and this "original Faust" have long since been inseparably linked. According to an old Transylvanian legend, Paracelsus, when aged, made a pact with the devil in order that he might become a young man again. According to another legend (and this is one of the paradoxes attending the figure of Paracelsus) his tomb, like that of a saint, became in times of great stress—for instance, when the cholera was raging in Europe—a miraculous place of pilgrimage, whither thousands upon thousands of people went to pray. Even the manner of his death was not untouched by rumour. One story has it that his enemies hurled him from a cliff after he had eaten a luxurious meal; another that he threw himself down a flight of stairs in a state of heavy drunkenness; a third even speaks of violent death by a mysterious poison made of diamond powder. Other legends—for it is characteristic of fairytales to contradict one another—make him immortal, endowing him with supernatural knowledge and the secret of eternal life. For how could this Paracelsus, who allegedly transformed brass coins into gold, who called the philosophers' stone his own, who possessed all the rejuvenating essences, who had commerce with witches and nymphs, who could resurrect the dead and who was able to perform his endless journeys only because he rode a white horse given him by the devil in person—how could this wonder-worker be mortal like any common man?

And the truth is that he did not die. The unity of his conception of the world corresponded to the integrity of his being. Like every true genius, he himself was a free cosmos obedient only to his own law, and ultimately subject only to the commandments of God. And because every totality is infinity and transcends space and time, Paracelsus has always stood outside time. Of this his immortality is only a symbolic expression. The bold sentence from *Paragranum* which he hurls against his adversaries—"But

I shall put forth leaves, while you will be dry fig trees"—
has come true. He stands like a tree with spreading
branches, and with each year that passes the leaves he puts
forth seem richer and greener. Always and everywhere
living and active in his power to fructify our souls, he is
still living among us today. And because fundamentally the
living can be revealed only in itself, and only to those whose
intuition is receptive to it, let his own words, as transcribed
in the following pages, bear eloquent witness to his living
greatness.

PARACELSUS:
SELECTED WRITINGS

CREDO

I am different, let this not upset you. *I/12, 403**

I am writing this to prevent you from being misled in any point; please read and reread it with diligence, not with envy, not with hatred, for you are students of medicine. Also study my books, and compare my opinions with the opinions of others; then you may be guided by your own judgment. *I/8, 158*

I have thus far used simple language, and I cannot boast of any rhetoric or subtleties; I speak in the language of my birth and my country, for I am from Einsiedeln, of Swiss nationality, and let no one find fault with me for my rough speech. My writings must not be judged by my language, but by my art and experience, which I offer the whole world, and which I hope will be useful to the whole world. *I/10, 199*

By nature I am not subtly spun, nor is it the custom of my native land to accomplish anything by spinning silk. Nor are we raised on figs, nor on mead, nor on wheaten bread, but on cheese, milk, and oatcakes, which cannot give one a subtle disposition. Moreover, a man clings all his days to what he received in his youth; and my youth was coarse as compared to that of the subtle, pampered, and over-refined. For those who are raised in soft clothes and in women's apartments and we who are brought up among the pine-cones have trouble in understanding one another well. *I/11, 151–52*

To begin with, I thank God that I was born a German, and praise Him for having made me suffer poverty and hunger in my youth, and I rejoice when the day's labour is over and I can rest. I also thank God that He so kindly

---

* References so printed relate to the source, in the Sudhoff-Matthiessen edition, of the paragraph or paragraphs they follow; to wit, the source here is to be found in Part I, volume 12, page 403, of that edition. See pp. 307ff. for key.

1/13, 249

commended me to the Virgin, under whose wings I am protected by the Holy Trinity.

I am resolved to pursue the noblest and highest philosophy and to let nothing divert me from it. . . . I shall not be concerned with the mortal part of man, and I shall meditate only upon that within him which does not die; for that is what we hold to be the highest philosophy.

1/1, 298

Ever since my childhood I have pursued these things and learned them from good teachers, who were thoroughly grounded in *adepta philosophia* and well versed in the arts. First, from Wilhelmus von Hohenheim, my father, who has never forsaken me, and later from a great number of others whom I shall not name here, also from many writings of ancients and moderns of diverse lands, who laboured mightily.

1/10, 354

For many years I studied at the universities of Germany, Italy, and France, seeking to discover the foundations of medicine. However, I did not content myself with their teachings and writings and books, but continued my travels to Granada and Lisbon, through Spain and England, through Brandenburg, Prussia, Lithuania, Poland, Hungary, Wallachia, Transylvania, Croatia, the Wendian Mark, and yet other countries which there is no need to mention here, and wherever I went I eagerly and diligently investigated and sought after the tested and reliable arts of medicine. I went not only to the doctors, but also to barbers, bathkeepers, learned physicians, women, and magicians who pursue the art of healing; I went to alchemists, to monasteries, to nobles and common folk, to the experts and the simple. . . . I have oftentimes reflected that medicine is an uncertain and haphazard art scarcely honourable to practise, curing one, and killing ten. . . . Many times I abandoned medicine and followed other pursuits, but then again I was driven back to it. Then I remembered Christ's saying: The healthy need not a physician, but only the sick. And so I made a new resolve, interpreting Christ's words to mean that the art of medicine is true, just, certain, perfect, and whole, and there is nothing in it that should be attributed to the deception of spirits or chance, but that it is an art tested in need, useful to all the sick and beneficial in restoring their health.   *I/10, 19–20*

This is my vow: To perfect my medical art and never to swerve from it so long as God grants me my office, and to oppose all false medicine and teachings. Then, to love the sick, each and all of them, more than if my own body were at stake. Not to judge anything superficially, but by symptoms, nor to administer any medicine without understanding, nor to collect any money without earning it. Not to trust any apothecary, nor to do violence to any child. Not to guess, but to know. . . .   *I/6, 181*

To give to each nation its own type of medicine, the theoricam best suited to it, as it behooves. For I can well realize that my prescriptions may turn out to be ineffectual among the foreign nations, and that foreign recipes may turn out to be ineffectual in our nation. That is to say, I write for Europe, and I do not know whether Asia and Africa may profit by it.   *I/11, 26*

There is nothing in me except the will to discover the best that medicine can do, the best there is in nature, the best that the nature of the earth truly intends for the sick. Thus I say, nothing comes from me; everything comes from nature of which I too am part.   *I/7, 154–55*

I have been criticized for being a wayfarer as though this made me the less worthy; let no one hold it against me if I defend myself against such allegations. The journeys I have made up until now have been very useful to me, because no man's master grows in his own home, nor has anyone found his teacher behind his stove.   *I/11, 141*

I am Theophrastus, and greater than those to whom you liken me; I am Theophrastus, and in addition I am *monarcha medicorum*, monarch of physicians, and I can prove to you what you cannot prove. I will let Luther defend his cause, and I will defend my cause, and I will defeat those of my colleagues who turn against me; this I shall do with the help of the arcana. . . . It was not the constellations that made me a physician: God made me. . . . I need not don a coat of mail or a buckler against you, for you are not learned or experienced enough to refute even one word of mine. I wish I could protect my bald head against the flies as effectively as I can defend my monarchy. . . . I will not defend my monarchy with empty talk but with arcana. And I do not take my medicines from the apothecaries; their shops are but foul sculleries, from which comes nothing but foul broths. As for you, you defend your kingdom with belly-crawling and flattery. How long do you think this will last? . . . Let me tell you this: every little hair on my neck knows more than you and all your scribes, and my shoebuckles are more learned than your Galen and Avicenna, and my beard has more experience than all your high colleges.

I/8, 63–65

I cannot help being indignant at your simplicity, for you do not understand the origin of surgery. To believe you, I am a surgeon and not a physician; how can you think so when everyone knows that I administered medical treatment (I am not writing this to boast of it) to eighteen princes whom you had given up? And when I have also tended innumerable persons stricken with fever, and cured them of forty kinds of disease which I found in them, in the Netherlands, in the Romagna, in Naples, and in Venetian, Danish, and Dutch wars? Is there no physician to reveal the lies of the scribes, to denounce their errors and abuses, to bring them to an end? Will you turn to ridicule the experience that I have acquired with so much diligence?

I/7, 374–75

If they hate me for writing otherwise than their own authors, that is the fault of their own ignorance, not of mine. . . . The art of medicine does not cry out against me, for it is imperishable and established upon foundations so imperishable that heaven and earth shall pass away before the art of medicine shall die. And since the art of medicine leaves me at peace, why should I be perturbed by the outcries of mortal physicians, who cry only because

I overthrow and wound them? . . . They are more eager to obscure their own errors than to fight in behalf of what the patients need, that is to say, the art, erudition, experience, piety, in which I seek the foundations and sources of my own writing.

I/8, 53

But since such useless rabble befoul the art of medicine with their bungling, and seek nothing but their own profit, what can it avail that I admonish them to love? I for my part am ashamed of medicine, considering what an utter fraud it has come to be.

I/11, 148

How can I fail to be horrified that a servant should be no servant but a master? They see to their own profit and take delight in letting me starve and perish. They lie about me to the patients, they receive patients behind my back, without my will and knowledge, treat them for half the money, say that they know my art, that they have watched me do it. . . . This has been done to me by doctors, barbers, bathkeepers, students, servants, and boys—should this make me as sweet as a lamb? It seems more likely that it should end by making me into a wolf! And with all this, I must walk on foot while they ride. The only thing that comforts me is that I remain where I am, while they run away and their falsity is exposed . . . for the cheat is discredited when the truth is told.

I/11, 153–54

I have also employed barbers, bathkeepers, and others of that kind, indeed I maintained them at great cost and trusted them fully. As soon as they learned how to make a plaster, etc., they left my service stealthily and secretly and, as is the habit of deserters, claimed the praise for themselves; they did not walk but ran away from me, and boasted of having mastered excellent arts. . . . I do not say this of all my apprentices; those to whom I am not referring here I regard as experienced, but I set small store by the others.

I/7, 138

This is why I expect thanks from no one. For my medical teachings will give rise to two parties. The first will befoul them; these are not of a breed to thank God or me, but rather will curse me wherever possible. The others will thrive so well that for sheer joy they will forget to thank me. This is the fate of the scientist—the greater his services, the greater the ingratitude . . . and not only ingratitude, but the more he teaches, the more his disciples will one day abuse him.

I/6, 460

This has been my cross and remains my cross. . . . There has been no one to give me support and protection. For all manner of men have persecuted and accused me and obstructed my path, and discredited me, so that I have enjoyed little esteem among men; but I have rather been despised and forsaken.

II/1, 84

I am not an apostle or anything like an apostle, but a philosopher in the German manner.

II/1, 76

Here I have no wish to philosophize or speak of the afterlife, except in so far as this can be done in the light of nature. I await the consummation of my hope; let me first achieve my own salvation through my faith in the Saviour, and then it will be time to impart it to others.

I/12, 348

Although I have spoken here in a heathen way, as many might think, although I called man an animal, it is not concealed from me and I know full well that the difference between man and animal lies solely in the countenance and the spirit. To this I must bear witness before God.

I/12, 17

Why should my Father's light be judged and looked upon as heathenish, and I as a heathen, when I am a Christian and walk in the light of Christ, both old and new? . . . And since I love them both, and see the light of each, as God ordained everyone to do, how can I be a heathen? . . . I have written in the Christian spirit and I am not a heathen . . . and I would defend myself as a Christian by saying that . . . I will not be called a sorcerer, or a heathen, or a gypsy, but profess myself as a Christian in my writings, and let the false Christians sweat with their own sour dough.

I/12, 10–12

Desiring to write like a Christian, I have omitted the four *entia*, i.e., the active principles of the stars, the poisons, nature, and the spirit, and I have not described them. For this is not Christian style but heathen style. But the last principle is Christian, and with it I shall conclude. And the heathen conception that we describe in the four *entia* ought not to harm our faith, but only to make our minds keener.   *I/1, 175–76*

So I have deemed it good to describe not only the natural man . . . but also, and with more delight, to go further and describe the eternal man, the heavenly man in the new birth, so that the old man may see and observe what man is, and learn to guide himself accordingly and learn what this reborn man can do, here on earth, and after this life, in the eternal life.   *I/12, 332*

The time for writing is ripe, for I must spare nothing of what I have spoiled. The field has not yet been plowed: . . . the time of geometry is ended, the time of artistry is ended, the time of philosophy is ended, the snow of my misery has gone; the time of growth is ended. The time of summer is here; whence it comes I know not, whither it goes, I know not: it is here! . . . And so also is come the time to write on the blessed life and the eternal.   *I/1, 82*

Fig. 5. Signature and impression of the signet ring of Paracelsus

Fig. 6. A Group of Great Alchemists and Physicians: (*reading down, left*) Hermes Trismegistus, Morienus Romanus, and Raimundus Lullus; (*right*) Geber (Djabir), Roger Bacon, and Paracelsus. Title-page of *Basilica chymica,* by Oswald Crollius (d. 1609), physician and alchemist

Read and read again, be not discouraged, but let the existence of so many terrifying diseases that no one can ignore induce you to follow the truth and not the idle chatterers. Then you will be a righteous judge! *1/9, 382*

I

MAN AND THE CREATED WORLD

Fig. 7. Creation

God is marvellous in his works. . . .

WHEN the world was still nothing but water, and the Spirit of the Lord moved upon the face of the waters, the world emerged from the water; water was the matrix of the world and of all its creatures. And all this became the matrix of man; in it God created man in order to give His Spirit a dwelling place in flesh.

1/9, 191

The matrix is invisible and no one can see its primal substance; for who can see that which was before him? All of us come from the matrix, but no one has ever seen it because it existed before man. And even though man comes from it, and men are born from it again and again, no one has seen it. The world was born from the matrix, as was man and all other living creatures: all this has come out of the matrix. . . . Before heaven and earth were created, the Spirit of God brooded upon the water and was carried by it. This water was the matrix; for it is in the water that heaven and earth were created, and in no other matrix.

13

By it the Spirit of God was borne, that is to say, that Spirit which lives in man, and which is lacking in other creatures. For the sake of this Spirit man has been created; the Spirit of God lives in man so that God need not live alone. Therefore the Spirit of God comes to dwell in man, and is *I/9, 190–91* of God and returns to God.

The world is as God created it. In the beginning He made it into a body, which consists of four elements. He founded this primordial body on the trinity of mercury, sulphur, and salt, and these are the three substances of which the complete body consists. For they form everything that lies in the four elements, they bear in them all the forces and faculties of perishable things. In them there are day and night, warmth and coldness, stone and fruit, and everything else, still unformed. In a piece of wood . . . there lie concealed the forms of animals, the forms of plants of every description, the forms of all instruments; and he who can carve them out finds them. Accordingly, the first body, the Yliaster, was nothing but a clod, which contained all the chaos, all the waters, all minerals, all herbs, all stones, all gems. Only the supreme Master could release them and form them with tender solicitude, so that other *I/13, 12–13* things could be created from the rest.

A potter is able to make a thousand different things from his clay, which, in a manner of speaking, comprehended diverse vessels and implements; or a woodcarver is able to carve out of wood whatever he pleases provided he can separate the wood from that which does not belong to it. Thus also God took out, drew out, and separated all His creatures from one mass and material, and He left no chips in the process, and He fashioned whatever He undertook to create in six days, into His ultimate matter. He selected that which belongs to the stars and made it into stars, from the darkness He took that which belongs to light and made it into light, and similarly with each thing according to its nature and in its own place. And thus there is nothing left for anyone to create because everything was adequately created, and the number is filled in all the creatures, races, and beings. . . . The earth is black, brown, and foul, there is nothing beautiful or pleasant in it; but all the hues—green, blue, white, and red—are concealed in it. There is none that is not in it. When spring comes and then the summer, all the hues sprout forth, and no one would suspect their presence in the earth if the earth itself did not produce them. Just as the noblest and most delicate colours arise from this black, foul earth, so various creatures sprang forth from the primordial substance that was only formless filth in the beginning. Behold the element of water in its un-differentiated state! And then see how all the metals, all the stones, all the glittering rubies, shining carbuncles, crystals, gold, and silver are derived from it; who could have recognized all these things in water . . . except for Him who created them in it? Thus God drew out of the basic substances that which He had put into them, and He assigned each created thing to its purpose and place. *I/9, 150–51*

At the beginning of each birth stood the birth-giver and begetter—separation. It is the greatest wonder of the philosophies. . . . When the *mysterium magnum* in its essence and divinity was full of the highest eternity, *separatio* started at the beginning of all creation. And when this took place, every creature was created in its majesty, power, and free will. And so it will remain until the end, until the great harvest when all things will bear fruit and will be ready for gathering. For the harvest is the end of all growth. . . . And just as the *mysterium magnum* is the wonderful beginning, so the harvest is the wonderful end of all things. *I/13, 393*

Matter was at the beginning of all things, and only after it had been created was it endowed with the spirit of life, so that this spirit might unfold in and through the bodies as God had willed. And thus the days of the creation and the order of all creatures were fulfilled. Only then was man

Fig. 8. The Creation of Adam

1/12, 14–15 created in the likeness of God, and endowed with His spirit.

Man was not born out of a nothingness, but was made from a substance. . . . The Scriptures state that God took the *limus terrae,* the primordial stuff of the earth, and formed man out of this mass. Furthermore they state that man is ashes and powder, dust and earth; and this proves sufficiently that he is made of this primordial substance. . . . But *limus terrae* is also the Great World, and thus man was created from heaven and earth. *Limus terrae* is an extract of the firmament, of the universe of stars, and at the

1/12, 33 same time of all the elements. . . .

The *limbus* is the primordial stuff of man. . . . What the *limbus* is the man is too. He who knows the nature of the *limbus* knows also what man is. . . . Now, the *limbus* is heaven and earth, the upper and lower sphere of the cosmos, the four elements, and everything they comprise; therefore it is just to identify it with the microcosm, for it too is the whole world.   *1/9, 193*

Heaven encompasses both spheres—the upper and the lower—to the end that nothing mortal and nothing transient may reach beyond them into that realm which lies outside the heaven that we see. . . . For mortal and immortal things must not touch each other, and must not dwell

Fig. 9. The Stages of Nature

together. Therefore, the Great World, the macrocosm, is closed in itself in such a way that nothing can leave it, but that everything that is of it and within it remains complete and undivided. Such is the Great World. Next to it subsists the Little World, that is to say, man. He is enclosed in a skin, to the end that his blood, his flesh, and everything he is as a man may not become mixed with that Great World. . . . For one would destroy the other. Therefore man has a skin; it delimits the shape of the human body, and through it he can distinguish the two worlds from each other—the Great World and the Little World, the macrocosm and man—and can keep separate that which must not mingle. Thus the Great World remains completely undisturbed in its husk . . . and similarly man

17

in his house, that is to say, his skin. Nothing can penetrate into him, and nothing that is in him can issue outside of him, but everything remains in its place.

1/9, 178

Man emerged from the first matrix, the maternal womb, of the Great World. This world—formed by God's hand along with all other creatures—gave birth to man in his flesh and placed him in a transient life. For this reason man became "earthly" and "carnal"; he received his material body from earth and water. These two elements constitute the body in its transient, animal life, which man as a natural being received from divine creation. . . . In his earthly life man consists of the four elements. Water and earth, of which his body is formed, constitute the dwelling place and the physical envelope of life. And I am not referring here to that life of the soul, which springs from the breath of God . . . but to the transient life, of the earthly kind. For we must know that man has two kinds of life—animal life and sidereal life. . . . Hence man has also an animal body and a sidereal body; and both are one, and are not separated. The relations between the two are as follows. The animal body, the body of flesh and blood, is in itself always dead. Only through the action of the sidereal body does the motion of life come into the other body. The sidereal body is fire and air; but it is also bound to the animal life of man. Thus mortal man consists of water, earth, fire, and air.

1/14, 597–98

Man is the child of two fathers—one father is the earth, the other is heaven. . . . From the earth he receives the material body, from heaven his character. Thus the earth moulds his shape, and then heaven endows this shape with the light of nature. Every man takes after his father; he is able to accomplish what is innate in him. And the son is empowered to dispose of his paternal inheritance.

1/9, 641

The world edifice is made of two parts—one tangible and perceptible, and one invisible and imperceptible. The tangible part is the body, the invisible is the Stars. The tangible part is in turn composed of three parts—sulphur, mercury, and salt; the invisible also consists of three parts—feeling, wisdom, and art. The two parts together constitute life.

I/12, 20

The mysteries of the Great and the Little World are distinguished only by the form in which they manifest themselves; for they are only *one* thing, *one* being. Heaven and earth have been created out of nothingness, but they are composed of three things—*mercurius, sulphur,* and *sal.* . . . Of these same three things the planets and all the stars consist; and not only the stars but all bodies that grow and are born from them. And just as the Great World is thus built upon the three primordial substances, so man—the Little World—was composed of the same substances. Thus man, too, is nothing but mercury, sulphur, and salt.

Fig. 10. The Hermaphrodite

I/8, 280

The body has four kinds of taste—the sour, the sweet, the bitter, and the salty. . . . They are to be found in every creature, but only in man can they be studied. . . . Everything bitter is hot and dry, that is to say, choleric; everything sour is cold and dry, that is to say, melancholic. . . . The sweet gives rise to the phlegmatic, for everything sweet is cold and moist, even though it must not be compared to water. . . . The sanguine

Fig. 11. The Man of the Zodiac

originates in the salty, which is hot and moist. . . . If the
salty predominates in man as compared with the three others,
he is sanguine; if the bitter is predominant in him, he is
choleric. The sour makes him melancholic, and the sweet, if
it predominates, phlegmatic. Thus the four tempers are
1/1, 211–12 rooted in the body of man as in garden mould.

The inner stars of man are, in their properties, kind, and nature, by their course and position, like his outer stars, and different only in form and in material. For as regards their nature, it is the same in the ether and in the microcosm, man. . . . Just as the sun shines through a glass—as though divested of body and substance—so the stars penetrate one another in the body. . . . For the sun and the moon and all planets, as well as all the stars and the whole chaos, are in man. . . . The body attracts heaven . . . and this takes place in accordance with the great divine order. Man consists of the four elements, not only—as some hold—because he has four tempers, but also because he partakes of the nature, essence, and properties of these elements. In him there lies the "young heaven," that is to say, all the planets are part of man's structure and they are the children of the "great heaven" which is their father. For man was created from heaven and earth, and is therefore like them! *1/8, 160–64*

Consider how great and noble man was created, and what greatness must be attributed to his structure! No brain can fully encompass the structure of man's body and the extent of his virtues; he can be understood only as an image of the macrocosm, of the Great Creature. Only then does it become manifest what is in him. For what is outside is also inside; and what is not outside man is not inside. The outer and the inner are *one* thing, *one* constellation, *one* influence, *one* concordance, *one* duration . . . *one* fruit. For this is the *limbus*, the primordial matter which contains all creatures in germ, just as man is contained in the *limbus* of his parents. The *limbus* of Adam was heaven and earth, water and air; and thus man remains like the *limbus*, he too contains heaven and earth, water and air; indeed, he is nothing but these. *1/8, 180*

Heaven imprints nothing upon us; it is the hand of God that has created us in His likeness. Regardless how we are made—in all our members the hand of God has been directly

I/9, 115   at work. God endowed us with our complexions, qualities, and habits when He endowed us with life.

Fig. 12. Creator and Creation

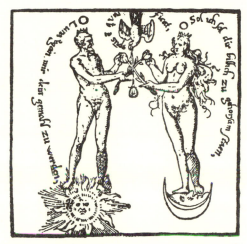

Fig. 13. Adam and Eve (*Coniunctio*)

God wills man as man, and woman as
woman, and He wills that both should
be of the human kind.   *1/1, 256*

God created man directly from the matrix. He took him
from the matrix and made a man of him. . . . And then He
gave him a matrix of his own—woman. . . . To the end
that henceforth there may be two of them, and yet only
one; two kinds of flesh, and yet only one, not two. This
means that neither of them is perfect alone, that only both
together are the whole man. . . . Thus the son is created
from the *limbus*—the father—but he is shaped, built, and endowed with his complexions in the matrix . . . just as the
first man was created in the macrocosm, the Great World.   *1/9, 193*

There are three different kinds of matrix: the first is the
water on which the spirit of God was borne, and this was the
maternal womb in which heaven and earth were created.
Then heaven and earth each in turn became a matrix, in
which Adam, the first man, was formed by the hand of God.
Then woman was created out of man; she became the

maternal womb of all men, and will remain so to the end of
the world. Now, what did that first matrix contain within itself? Being the kingdom of God, it encompassed the spirit of
God. The world encloses the eternal, by which it is at the

Fig. 14. The Creation of Eve

same time surrounded. Woman is enclosed in her skin as in
a house, and everything that is within it forms, as it were, a
single womb. Even though the female body was taken from
the male, it cannot be compared to it. It is true that in shape
it is similar to the male body, for woman too is formed as a
human being, and like man she carries God's image in her.

24

But in everything else, in its essence, properties, nature, and peculiarities, it is completely different from the male body. Man suffers as man, woman suffers as woman; but both suffer as creatures beloved by God.

1/9, 192

Just as heaven and earth close to form a shell, so the maternal body is a closed vessel. . . . An empty matrix in which no child is contained is like heaven and earth before they contained anything living. Since man is a child of the cosmos, and is himself the microcosm, he must be begotten, each time anew, by his mother. And just as he was created of the four elements of the world even in the beginning, so he will be created in the future again and again. For the Creator created the world once, and then He rested. Thus He also made heaven and earth and formed them into a matrix, in which man is conceived, born, and nourished as though in an outer mother, when he no longer rests in his own mother. Thus life in the world is like life in the matrix. The child in the maternal body lives in the inner firmament, and outside the mother's body it lives in the outer firmament. For the matrix is the Little World and has in it all the kinds of heaven and earth.

1/8, 327

Woman is like the earth and all the elements, and in this sense she must be considered a matrix; she is the tree which grows from the earth, and the child is like the fruit that is born of the tree. Just as a tree stands in the earth and belongs not only to the earth but also to the air and the water and the fire, so all the four elements are in woman—for the Great Field, the lower and the upper sphere of the world, consists of these—and in the middle of it stands the tree; woman is the image of the tree. Just as the earth, its fruits, and the elements are created for the sake of the tree and in order to sustain it, so the members of woman, all her qualities, and her whole nature exist for the sake of her matrix, her womb.

1/9, 209–10

God willed that the seed of man should not be sown in the body of the elements—not in the earth—but in woman; that his image should be conceived in her and born through her and not from the field of the world. And yet woman in her own way is also a field of the earth and not at all different from it. She replaces it, so to speak, she is the field and the garden mould in which the child is sown and planted, then growing up to be a man.

I/12, 46

He who contemplates woman should see in her the maternal womb of man; she is man's world, from which he is born. But no one can see from what force man actually is born. For just as God once created man in His likeness, so He still creates him today.

I/9, 194

How can one be an enemy of woman—whatever she may be? The world is peopled with her fruits, and that is why God lets her live so long, however loathsome she may be.

I/9, 29

Fig. 15. Venus

A woman is like a tree bearing fruit. And man is like the fruit that the tree bears. . . . The tree must be well nourished until it has everything by which to give that for the sake of which it exists. But consider how much injury the tree can bear, and how much less the pears! By that much woman is also superior to man. Man is to her what the pear is to the tree. The pear falls, but the tree remains standing. The tree continues to care for the other fruit in order itself to survive; therefore it must also receive much, suffer much, bear up with much, for the sake of its fruits, in order that they may thrive well and happily.

I/9, 200

Woman's season of blossoming occurs when she conceives. At this hour she is in bloom, and the blossoming is followed by the fruit, that is to say, the child. . . . When a tree blossoms, it is always because of the fruit that desires to ripen in it, and the tree in which no fruit lies hidden does not blossom. . . . If a virgin is ever to blossom, she must bear fruit. . . . For this is the nature of woman, that she is transformed as soon as she conceives; and then all things in her are like a summer, there is no snow, no frost, and no winter, but only pleasure and delight. *I/9, 197–98*

Just as a house is a work and is visible, and its master is also a work and is visible, so the master is a work of God, and the house a work of the master. In the same way it must be understood that we have the works visible before our eyes, and when we discover the master of the work, he is also visible to us. In things eternal, faith makes all the works visible; in things corporeal, but not visible, the light of nature makes all things visible. . . . Do not judge a thing that can become visible by its present invisibility. A child that is being conceived is already a man, although it is not yet visible. . . . It already resembles the visible man. *I/9, 257*

When the seed is received in the womb, nature combines the seed of the man and the seed of the woman. Of the two seeds the better and stronger will form the other according to its nature. . . . The seed from the man's brain and that from the woman's brain make together only one brain; but the child's brain is formed according to the one which is the stronger of the two, and it becomes like this seed, but never completely like it. For the second seed breaks the force of the first, and this always results in a change of nature. And the more different the two seeds are in their innate complexions, the more the change will be manifest. *I/1, 263–64*

When the seeds of all members come together in the matrix, this matrix combines the seed of the head with the seed of the brain, etc., in its own way . . . putting each in its proper place, and thus each single member is placed where it belongs, just as a carpenter builds a house from pieces of wood. Then every seed lies as it is supposed to lie in the mother, which is also called a microcosm. Only life is not there, nor is the soul. . . . But the seed of a single man does not yet make a complete man. God wills to make man out of two, and not out of one; he wills man composed of two and not of one alone. For if man were born of the seed of one individual, he would not change in nature. His child would

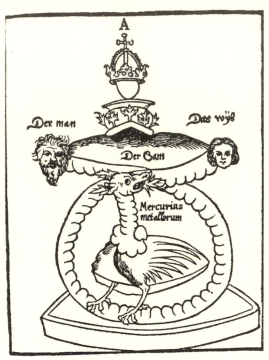

Fig. 16. The Seed

be just as he is, in the manner of a walnut tree, which is reborn of itself alone, and therefore is entirely like the one from which it is born. In all trees, the same always comes from the same; similarly all walnut trees bear the same nuts, without any difference. The same is true of man. If he had been born only of one individual, he would be like his father, and this father would be his father and his mother in one. Then there would be only people of one kind, and each would look like the other, and all would have the same nature. But the mixing of the seeds of man and woman results in so much change that no individual can be like the other. . . . Each individual's seed breaks the unity of the other, and that is why no man is like another.   *I/1, 262–63*

At first the herb grows from the root, then a flower grows from the herb, and in the end the seed grows from the flower; the seed is the vital sap, the *quinta essentia* of the herb. For nothing grows without a seed, nothing is born without a seed, nothing multiplies without a seed, and in all fruits of the earth the seed is the most precious, the most noble part, which should be most valued and prized.   *I/13, 371*

A good tree brings good fruits. If the mother is healthy like healthy earth, and if her body is fertile, then the tree too is good and bears good fruit. But for the children there is another matter of importance: a good fruit can be born only of a good seed. . . . A tree of the earth bears fruit again and again, without always requiring a new seed; the tree of woman only when a new seed is planted in it, namely, by man. Therefore much depends upon the seed; if it is worthless, the tree cannot improve it. What is true of the tree is also true of the seed; both must be fit. And if both are good, together they produce something good: the fruit.   *I/9, 213*

A bad seed produces a bad tree, which brings bad fruit. Only the evil seed is not the man himself, nor is the good seed; for the good seed is God, and the evil seed is the devil, and man is only the field. If a good seed falls into a man, it grows from him, since this man is its field, his heart is its tree, and his works are its fruits. Cannot a field that bears weeds be weeded and cleansed of this bad fruit, so that another, good seed can be planted in it? . . . Or cannot a good field be sown with bad seeds? Indeed it can! Every field is ordered by its seed, and no seed by its field. For the seed is the master of the field. Every man is like a field, neither entirely good nor entirely bad, but of an uncertain kind. . . . If a good seed falls into the field, and the soil receives it, it grows to be good. If a bad seed falls into the field and is received, it grows to be bad. Therefore it is not

29

the soil of the field that decides the matter; it is neither good nor bad. It is like a body of water, coloured by the colours that fall on the water.

God set a term to the formation of a child, namely forty weeks; similarly a time was set for the formation of cows, pigeons, and all other animals. During this span of time the seed develops into a child. After this manner: When conception has occurred, nature begins its work and orders the seeds; the seed of the head moves to the place of the head, the seed of the arms to its place, and everything occupies the place which it must occupy according to its nature. When everything is in its right place, the matrix rests, and does nothing more. Thereupon follows the action of material nature and makes the child grow, so that everything that has been thus arranged may develop into a proper human body: what belongs to the flesh develops into flesh, what belongs to the bones, into the bones, what belongs to the blood vessels, into blood vessels, what belongs to the internal organs, into internal organs. And thus the seed ceases to be seed, and becomes flesh and blood. . . . Then it is no longer subject to material action, and it becomes subject to that action which is given to man by God's grace; it endows the child with life and with every attribute of a living being—sight, hearing, touch, taste, smell, and the active principle of these senses. When life has thus been infused into the child according to God's dispensation, the child grows for a long time in the mother's body, until all its members gain their full strength, and they are no longer wanting in force and completeness, and they become quite solid. Then, in the end, the child is endowed with spirit, soul, reason, understanding, and all the attributes of the soul. Understand, therefore, how the received seed is at first formed, and correctly ordered, then develops into flesh and blood, then is given size and strength, in order to be able to bear the burden of earthly life; and finally, how it is endowed with spirit and soul. For as long as the child is still too weak to be able to bear the life of the earth, spirit is not given to it; only as its strength grows is it infused with spirit, and spirit is followed by the soul. For the soul does not move into any body in which the spirit does not dwell. . . . Thus the child grows in the union of spirit and body, until it no longer can do without the earth's air and the maternal food.—And then comes birth.

I/1, 270–72

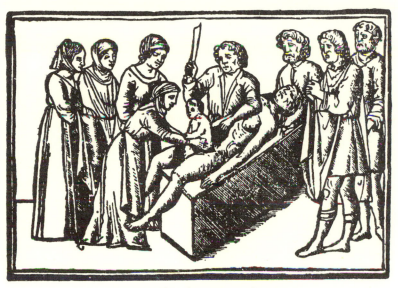

Fig. 17. The Caesarean Section

What has a man received from his father and his mother that he can boast of? For in his nature and in his qualities he is nothing but what they were, nothing but a hungry stomach and a wretched rudimentary intelligence, nothing but a naked image, at the mercy of death. What could man make of himself, or what could he do with himself, if he were nothing but a naked human body? He really possesses only what was given him outside this body, and beyond this, nothing. Only what God put into him, and what this gift contains, defines his action and his being.

I/1 315

Four things play a part in conception and birth: body, imagination, form, and influence. The "body" as ordained in the beginning must become a body and nothing else. For it is a law of nature that the oak tree must arise from an oak; and the same is true of the body of man. From the "imagination," and its objects, the child receives its reason. And just as heaven infuses the child with its motion, its good and evil qualities, sometimes strongly, sometimes weakly, so the imagination of man—like the stars—has a course, and makes the child's reason turn to higher or lower things. The third thing, the "form," compels the child to look like the one from whom it descends. And finally it is the "influence" that determines the health or sickness of the body. For in the same way as a strong architect erects good and solid buildings, and a weak one weak buildings, so it is in the conception of a child.

1/7, 203

Fig. 18. The Holy Virgin with the Child, as Patron Saint of Sailors

The imagination of a pregnant woman is so strong that it can influence the seed and change the fruit in her womb in many directions. Her inner stars act powerfully and vigorously upon the fruit, so that its nature is thereby deeply and solidly shaped and forged. For the child in the mother's womb is exposed to the mother's influence, and is as though entrusted to the hand and will of its mother, as the clay is entrusted to the hand of the potter, who creates and forms out of it what he wants and what he pleases.

1/11, 314

Thus the child requires no stars or planets: its mother is its star and its planet.

1/1, 179

God does not want man or woman to be like a tree which always grows the same fruit. . . . Nor does He want every man to multiply his race, but created many without and many with seeds; He made each one different from the other.

God left man free to propagate his kind; according to his will, he may beget a child, transmit his seed, or not. God planted the seed in all its reality and specificity deep in the imagination of man. . . . If a man has the will, the desire arises in his imagination, and the desire generates the seed. *1/1, 256–57* . . . But man himself cannot kindle the desire, it must be fanned by an object. That is to say, when a man sees a woman, she is the object, and it depends only upon him whether he wants to fasten to it or not. . . . God endowed man with reason, in order that he might know what the desire means. But he himself must decide whether to yield to it or not, whether to let it act on him or not, whether to follow his intelligence or not. God has entrusted the seed to man's reflective reason because the reflective reason encompasses both his intelligence and the object that inflames his fantasy. But all this takes place only if he himself wants it; otherwise there is no seed in him. . . . It is the same with woman. When she sees a man, he becomes her object, and her imagination begins to dwell on him. She does this by virtue of the ability that God has bestowed upon her. . . . It is in her power to feel desire or not. If she yields, she becomes rich in seeds; if not, she has neither seed nor urge. Thus God left the seed to the free decision of man, and the decision depends upon man's will. He can do as he wishes. And since this free decision exists, it lies with both, with man and with woman. As they determine by their will, so will it happen.—That is how matters stand regarding the birth of the seed. *1/1, 254–55*

Just as man originates in the Great World, and is inseparably bound to it, so has woman been created from man, and cannot separate from him. For if Lady Eve had been formed otherwise than from the body of man, desire would never have been born from both of them. But because they are of one flesh and one blood, it follows that they cannot let go of each other. *1/12, 44*

Just as there is love among cattle, which come together

Du folt mit vnkeüfch fein

Fig. 19. The Ten Commandments: "Thou Shalt Not Commit Adultery."

couple by couple, female with male, so also among men such love is of the animal kind, and is inherited from the animal. This love has its usefulness, and its rewards, but it remains animal, and it is mortal, it does not endure, and it reflects only the reason and aspiration of instinctual man. It does not know higher goals. It is because of this animal love that people can be friendly or hostile, well or ill disposed toward one another, exactly as animals are fierce and angry, envious and hostile toward one another. Just as toads and snakes always behave according to their nature, so do men. And just as dogs and cats hate each other, so nations fall into conflicts. All this is rooted in the animal nature. When dogs bark and snap at one another, it is because of envy or greed, because each of them wants to have everything for himself, wants to devour everything himself and begrudges everything to the other; this is the way of beasts. In this respect, man is the child of dogs. He, too, is burdened with envy and disloyalty, with a violent disposition, and each man grudges the other everything. Just as dogs fight over a bitch, so the courtship of men is doglike in nature. For such behaviour is also found among the beasts, and it is the same among them as among men.

I/13, 318

When a man and a woman who belong to each other and

34

have been created for each other come together, no adultery
will take place because they form *one* being in their structure, which cannot be broken. But if these two do not come
together, there is no steadfast love, their love sways like a
reed in the wind. When a man courts many women, he has
not found the proper wife to complement him; similarly, a
woman who carries on amorous intrigues with other men
has not found the proper husband. But God has created each
man's instincts in such a way that he need not become an
adulterer. Therefore,
for those who are not
fit for each other,
the commandment is
to observe their mar-
riage as if they be-
longed together. For
there are two kinds of
marriage—the one that
God makes, and the
one that man himself
makes. In the first kind
of marriage, husband
and wife observe the
commandment of their

Fig. 20. The Ten Commandments:
"Thou Shalt Not Covet Thy
Neighbour's Wife."

own accord; in the second, they do not, but are compelled to
observe it.   *I/9, 304*

Chastity endows a man with a pure heart and power to
study divine things. God himself, who bids us do this, gave
man chastity. But he who is unable to be his own master does
better not to live alone.   *I/9, 148*

Let us suppose that there are one hundred men and one
thousand women in the world, and that each woman wants
a man, and does not want to do without one. But there are
only one hundred men; thus only one hundred women are
provided for, and for nine hundred there is no provision.
Whereupon it may happen that the women pursue the men
in such a way that adultery will result. . . . Would it not

be preferable to give each man ten women as wives instead of one, and thus to save the other nine from becoming whores? For God ordained that marriage be sacred, but He did not prescribe the number of wives, neither a high nor a low one: He commanded: thou shalt be faithful to thy marriage vow and thou shalt not break it. Now, it so happens that God has always created many more women than men. And He makes men die far more readily than women. And He always lets the women survive and not the men. Therefore it would be just not that three men should marry one woman, but that three women should marry one man, so that no path be opened to fornication. And if there is such a surplus of women, let it be taken care of by marriage, so that the meaning of God's commandment may be heeded. . . . If this cannot be achieved by giving each man one wife, he should have two, or whatever number may be required to take care of the surplus. And all this should be done in a just way, not in the spirit of partisanship; treat the other man just as you want to be treated yourself. . . . Why then issue laws about morality, virtues, chastity, and so forth? No one but God can give commandments that are permanent and immutable. For human laws must be adapted to the needs of the times, and accordingly can be abrogated and replaced by others.

I/14, 260

Man is the Little World, but woman . . . is the Littlest World, and hence she is different from man. She has a different anatomy, a different theory, different effects and causes, different divisions and cares. . . . For the world is and was the first creature, man the second, and woman the third. Thus the cosmos is the greatest world, the world of man the next greatest, and that of woman the smallest and least. And each world—the cosmos, man, and woman— has its own philosophy and "art." The tooth of time gnaws at the world, as also at man and woman, and with respect to their transience all three of them—despite their diversity —are creatures of the same philosophy, astronomy, and theory. Also what they bring forth is transitory, and therein they do not differ. But the manner in which they bring it forth is different in the cosmos, in man, and in woman. And because the ways and means are different, the result is different in form. . . . But even though these three empires are separated from one another, they are borne by the same spirit . . . for this spirit encompasses them all.   *I/9, 178–79*

Fig. 21. Heaven and
Earth

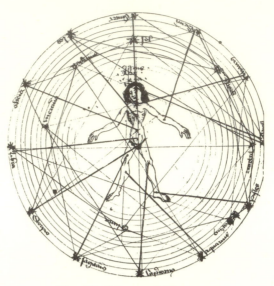

Fig. 22. Man and Heaven

I/12, 164

The centre of all things is man, he is the middle point of heaven and earth. . . .

The whole world surrounds man as a circle surrounds one point. From this it follows that all things are related to this one point, no differently from an apple seed which is surrounded and preserved by the fruit, and which draws its sustenance from it. . . . Similarly, man is a seed and the world is his apple; and just as the seed fares in the apple, so does man fare in the world, which surrounds him. . . . Each thing has its own origin; partly in the eternal, and partly in the temporal. And wisdom, whether it be heavenly or earthly, can be achieved only through the attractive force of the

I/12, 164–67   centre and the circle.

Let man consider who he is and what he should and must become. For the *compositio humana* is prodigious, and its oneness is formed of a very great diversity. . . . Man needs more than common intelligence to know who he is; only he who studies himself properly and knows whence he comes

38

and who he is will also give profound attention to the eternal.   *1/12, 297*

Everything that comes from the flesh is animal and follows an animal course; heaven has little influence on it. Only that which comes from the stars is specifically human in us; this is subject to their influence. But that which comes from the spirit, the divine part of man, has been formed in us in the likeness of God, and upon this neither earth nor heaven has any influence.   *1/12, 18*

You should look upon man as a part of nature whose end lies in heaven. In the heavens you can see man, each part for itself; for man is made of heaven. And the matter out of which man was created also indicates to you the pattern after which he was formed. . . . External nature moulds the shape of internal nature, and if external nature vanishes, the inner nature is also lost; for the outer is the mother of the inner. Thus man is like the image of the four elements in a mirror; if the four elements fall apart, man is destroyed. If that which faces the mirror is at rest, then the image in the mirror is at rest too. And so philosophy is nothing other than the knowledge and discovery of that which has its reflection in the mirror. And just as the image in the mirror gives no one any idea about his nature, and cannot be the object of cognition, but is only a dead image, so is man, considered in himself: nothing can be learned from him alone. For knowledge comes only from that outside being whose mirrored image he is.   *1/8, 71–72*

Heaven is man, and man is heaven, and all men together are the one heaven, and heaven is nothing but one man. You must know this to understand why one place is this way and the other that way, why this is new and that is old, and why there are everywhere so many diverse things. But all this cannot be discovered by studying the heavens. . . . All that can be discovered is the distribution of their active influences. . . . We, men, have a heaven, and it lies in each of us in its entire plenitude, undivided and corresponding to each man's specificity. Thus each human life takes its own course, thus dying, death, and disease are unequally distributed, in each case according to the action of the heavens. For if the same heaven were in all of us, all men would have to be equally sick and equally healthy. But this is not so; the unity of the Great Heaven is split into our diversities by the various moments at which we are born. As soon as a child is conceived, it receives its own heaven. If all children had been born at the same moment, all of them would have had the same heaven in them, and their lives would have followed the same course. Therefore, the starry vault imprints itself on the inner heaven of a man. A miracle without equal!

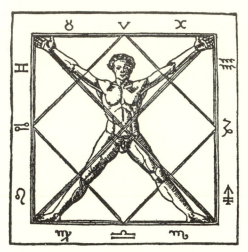

1/8, 100–101

Fig. 23. Man and Zodiac

Just as the firmament with all its constellations forms a whole in itself, likewise man in himself is a free and mighty firmament. And just as the firmament rests in itself and is not ruled by any creature, the firmament of man is not ruled by other creatures, but stands for itself and is free of all bonds. For there are two kinds of created things: heaven and the earth are of one kind, man is of the other. . . . Everything that astronomical theory has profoundly fathomed by studying the planetary aspects and the stars . . . can also be applied to *1/1, 202–3* the firmament of the body.

The light of nature in man comes from the stars, and his flesh and blood belong to the material elements. Thus two influences operate in man. One is that of the firmamental light, which includes wisdom, art, reason. All these are the children of this father. . . . The second influence emanates from matter, and it includes concupiscence, eating, drinking, and everything that relates to the flesh and blood. Therefore one must not ascribe to the stars that which originates in the blood and flesh. For heaven does not endow one with concupiscence or greed. . . . From heaven come only wisdom, art, and reason. I/12, 22

As great as the difference in form and shape between the two bodies, the visible and the invisible, the material and the eternal, is the difference between their natures. . . . They are like a married pair, one in the flesh, but twofold in their nature. . . . And because this is so, a contradiction dwells in man. . . . Namely, the stars in him have a different disposition, a different mind, a different orientation than the lower elements; and on the other hand, these elements in turn have a different wisdom and a different disposition than the stars in man. For instance: the elemental, material body wants to live in luxury and lewdness; the stars, the ethereal body, the inner counterpart of the upper sphere, want to study, learn, pursue arts, and so forth. As a result there arises an antinomy in man himself. The visible, ma-

Fig. 24. Man and Zodiac

terial body wants one thing, and the invisible, ethereal body wants another thing, they do not want the same thing. . . . Therefore there dwells in each of these bodies an urge to exceed that which is given to it, and neither wants to follow a middle course and act with measure. Both strive to exceed their bounds, and each wants to expel the other; thus en-

1/12, 62–63

mity arises between them. For everything that exceeds its measure brings destruction in its train.

Everything that man accomplishes or does, that he teaches or wants to learn, must have its right proportion; it must follow its own line and remain within its circle, to the end that a balance be preserved, that there be no crooked thing,

1/11, 19

that nothing exceed the circle.

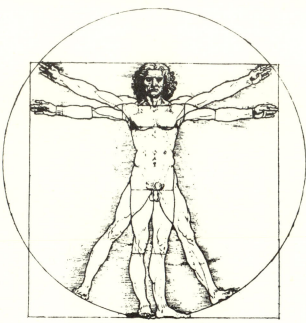

Fig. 25. Man in Equilibrium

Blessed and thrice blessed is he who observes the right measure and needs none of the help devised by men, but

1/11, 219

follows the path that God prescribed to him.

God could surely have created man out of nothingness by merely saying: "So be it!" This he did not do, but took him from nature, placed him in nature, left him to nature, and subjected him to nature as her child. But He also subjected nature to him, indeed as a father. . . . Thus nature is subject to man, she belongs to him as to one of her blood; he is her child, her fruit, which was made of her in the body of

1/10, 653

the elements . . . and in the ethereal body.

In nature we find a light that illumines us more than the sun and the moon. For it is so ordered that we see but half of man and all the other creatures, and therefore must explore them further. . . . Nor should we become drowned in our daily work, for whosoever seeks . . . shall find. . . . And if we follow the light of nature, we learn that there exists another half of man, and that man does not consist of blood and flesh alone . . . but also of a body that cannot be discerned by our crude eyesight.

I/9, 254–55

The moon emits light, yet by this light colours are not discernible; but as soon as the sun rises, all the colours can be distinguished. Similarly nature has a light that shines like the sun; and as the light of the sun exceeds the light of the moon, so the light of nature far exceeds the power of the eyes. In its light all things invisible become visible; remember always that the one light outshines the other.

I/9, 253

Know that our world and everything we see in its compass and everything we can touch constitute only one half of the cosmos. The world we do not see is equal to ours in weight and measure, in nature and properties. From this it follows that there exists another half of man in which this invisible world operates. If we know of the two worlds, we realize that both halves are needed to constitute the whole man; for they are like two men united in one body.

I/9, 258

The sun can shine through a glass, and fire can radiate warmth through the walls of the stove, although the sun does not pass through the glass and the fire does not go through the stove; in the same way, the human body can act at a distance while remaining at rest in one place, like the sun, which shines through the glass and yet does not pass through it. Hence nothing must be attributed to the body itself but only to the forces that flow from it—just as the smell of an animal is suffused while the animal's body may be at rest.

I/9, 325

Nature emits a light, and by its radiance she can be known. But in man there is still another light apart from that which is innate in nature. It is the light through which man experiences, learns, and fathoms the supernatural. Those who seek in the light of nature speak from knowledge of nature; but those who seek in the light of man speak from knowledge of super-nature. For man is more than nature; he is nature, but he is also a spirit, he is also an angel, and he has the properties of all three. If he walks in nature, he serves nature; if he walks in the spirit, he serves the spirit; if he walks with the angel, he serves the angel. The first is given to the body, the others are given to the soul, and are its jewel.

1/14, 115

The book in which the letters of the mysteries are written visibly, discernibly, tangibly, and legibly, so that everything one desires to know can best be found in this self-same book, inscribed by the finger of God; the book compared with which, if it is correctly read, all other books are nothing but dead letters—know that this book is the book of man, and should not be sought anywhere but in man alone. Man is the book in which all the mysteries are recorded; but this book is interpreted by God.

1/14, 547–48

If you would gain understanding of the whole treasury that the letters enclose, possess, and encompass, you must gain it from far off, namely, from Him who taught man how to compose the letters. . . . For it is not on paper that you will find the power to understand, but in Him who put the words on paper.

1/12, 193–94

Man is born of the earth, therefore he also has in him the nature of the earth. But later, in his new birth, he is of God and in this form receives divine nature. Just as man in nature is illumined by the sidereal light that he may know nature, so he is illumined by the Holy Ghost that he may know God in His essence. For no one can know God unless he is of divine nature, and no one can know nature unless he is of nature. Everyone is bound to that in which he originates and to which he must at some time return.

1/12, 326

The light of nature is a steward of the Holy Light. What harm comes to the natural tongue because the fiery tongue has spoken? Or how does the fiery tongue offend against the natural one? It is the same as with a man and a woman, who both give birth to a child; without both this could not be. Similarly, both lights were given man, to dwell within him. *I/12, 11*

How marvellously man is made and formed if one penetrates into his true nature . . . and it is a great thing—consider for once, that there is nothing in heaven or in earth that is not also in man. . . . In him is God who is also in Heaven; and all the forces of Heaven operate likewise in man. Where else can Heaven be rediscovered if not in man? Since it acts from us, it must also be in us. Therefore it knows our prayer even before we have uttered it, for it is closer to our hearts than to our words. . . . God made His Heaven in man beautiful and great, noble and good; for God is in His Heaven, i.e., in man. For He Himself says that He is in us, and that we are His temple. *I/9, 219–20*

Thoughts are free and are subject to no rule. On them rests the freedom of man, and they tower above the light of nature. For thoughts give birth to a creative force that is neither elemental nor sidereal. . . . Thoughts create a new heaven, a new firmament, a new source of energy, from which new arts flow. . . . When a man undertakes to create something, he establishes a new heaven, as it were, and from it the work that he desires to create flows into him. . . . For such is the immensity of man that he is greater than heaven and earth. *I/12, 183*

Fig. 26. Astrolabe

II

MAN AND HIS BODY

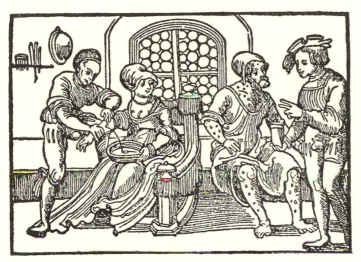

Fig. 27. Barber Shop: (*left*) a blood-letting; (*right*) the assistant dispenses a remedy against a skin disease and explains how to apply it

Medicine should be based upon truth and not upon verbal sleight-of-hand. *1/6, 316*

THE physician comes from nature, from nature he is born; only he who receives his experience from nature is a physician, and not he who writes, speaks, and acts with his head and with ratiocinations aimed against nature and her ways. *1/6, 52*

The physician is only the servant of nature, not her master. Therefore it behooves medicine to follow the will of nature. *1/7, 150*

He who would be a good physician must find his faith in the rational light of nature, he must work with it, and not undertake anything without it. . . . For Christ would have you draw your faith from knowledge and not to live without knowledge. . . .If you desire to apply an art, let it be only in the light of nature, and not in superficial action.

God has given to each man the light that was his due; so

1/1, 300

that he need not go astray.

Who possesses a truth unless he has received it of a master? No one! We have the truth of the soul from God, otherwise we would not have it. Similarly we have the truths of philosophy from nature; she has taught us these without idle talk. . . . Just as Christ offered his person to our eyes, so we have personal teachers in nature. . . . They are born through seeing and touching, and not through nonseeing.

1/8, 306

For seeing and touching beget the truth.

No disease comes from the physician, nor any medicine. But he can aggravate the course of the disease, and he can also improve it. What teacher can be better in this respect than nature herself? Nature possesses the knowledge and makes the meaning of all things visible; it is nature that teaches the physician. Since nature alone possesses this knowledge, it must also be nature that compounds the recipe. . . . The art of healing comes from nature, not from the physician. Therefore the physician must start from na-

1/8, 70

ture, with an open mind.

It must not surprise the physician that nature is more than his art. For what can equal the forces of nature? He who has no expert knowledge of them has not mastered the art of medicine. In one herb there is more virtue and force than in all the folios that are read in the high colleges and that are

1/2, 8

not fated to live long.

Every physician must be rich in knowledge, and not only of that which is written in books; his patients should be his book, they will never mislead him . . . and by them he will never be deceived. But he who is content with mere letters is like a dead man; and he is like a dead physician. As a man and as a physician, he kills his patient. Not even a dog killer can learn his trade from books, but only from experience. And how much more is this true of the physician!

1/11, 85, 591

From his own head a man cannot learn the theory of medicine, but only from that which his eyes see and his fingers touch. . . . If a man were brought up in a monastery and had never known anything but the customs of the monastery, and never experienced anything but what takes place in the monastery, and the monastic customs and ways, he would know nothing except these very monastic customs. If he should then encounter other customs, he would not know what to do, for he knows only his own tune. . . . He would not have anything to say except what he had learned in his

Fig. 28. Autopsy

monastery; moreover, this monastic doctrine originated only in speculation . . . and was contrived only by men. . . . Consequently, our monastic scholar remains inexperienced and can never get to the fundament of things, whence everything comes; for this can never be discovered by pure theory. *I/11, 24–25*

Theory and practice should together form one, and should remain undivided. For every theory is also a kind of speculative practice and is no more and no less true than active practice. But what would you do if your speculation did not jibe with findings based on practice? Both must be true or both must be untrue. Look at the carpenter: first he builds his house in his head. But whence does he take this structure? From his active practice. And if he did not have this, he could not erect his structure in his mind: thus, both theory and practice rest upon experience.

1/6, 314

Practice should not be based on speculative theory; theory should be derived from practice.

1/11, 183

Experience is the judge; if a thing stands the test of experience, it should be accepted; if it does not stand this test, it should be rejected.

1/11, 190

Every experiment is like a weapon which should be used according to its specific function—as a spear is used to thrust, or a club to batter. It is the same with experiments. And just as a club is not suitable for thrusting, and a spear for battering, so the nature and manner of the experiments must not change. Hence it is very important to discover the true active forces in experiments, in order to know in what form they can best be applied. The proper use of experiments requires an experienced man, who is skilled in thrust and blow, so that he can apply and master them, each according to its nature.

1/6, 456

These are the qualifications of a good surgeon:
Regarding his innate temper:
A clear conscience,
Desire to learn and to gather experience,
A gentle heart and a cheerful spirit,
Moral manner of life and sobriety in all things,
Greater regard for his honour than for money,
Greater interest in being useful to his patient than to himself,
He must not be married to a bigot.

. . .

He should not be a runaway monk,
He should not practise self-abuse,

He must not have a red beard,

He must not act without judgment,

He must not accept belief without understanding,

He must not scorn the workings of chance,

He must not boast of knowing anything without experience,

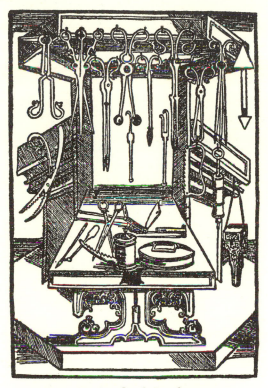

Fig. 29. Medical Implements

He must never boast or praise himself,

He must despise no one.

Regarding knowledge of the body:

He should know all the properties of the flesh,

He should know the bones of the body,

He should know the blood vessels,

He should know the veins and arteries of the whole body,

Fig. 30. Barber-Surgeon at Work

He should know the length and breadth of all the
    organs,
He should know the relations between the different
    parts of the body,
He should know the articulations of nature and all
    her properties,
He should know what injury can befall each organ,
He should know how injury affects each organ,
He should know the needs of each organ in the body,
And he should know where death is and where life is.
Regarding the practice of his art:
He should know all the vulnerary herbs,
He should know all the tissue-forming remedies,
He should know all the essences,
He should know the course of all surgical diseases,
He should know how diseases are cured by time and
    by accidents.

.   .   .

He should know what to forbid the patient and what
    to permit him . . .
He should know the effect of each remedy,
He should know plaster for wounds,
He should know lotions for wounds,
He should know etc.

1/5, 476

The right path does not consist in speculation, but leads
deep into experience. From experience the physican receives his help, and upon it rests all his skill. He must have
rich knowledge based on experience, for he is born blind,
and book knowledge has never made a single physician. For
this purpose he needs not human, but divine things, and
therefore he should not treat truth lightheadedly. He does
not act for himself, but for God, and God bestows His
grace upon him so that he may come to the assistance of his
fellow men in their needs. Medicine does not serve man's

self-conceit but his pressing needs. And you must not abuse medicine to inflict damage on your fellow man, just as it is not meet to misuse the fruits of the earth. For it is not you who acts through medicine, but God, just as it is He who *I/7, 202* makes the corn grow, and not the peasant.

Your eyes, which take delight in experience, are your masters; for your own fantasies and speculations cannot advance

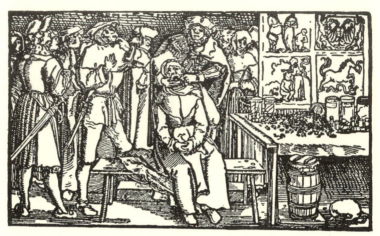

Fig. 31. The Forerunner of the Dentist: he extracted teeth with his fingers

you so far that you can boast of being a physician. Nor can you acquire the art of medicine by sophisms, or after the manner of the sophists, those pseudo-scientists, who imagine that their own wisdom reaches as far as the end of the earth and the sea and all the elements. And not only do they maintain this; they also believe that their speculation reveals how God comports Himself in Heaven and what is in His heart. But no physician should build on such a precarious founda-
I/11, 29 tion, and must never rely on such things.

The art of medicine cannot be inherited, nor can it be copied from books; it must be digested many times and many times spat out; one must always rechew it and knead it thoroughly, and one must be alert while learning it, one *I/10, 225* must not doze like peasants turning over pears in the sun.

Prolix writing has no place in medicine; concise writing and great intelligence, brief treatises but great force —that is the standard by which the physician is measured. The longer the book, the less the intelligence; the longer the prescriptions, the poorer their virtue. Therefore each physician should achieve great things by means of small things. For nature is so excellent in its gifts that . . . it better befits a man to know one herb in the meadow, but to know it thoroughly, than to see the whole meadow without knowing what grows on it. *1/6, 289*

It is better to know and to understand one remedy than to rummage through the great libraries of the monasteries, where of a thousand pages barely one is understood . . . nature does not call for long recipes. *1/6, 144*

Regardless how much knowledge or skill a physician may have, he can be surprised by an anomaly—like a white raven —which confounds all the books; and all his experience, everything he has learned at the sickbed, is suddenly gone. Therefore study each day without respite, investigate and observe diligently; despise nothing, and do not lightly put too much trust in yourself. Do not be arrogant when in fact you are helpless, and do not regard yourself as a master at the outset; for no one can achieve mastery without labour. Also, learn from those who are more experienced than you, for who can pretend to know everything? Who can be everywhere and know where all things lie? Therefore travel and explore everything, and whatever comes your way, take it without scorn, and do not be ashamed to do so on the ground that you are a doctor, a master. *1/5, 425*

The physician does not learn everything he must know and master at high colleges alone; from time to time he must consult old women, gypsies, magicians, wayfarers, and all manner of peasant folk and random people, and learn from them; for these have more knowledge about such things than all the high colleges. *1/14, 541*

The arts are not all confined within one man's country; they are distributed over the whole world. They are not found in one man alone or in one place, but must be gathered together, sought out, and taken where they happen to be. . . . Or is it not so? Art pursues no one, it must rather be pursued. Therefore, it is only just that we should seek art, and not that art should seek us. . . . If we would go to God, we must go to Him, for He says, Come to me, all. Now, since this is so, we must pursue what we wish to find. If a man would see a specific person, or a country, or a city, if he would study the customs of a place or the nature of the heavens and the elements, he must pursue them, for they will not come to him. And this is true of anyone who wishes to see and experience anything whatsoever.

I/11, 141–42

Fig. 32. The Doctor: uroscopy

The physician should prescribe physic composed in accordance with the patient's blood and flesh, with his country's ways and his innate nature—harsh, crude, hard, gentle, mild, virtuous, friendly, tender, etc. But this is not the essence of his art; the
I/11, 152–53 long and short of it is what he truly accomplishes.

The physician must give heed to the region in which the patient lives, that is to say, to its type and peculiarities. For one country is different from another; its earth is different, as are its stones, wines, bread, meat, and everything that grows and thrives in a specific region. This means that each country, in addition to the general properties common to the whole world, also has its own specific properties. The physician should take this into account and know it, and accordingly he should also be a cosmographer and geographer, well versed in these disciplines.

I/4, 501–2

How can a man become a good geographer of cosmographer if he always sits by the fireside? Does not the sight of a thing give the eyes a true foundation? Then let the foundation be made solid. What can the roaster of pears experience in his chimney corner? And what can the carpenter learn

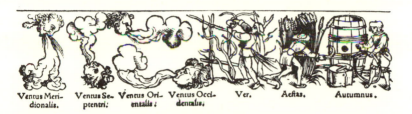

Ventus Meri-dionalis.   Ventus Se-ptentri: Ventus Ori-entalis: Ventus Occi-dentalis.   Ver.   Aeftas.   Autumnus.

Fig. 33. Winds and Seasons

without the knowledge acquired by his eyesight? Or what can be proved without the help of the eyesight? Did not God reveal Himself to our eyes, and does He not call us to witness that our eyes have seen Him? How then should an art or anything else deprive itself of the testimony of the eyes? . . . The diseases migrate hither and thither throughout the broad world, and do not stay in one place. If a man desires to recognize many various diseases, he must travel from place to place; if he travels far, he will experience a great deal and he will learn to recognize many things.

I/11, 142

He who would explore nature must tread her books with his feet. Holy Scripture is explored through its letters, but nature is explored from country to country; it has as many pages as there are countries. This is the code of nature, and thus must her leaves be turned.

I/11, 145–46

Medicine rests upon four pillars—philosophy, astronomy, alchemy, and ethics. The first pillar is the philosophical knowledge of earth and water; the second, astronomy, supplies its full understanding of that which is of fiery and airy nature; the third is an adequate explanation of the properties of all the four elements—that is to say, of the whole cosmos—and an introduction into the art of their transformations; and finally, the fourth shows the physician those virtues which must stay with him up until his death, and it should *I/8, 55–56*   support and complete the three other pillars.

Fig. 34. An Itinerant Quack

The physician should be versed in all branches of philosophy, physics, and alchemy as well, as thoroughly, as profoundly as possible, and he should not lack any knowledge in all these fields. What he is should stand on solid ground, founded in truthfulness and highest experience. For of all men, the physician is supreme in the study and knowledge of nature and her light, and that is what enables him to be a *I/10, 277–78*   helper of the sick.

What is a pearl to the sow, since all she can do is eat? I praise the art of alchemy because it reveals the mysteries of medicine and because it is helpful in all desperate illnesses. But what shall I praise in those who have no idea of the mysteries of nature that are placed in their hands? I also praise the art of medicine; but how can I praise those who are physicians and not alchemists at the same time? If the art of medicine were found among those who are only alchemists, they would not understand it, and if it were found among those who are only physicians, they would not be able to make use of it, for they do not hold in their hands the key to the mysteries. Thus I can only praise him who knows how to induce nature to be helpful, that is to say, is able to recognize what lies hidden in nature. For never must knowledge and preparation, that is to say, medicine and alchemy, be separated from each other. *1/10, 66–67*

Know that philosophers are of two kinds, the philosopher of heaven and the philosopher of the earth. Each sphere constitutes only one aspect of the physician, and in itself neither makes the whole physician. He who has knowledge of the lower spheres is a philosopher, he who has knowledge of the upper spheres is an astronomer. But both have one intellect and one art, and both have a share in the mystery of the four elements. . . . Just as in heaven there is a Saturn of fiery nature, so on earth there is one of earthly nature; and just as there is a sun in the water, so is there one in heaven. In man each thing is fourfold. What lies in the remotest corner of the earth, casts its shadow on man, and man is suffused with what lies in the depths of the sea. . . . What is the difference between the sun, moon, Mercury, Saturn, and Jupiter in heaven, and the same planets in man? The difference is only one of form. That is why there are not four arcana but only one arcanum; however, it has four aspects, just as a tower has four sides, according to the four winds. And just as a tower cannot be lacking in one side, so a physician must not lack any of these aspects. For one aspect does not yet make a whole physician, nor two, nor three; all four are needed. Just as the arcana consist of four parts, so the whole physician must comprise all the four aspects. *1/8, 77*

Medicine should be taught so cleanly and clearly in the language of the homeland that the German should under-

Fig. 35. Sickness and Celestial Constellation

stand the Arab, and the Greek the German; its art and wisdom should be of such a nature that all those versed in it should enjoy marvellous respect, and that all should pay tribute to this high art. For whom does heaven distinguish if not the physician who studies it? And whom the earth, if not its philosopher? The mysteries of the firmament are revealed by the physician; to him the mysteries of nature are manifest, and he communicates them to other learned men. Thus philosophy comprises knowledge of all the organs and limbs, health and sickness. The condition of urine must be read from the outer world, the pulse must be understood in relation to the firmament, physiognomy to the stars, chiromancy to the minerals, the breath to the east and west winds, fever to earthquakes, etc.—If the physician understands things exactly and sees and recognizes all illnesses in the macrocosm outside man, and if he has a clear idea of man and his whole nature, then and only then is he a physician. Then he may approach the inside of man; then he may examine his urine, take his pulse, and understand where each thing belongs. This would not be possible without profound knowledge of the outer man, who is nothing other than heaven and earth. It would be bold and presumptuous to approach the study of man without such knowledge and to defend the sandy ground of speculation, which is more unstable than a reed in the wind. *I/8, 76*

He who studies the sun and the moon and knows with his eyes closed how the sun and the moon look, bears them within himself in the same form as they shine in heaven. Philosophy teaches that they are intangibly imprinted upon man, just as in the firmament, one like a mirrored image of the other. Just as a man can see himself reflected exactly in a mirror, so the physician must have exact knowledge of man and recognize him in the mirror of the four elements, in which the whole microcosm reveals itself. *I/8, 71*

The physician should speak of that which is invisible. What is visible should belong to his knowledge, and he should recognize the illnesses, just as everybody else, who is not a physician, can recognize them by their symptoms. But this is far from making him a physician; he becomes a physician only when he knows that which is unnamed, *1/8, 177* invisible, and immaterial, yet efficacious.

A good physician must be a born physician. Therefore no one should be surprised that the medical faculty is full of students who contribute nothing to its good reputation, but only harm it and make it an object of contempt. A tree that has once borne fruit cannot be changed. And no more than an apple can be changed into a pear, will such people ever *1/6, 356* become good physicians. A life-long calling must be innate.

There are three kinds of physician. The first kind is born of nature, through the meeting of celestial constellations—

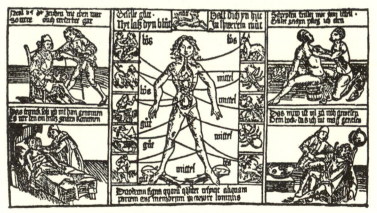

Fig. 36. Blood-Letting Chart

as also musicians, orators, and artists are born. The second kind is taught by men introduced to medicine and trained in it, to the extent that man in general and they in particular are capable of learning. The third kind is that given by God, and is directly taught by God. As Christ says, each scribe will receive his knowledge from God; that is to say, what we can

Fig. 37. Cosmas and Damian, Patron Saints of Medicine

do, we have from God. Now, although medicine has masters of three kinds, they need not agree in their theory and arguments; for in their work they will all meet, and will be directed to the same end. . . . Thus man teaches according to his abilities, but God teaches according to his will. And it is established that, in all things, the man who desires to transmit his knowledge to others must take this knowledge from God and from nature. . . . Whosoever teaches from another source is steeped in error.

1/11, 131

The physician was created by God, not by man. Therefore let him act in good faith and without lying. He can help only him who has grace.

1/9, 193

Whereas God created the physician . . . and appointed him to be useful to other men, it is good for him to know, in order to accomplish such special works, that he has no other duty but to drive out disease. If this is his office, he must act like God, his Lord, who appointed him. God took away the disease of the Great World, and that is why every year the flowers grow, every year the snow falls, and so on. All these things would have died if God Himself had not been their physician and had not taken away the disease of the winter. To take away the diseases of the Little World, those of man, he ordained the physician. If the physician is thus a god of the Little World, appointed as God's deputy, on what foundation should he build, and from whom shall he learn if not from the oldest physician, from God? Him he should imitate, follow His example and His actions, and he should not overestimate himself as a physician, but consider himself only the disciple of this Highest Physician.

1/7, 272

To you Christians let God be the highest and first physician, the most powerful, and not the least important; nothing takes place without Him. The heathen and the infidels call to man for help. But as for you, call upon God, and He will send you him who will make you healthy again—whether he be a saint, a physician, or He Himself.

1/1, 229

Sad would be the condition of a jurist who did not know the emperor's power, will, and laws; and how sad the condition of a Christian desirous of being Christian, who did not know the Christian articles of faith. Such Christians would be worthless good-for-nothings. Take, for example, a bird; how could it fly if it did not have its wings and feathers? How could anyone be a physician . . . if he were not properly equipped for it? The Holy Scriptures say that faith without works is dead—is then not mere reputation without works dead? Is then not the physician without medicine dead? There must always be two sides to each thing, dependent on and bound to each other; for so did God ordain; both faith and works . . . physician and medicine, master and mastery. Neither can stand alone. The two must always be together. Therefore it is said: Woe to him who is alone! For if he falls, no one is there to raise him!

I/11, 120

Only he who has no fear of God's works is wise. In him who fears medicine there lives knowledge neither of God nor of medicine. For where the wisdom given by God is lacking, in that place He who gives it is absent too. Therefore, if you want to become a physician, seek out medicine at its fountainhead. . . . Study all the books that exist on that subject! That which is in agreement with the light of nature has force and durability. But that which is in disagreement with it is like a labyrinth that has neither sure entrance nor exit.

I/11, 269–70

It is the physician who reveals to us the diverse miraculous works of God. And having revealed them he must use them in the right way, not in the wrong way; in the true, not in the false way. What is in the sea that he should not bring to the light of day? Nothing. He should make it manifest; and not only what is in the sea, but also what is in the earth, in the air, in the firmament . . . so that many people may be able to see the works of God and recognize how they can be used to cure disease. But if they are not brought to light, it is a sign that the intelligence capable of discovering them is still lacking. For what reason is the physician's calling practised with so much stupidity and so little art, although he fancies himself so important and so superior? And how is it that blindness and shortsightedness prevail in many other trades? For physicians do not know the constellation of the Whale—the monster of the sea—and similarly in the other disciplines it is not known what the apocalyptic beast is, and what is Babylon: everywhere the same blindness prevails. . . . This blindness is the death of the soul, just as the physician's blindness can be the death of his patient. Christ says curious things in marvellous language.

Fig. 38. Cranial Operation

Medical science too is full of mysteries, and must be studied like the words of Christ. These two callings—the promulgation of the word of God and the healing of the sick—must not be separated from each other. Since the body is the dwelling place of the soul, the two are connected and the one must open access to the other.

I/9, 70

There are two kinds of physician—those who work for love, and those who work for their own profit. They are both known by their works; the true and just physician is known by his love and by his unfailing love for his neighbour. The unjust physicians are known by their transgressions against the commandment; for they reap, although they have not sown, and they are like ravening wolves; they reap because they want to reap, in order to increase their profit, and they

I/11, 147

are heedless of the commandment of love.

So great is the ill-will among physicians that each denies honour and praise to the other; they would rather harm a patient and even kill him than grant a colleague his meed of praise. From this, everyone can judge why a man has become a physician: not out of love for the patient, which should be the physician's first virtue, but for the sake of money. Where money is the goal, envy and hatred, pride and conceit, are sure to appear—and may God protect and preserve us all from such temptations!

God gave to the herbs power and virtue to free man from his infirmity, to the end that he might not too soon be conquered by death, but sojourn a little longer in this world, from which death has power to snatch him. For just as the herb and the remedy hidden in it were created before man, so God's mercy preceded his sternness. In the very beginning He sent death to man, but He

1/10, 279

Fig. 39. The Physician

also gave him His mercy and medicine, whereby to protect his life span against the wrath of death up until the last minute. . . . Therefore the Scriptures say that God created the physician and endowed him with his mercy that he might help his fellow men. And He created the remedies of the earth, that is to say, He breathed His mercy into the herbs by means of which the physician can help the patient. . . . The wise man who recognizes God's mercy will not scorn it, but willingly accept it. For all hope is directed toward God's

1/9, 602

mercy.

Man's frivolity is the cause of much disappointment, and we have no right to accuse anyone but ourselves. No one wants to learn his trade to perfection; everyone wants to fly before he has grown wings. The disappointment occurs when man does not know his trade. The frivolity inherent in man is to undertake a piece of work, in the knowledge that he is unequal to it. . . . Medicine is an art that should be applied only with great assiduity, great experience, and great fear of God. For he who does not fear God steals and

1/11, 150–51

murders for ever and ever.

The difference between a physician and the rest of men is this, that the others need think only of themselves, while the physician must care not only for himself but also for others. His office consists of nothing but compassion for others. But his compassion does not originate in him any more than the efficacy of the remedy emanates from him. And because there is nothing that comes from him—although he accomplishes it as though it were his work—his office is not to murder and injure, to strangle and cripple, but to cure the patient by the charity and love with which God has endowed man. A physician is uncharitable if he does not understand the nature of his office here below and does not live up to the responsibilities of his office. What is the meaning of an office to which one is appointed by God, if not to

1/8, 264–65

carry out and fulfil the will of God?

To teach and do nothing is little. To teach and do, that is great and whole. . . . A stonecutter who teaches his apprentices with his hands rather than with his tongue teaches and acts at the same time, and it is impossible for him to teach what he himself cannot also do. If he tried to teach what his hands cannot accomplish, nothing good would come out of it, nothing but uncertainties and failures. And if it is important to know how the stonecutter sets stone upon

1/7, 76

stone, how much truer this is of the physician's calling!

When Christ spoke and taught, his words were always accompanied by deeds. It should be the same in medicine. Those who spend their time in idle chatter and disputes and do no work speak vain words, for which they will be held to account. . . . Words and deeds should be wedded to each other. A theoretician of theology may talk about God and put the works aside, but a physician has no right to act thus; like a saint, he must prove himself by words and deeds. He whose words are efficacious is a saint. Simi-

Fig. 40. Operating on a Cataract

larly, only he whose remedies are efficacious is a physician. . . . There should be nothing in medicine except what results from both word and deed, because medicine is a true art, and truth lies only in the deed and not in idle talk. . . . Therefore study and learn that words and deeds are but one thing; if you fail to understand this, you are not a physician. *I/10, 281–82*

If an unbeliever becomes a physician, he will not strive for the kingdom of God any more than before he became a physician; it will thus be manifest that without God no proper work can be done. The spirit bloweth where it listeth, it is subject to no one, it is endowed with free will. Therefore the physician must rest his foundations on the spirit, for without it he is nothing but a pseudo-physician, deluded and lost in error. If he wants to attain the truth of his art, he must follow the path of God. If he does not, he may study forever, yet he will not attain to the truth. *I/11, 173*

Fig. 41. The Physician at the Sick-Bed

The art of medicine is rooted in the heart. If your heart is false, you will also be a false physician; if your heart is just, you will also be a true physician.

1/8, 266

No one requires greater love of the heart than the physician. For him the ultimate instance is man's distress. Privilege and lineage pale to nothingness, only distress has meaning.

1/8, 322

The physician should be pure and chaste, that is to say, a whole man in the sense that his mind is free from lewdness, conceit, and any evil thought. For all physicians who stand on evil ground produce lying works and fraudulent achieve-

72

ments; everything about them is false. They fatten on lies. But this is no proper soil for the medical art, which may rest only upon truth. Only what flows from the truth is pure and chaste, and only such fruits are of permanent value as are pure and chaste, and bear no stain of conceit, envy, lechery, lewdness, overweening pride, pomp, splendour, vanity, self-praise.

I/8, 210

Every disease has its own remedy. . . . God has ordained that we should love our neighbour as ourselves and Him above all else. Now, if you would love God, you must also love His works; if you would love your neighbour, you must not say, You cannot be helped. You must admit that you cannot do it and that you do not understand his illness. Only such truthfulness can free you from the curse that is decreed against those who are false. Therefore take good care . . . to continue your studies until you discover the art which is the foundation of good works.

I/11, 129–30

In medicine we should never lose heart, and never despair. For each ill there is a remedy that combats it. Thus there is no disease that is inevitably mortal. All diseases can be cured, without exception. Only because we do not know how to deal with them properly, because we are unable to understand life and death in their essence, can we not defend ourselves against them.

I/2, 430

Therapeutics is the noblest pearl and the supreme treasure, and it holds first place in medicine; and there is nothing on earth that can be valued more highly than the curing of the sick. . . . It is a commandment of God that you shall love Him, this is the supreme good, and there is nothing that man may prize above it. The next commandment says thou shalt love thy neighbour as thyself, and it follows immediately upon the first. Now by what manner on earth can greater love be shown a neighbour, than when a man motivated by true love discovers the curative virtues of remedies, in order to avert the great sufferings, the diseases, and the death that threatens his neighbour?

I/10, 350

A man without a woman is not whole, only with a woman

is he whole. Because woman was created from earth and he too is of earth, both are of earth and form together one whole. . . . Similarly, man and remedy derive from the same substance, and both together form a whole, that is to say, a whole man. . . . In this sense, the disease desires its wife, that is, the medicine. The medicine must be adjusted to the disease, both must be united to form a harmonious whole, just as in the case of man and woman. If the physician *1/1, 362–63* finds such a remedy, he is complete.

The physician must take good care of his hand . . . for in it he possesses the noblest and most precious object, most prized by the Creator. But if he does not know the world, nor the elements or the firmament, how should he discover the nature of man, who is everything that is in heaven and on earth, indeed, who is himself heaven and earth, air and water? God who created all things also created both worlds *1/9, 220* and to both He gave their remedies and their physicians.

Fig. 42. Blood-Letting

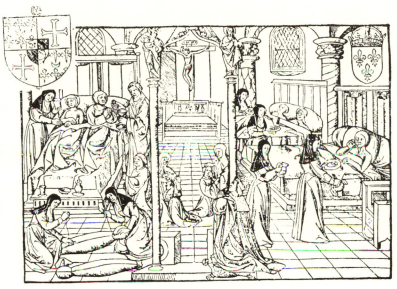

Fig. 43. Hospital

That which injures the body destroys
the house of the Everlasting.   *1/9, 257*

There are two realms into which diseases can penetrate
and spread. The first is that of matter, that is to say, the
body; it is here that all diseases lurk and dwell . . . the
other realm is not material, it is the spirit of the body, which
lives in it intangible and invisible, and which can suffer from
exactly the same diseases as the body. But because the body
has no share in this life, it is the *ens spirituale*, the spiritual
active principle, from which the disease springs. . . . Therefore there are two kinds of disease: the spiritual and the material.   *1/1, 216–17*

The *entia*, the active principles or influences, which govern our bodies and do violence to them are the following.
The stars have a force and efficacy that has power over our
body, so that it must always be ready to serve them. . . .

This virtue of the stars is called *ens astrorum*, and it is the first *ens* to which we are subjected. The second power that governs us and that inflicts diseases upon us is *ens veneni*, the influence of poison. Even if the stars are sound and have done no injury to the subtle body in us, this *ens* can destroy us; therein we are subject to it and cannot defend ourselves against it. The third *ens* is a power that injures and weakens our body even when the two other influences are beneficent; it is called *ens naturale*, the natural constitution. If it goes astray or disintegrates, our body becomes sick. From this many other diseases, indeed all diseases, can arise, even if the other *entia* are sound. The fourth *ens*, the *ens spirituale* —the spiritual entity—can destroy our bodies and bring various diseases upon us. And even if all four *entia* are propitious to us and are sound, yet the fifth *ens*, the *ens Dei*, can make our bodies sick. Therefore none of the *entia* deserves as much attention as this last one; for by it one can recognize the nature of all other diseases. . . . Note moreover that the various diseases do not come from one cause, but *I/1, 173–74* from five.

Even while still in the womb, unborn, man is burdened with the potentialities of every disease, and is subject to them. And because all diseases are inherent in his nature, he could not be born alive and healthy if an inner physician were not hidden in him. But wherever diseases are, there are also physicians and medicine! Each natural disease bears its own remedy within itself. Man has received from nature both the destroyer of health and the preserver of health. And just as the destroyer strives continuously to destroy and to kill man, so the preserver works with equal vigour and zeal to preserve him; what the first strives to shatter and destroy, the innate physician repairs. The destroyer finds in the body the instruments that help him in his destructive work. . . . Just as in the outside world a mason can wreck and has tools for this purpose, just as another mason has tools for building, so both—the destroyer and the preserver—have tools for wrecking and tools for building. . . . The body possesses the high art of wrecking and also of restoring.   *1/11, 196–97*

Who can protect himself from harm and disaster if he does not know his enemy? No one. Hence it is indispensable to know him. For there are enemies of many kinds, and it is necessary to know the evil as well as the good. Who can know what joy is, if he has never been sad or in pain? And who can properly discover what God is if he knows nothing of the devil? Just as God reveals to us the enemy of our soul, namely, the devil, so He also reveals to us the enemy of our

Capita.   Cerebra.   Oculi.   Pedes cum Tibijs.   Corda.   Vbera.   Testiculi.

Fig. 44. Organs and Parts of the Body

life, namely, death. And furthermore, He reveals to us the enemy of our body, the enemy of our health, the enemy of medicine, and the enemy of all natural things. But at the same time He reveals to us by what means this enemy can be disarmed. For there is no sickness against which some remedy has not been created and established, to drive it out and cure it. There is always some remedy, a herb against one disease, a root against another, a water against one, a stone against another, a mineral against one, a poison against another, a metal against one, something else against another.   *1/11, 323*

The nature and force of a disease must be discovered by their cause and not by their symptoms . . . for we must not merely extinguish the smoke of the fire but the fire itself. If we want the earth to produce better grass, we must plow it, and not merely tear out the bad grass. Similarly the physician . . . should direct his thought to the origin of the disease, and not only to that which his eyes see. For in this he would see but the symptoms and not the origin; similarly

I/10, 274

smoke is only the symptom of the fire, not the fire itself.

God alone preserves the body in life; He wants us to have a long life, and therefore provides us with many kinds of help and support. He even forces and compels our enemies to strengthen our life. God help us to gain salvation and good fortune from our enemies and those who hate us . . . whencesoever comes our help, it is always from God. . . . Behold the thistle amidst its thorns! It hates us so much that the thorns forbid us to touch the flower. And if we touch it, they prick us strongly and refuse us admission, to prevent us from obtaining the medicine that lies hidden in it. . . . But who for that reason would reproach the thistle which is otherwise so beneficent to us? Even though it hates our bodies, it must help them recover health. . . . And even if the devil himself told us that silver and gold bring us salvation and medicine, or have power to free us from prisons and dungeons, even this would be in fulfilment of God's com-

I/9, 329–31

mand.

There where diseases arise, there also can one find the roots of health. For health must grow from the same root as disease, and whither health goes, thither also disease must

I/9, 226

go.

Just as the sun and the moon are separated from each other, although they formerly were one thing, so health and disease were one thing, and later they were separated from each other, as the sun was from the moon. And just as these wane and wax in the sphere of heaven, and now one or the other appears, so also are all the stars woven into the body—this you should know—and similarly distributed, and the same is true of the forms in which health and disease are manifested. For all of them must be present in the body in order that the "inner firmament" may be whole and that the

I/7, 289

number of the parts may be full.

It is well known and evident that in the course of time heaven brings many diseases . . . and that no healthy person can protect itself from them. A healthy man must submit to heaven and every day he must await what it sends

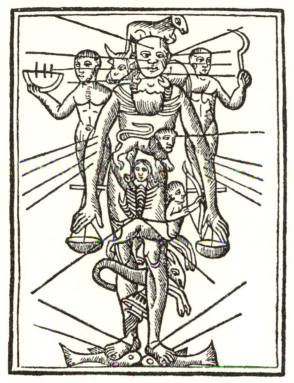

Fig. 45. Blood-Letting Chart

him. For the course of the heavens is wonderful, and just
as wonderfully are men placed in nature.   *I/10, 48*

Just as time can bring rain, roses, flowers, and shape all
things from their beginnings to their end, and no one can stop
it, so can it also make diseases break out at will. The physician must never forget that time can do this, or he will be
unable to discover what is possible and what is impossible,
and to understand what he can nevertheless undertake to
inspire people with respect for the medical art that God has
created, and to prevent the disease from getting worse, for
this cannot be the intention of God. Time is a brisk wind,
for each hour it brings something new. Just as the people's
thoughts change every hour, and are different twelve times
a day, and no one knows them except God alone, so is it

79

Fig. 46. Disease as a Scourge of God

with time. Again and again it brings something new, but who can understand and measure its sharp breath, its mystery and its design? Therefore the physician must not think himself too important; for over him there is a master—time —which plays with him as the cat with the mouse. *I/4, 495–96*

Health and sickness are granted by God; nothing comes from man. . . . You should divide the diseases of men . . . into those which arise in a natural way, and those which come upon us as God's scourges. For take good note of it: God has sent us some diseases as a punishment, as a warning, as a sign by which we know that all our affairs are naught, that our knowledge rests upon no firm foundation, and that the truth is not known to us, but that we are inadequate and fragmentary in all ways, and that no ability or knowledge is ours. *I/1, 226*

Because it is God who has given us disease, He could, when the time were proper and the limit of our purgatory had come, take it away from us, even without the physician. If He fails to do so, it is only because He does not want this to be accomplished without the help of man. If He works a miracle, He does it only in the human way and through man; if He makes us healthy by a miracle, He does it through a man. *I/1, 228*

Every disease is a kind of purgatory. The physician should know this and bear it in mind, lest he presume to determine in advance the time of recovery or the efficacy of his remedies; for this lies solely in God's hands. If Providence has decided otherwise than you physicians intend, you will not be able to cure the patient by any remedy. But if the hour of Providence has struck, you will succeed in curing him. Note that if a patient comes to you and recovers through your remedy, God has sent him to you; but if he does not recover, he was not sent by God. Only when the hour of recovery strikes for the patient, does God send him to the physician, not before. All those who go to Him before go in vain. . . . God has created remedies against the diseases, and He has also created the physician; but He holds them back until the hour predestined for the patient. Only when the time has been fulfilled, and not before, does the course of nature and art set in.

I/1, 227

Often the remedy is deemed the highest good because it helps so many. But is not He who created it for the sake of the sick body more than the remedy? And is not He who cures the soul, which is more than the body, greater? Here then lies the supreme good; it is more than that which takes the disease away from the body and preserves the body.

II/1, 113–14

Man and all creatures here on earth are subject to God: it is He who decrees fortune and misfortune for them. And to the end that you may well understand this, take good note that there are two kinds of chastisement administered by God: the first He sends you in your lifetime, the other after death.

I/1, 229

God is the master who measures the disease and the stars. He has ordered everything according to His wisdom; who can fathom it?

II/1, 225

The patient who pins his hope on the medicament is not a Christian; but he who puts his hope in God is a Christian.

I/1, 229

Fig. 47. Lungs, Heart, and
Diaphragm

Fig. 48. The Apothecary

No disease is so great that God has
not created a remedy against it. . . .   *1/8, 269*

The difference between the two medical arts—the heavenly and the worldly—consists in this: the adepts and nonadepts of worldly medicine are subject to the order and forces of nature, while those of heavenly medicine can dispense with herbs and the stars. . . . All active virtues come from the word of God, and His words have such power that all nature with its forces cannot accomplish as much as a single one of His words. This divine power is the heavenly medicine; it accomplishes what no natural force can accomplish. . . . There is no field on earth in which heavenly medicine grows or lies hidden, other than the resurrected flesh or the "new body" of man; only in the "new body" have all its words force and efficacy here on earth. This heavenly medicine works according to the will of the man of the "new birth"; in him lie all the active virtues. For it does not operate in the mortal body, but only in the eternal body.

1/12, 348–49

What sense would it make or what would it benefit a physician if he discovered the origin of the diseases but could not cure or alleviate them? And since the fit manner of preparation is not to be found in pharmaceutics, we must explore further; that is to say, we must learn from alchemy. In it we find the true cause and everything that is needed. Although alchemy has now fallen into contempt and is even considered a thing of the past, the physician should not be influenced by such judgments. For many arts, such as astronomy, philosophy, and others, are also in disrepute. I am directing you, physicians, to alchemy for the preparation of the *magnalia,* for the production of the *mysteria,* for the preparation of the *arcana,* for the separation of the pure from the impure, to the end that you may obtain a flawless, pure remedy, God-given, perfect, and of certain efficacy, achieving the highest degree of virtue and power. For it is not God's design that the remedies should exist for us ready-made, boiled, and salted, but that we should boil them ourselves, and it pleases Him that we boil them and learn in the process, that we train ourselves in this art and are not idle on earth, but labour in daily toil. For it is we who must pray for our daily bread, and if He grants it to us, it is only through our labour, our skill and preparation.

1/10, 277

The first and highest book of medicine is called *Sapientia.* Without this book no one will achieve anything fruitful. . . . For this book is God himself. In Him who has created all things lies also wisdom, and only He knows the primal cause of all things. . . . Without Him everything is mere foolishness. . . . For what is wisdom but the ability to recognize and know our talents and our calling? But we cannot do this by ourselves, no more than we have power over day and night, summer and winter. . . . Although the remedy is given by nature . . . it must be revealed to us by the all-highest book, so that we may learn what is in it, how it is made, how it is obtained from the earth, and how and to what patients it should administered. . . . The remedy must flow from the spirit that dwells in man . . . therefore the first teaching is—and every inquiry must begin with it—that we should above all seek the kingdom of God. There lies the treasure, the school that leads to the primal causes of wisdom within each man's sphere of action. . . . For what is there more noble than that we should pray and implore God's grace? . . . No one, then, should be surprised if I say that God is the first book; and who can recognize a work better than he who has accomplished it? He alone can state and show its virtues. And who else has created the remedy but God? It flows from Him as warmth flows from the sun, which also makes the flowers grow. No differently should our wisdom flow from God. What has ever been discovered in the wide world that has not come to us from God? He holds everything in His hand, and we should accept it from Him.

The second book of medicine—of this too you must take note!—is the firmament. But this book must be studied after the first. . . . For it is possible to write down all medicine in the letters of one book, to the end that everyone may learn it by reading the book, and the firmament is such a book containing all the virtues and propositions . . . and he who has not penetrated into this book cannot be a physician or be called a physician. Just as a man reads a book on paper, so the physician is compelled to spell out the stars of the firmament in order to know his conclusions. For just as every word has special virtues but does not embody the whole sentence, and acquires its complete meaning only when it is supplemented by other words and the sentence is rounded into a whole, so the stars in heaven must be taken together in order that we may read the sentence in the firmament. . . . It is like a letter which has been sent to us from a hundred miles off, and in which the writer's mind speaks to us; as though in such a letter, the firmament speaks to us. . . . This is the way to study medicine, this is the book of the highest school of medicine.

I/11, 171–76

The book of medicine is nature itself. And just as you see yourself in a mirror, so you must rediscover all your sciences in nature, with exactly the same certainty and with as little illusion as when you see yourself in a mirror.

I/1, 354–55

Marvellous virtues are inherent in the remedies. One would hardly believe that nature contained such virtues. . . . For only a great artist is able to discover them, not one who is only versed in books, but only one who has acquired his ability and skill through the experience of his hands.

. . . It is an important art, and therefore it cannot be clearly described, but can only be learned by experience. . . . These remedies must not be known merely as physics, they must be termed arcana, occult healing substances. They have such noble and lofty advantages and operate in so

Fig. 49. Male Herb and Female Herb

marvellous a manner that only with difficulty can our minds conceive and know from what properties and virtues their efficacy is derived.

I/2, 430

Why is the world made in such a way that one herb is female and another male? The reason for this is that the diseases too are different. If they were all identical, why should nature have divided the remedies into these two species? But because there exist two worlds, the world of woman and the world of man, there are also two kinds of remedies. And just as man and woman are different in their infirmities, so their remedies differ.

I/9, 182

Just as flowers grow from the earth, so the remedy grows in the hands of the physician. If he is a good physician, the remedy is like a root which grows a stem, which in turn unfolds into a flower, and which in the end becomes a fruit. For the physician's art is like the earth, which also conceals such potentialities in itself. . . . In the winter, no herb nor any flower grows in your garden; everything remains hidden in the earth, and you do not see and do not know what lies in it. Nevertheless you are sure that herbs, flowers, and all kinds of plants lie in it, although you cannot see them. It is no different with the remedy you hold in your hands. At first you do not see what it contains, but you know with certainty that something is in it, like a seed that is different from the fruit that grows out of it. The earth makes the seed ripen into a fruit. And if the seed did not bear fruit, it would be worthless. Similarly, the remedy is nothing but a seed which you must develop into that which it is destined to be.

I/7, 265

If the physician is to understand the correct meaning of health, he must know that there are more than a hundred, indeed more than a thousand, kinds of stomach; consequently, if you gather a thousand persons, each of them will have a different kind of digestion, each unlike the others. One digests more, the other less, and yet each stomach is suitable to the man it belongs to. . . . Therefore the various dietary prescriptions should be observed not only for the sake of recovery from illness but also for the sake of preserving one's health. There are a hundred forms of health in the liver; each man has a different one. It follows that no one drinks the same amount as another, that no one has the same thirst as another; this is explained by the diverse kinds of health, which must not be described as illnesses. . . . A man who lifts fifty pounds may be just as able-bodied as a man who can lift three hundred pounds.

I/6, 154

A man should be awake from about four in the morning until about eight in the evening, and then he should sleep. This time between eight and four—it may be somewhat

shorter or longer according to the particular disposition—
is needed for sleep. If a man does not observe this rule, if he
is not awake at about four o'clock but for instance only at
about ten, and stays awake all night instead, the order of
nature is violated. For the sun wants everything to be awake
and wants man, too, to be awake while it gives its warmth.
But when it sets, man should lie down and rise again with
the sun, and lie down again to rest with it, and so on. All

Hyems.   Septētrio. Meridies,   Oriens. Occidens. Aërepidimitus,   Tyriaca.

Fig. 50. Winter Medicine

prescriptions concerning sleeping and waking hours should
be based on this order. If they are not observed unknown illnesses break upon us.

If we would obey nature in its essence, all things must
stand in their order, according to number, weight, measure,
and revolution; the measure must nowhere be exceeded.
. . . Two unequal weights on the scales of nature break
its balance; either one is too heavy or the other too light, or
the scales are worthless. To fill your belly all week long, but
to abstain from all food except bread and water on Fridays
and Saturdays, or to take your fill of meat throughout the
year, and not touch anything during Lent, is to put unequal
weights on the scales of nature. And this is true not only of
eating, but also of work and leisure and everything else.

Purgatio.   Conftipatio.   Coitus.   Sperma.   Mundificatiuâ.   Ebrietas.   Foca.

Fig. 51. Human Circumstances

. . . Therefore the physician should know that he must distribute, prescribe, and weigh all things in such a way that nature should not be burdened too much on one side and too little on the other.

I/4, 534–36

When ordering a diet, the physician should consider not only the age or youth of the patient, but also the customs, peculiarities, and nature of his country; the patient's diet should be established accordingly. For the nature and customs of the country should be followed and not transgressed, and the physician should keep in mind what food and what drink this nature requires in each case, and how much and how often it wants food; and the seasons of the year should

| Balneū aquæ frigi dæ, & Cameræ. | Aqua dele ctabilis. | Aqua calida. | Aqua frigida. | Aqua in balneis frigi. bibita. | Philothriū. |

Fig. 52. Bathers

also be taken into account. For the summer diet is not fitting in the winter, nor the winter diet in summer. Each diet has its own time, and corresponds to the customs and habits of that season.

I/4, 521

Remedies should not be administered according to their weight, but according to other measurements. Who can weigh the brilliance of the sun, who can weigh air or the *spiritum arcanum?* No one. . . . The remedy should operate in the body like a fire . . . and its effect on the disease should be as violent as that of fire on a pile of wood. This mystery of fire should also apply to what you call dosage. How would it be possible to weigh the amount of fire needed to consume a pile of wood or a house? No, fire cannot be weighed! However, you know that one little spark is heavy enough to set a forest on fire, a little spark that has no weight at all. . . . Just as the spark acts on the wood, and becomes great or small according to the amount of it, so you must act when dealing with remedies. You must administer them to the patient in accordance with the extent of the illness. But who would indicate a definite weight for

1/7, 300–301 this? No one!

Just as gold is of little use if it has not gone through fire, so there is little virtue or use in a remedy that has not been

Auripigmentū.　　Inunctio olei.　　Fricatio.　　Bilinalua. Veſtis linea. Veſtis ſerica. Oleū uiol.

Fig. 53. Prescriptions for Bathing

purified in fire. For all things must go through fire in order

1/8, 198 to attain to a new birth, in which they are useful to man.

The art of prescribing medicine lies in nature, which compounds them herself. If she has put into gold what belongs to gold, she has done likewise with violets. . . . Therefore understand me correctly: the virtue that is inherent in each thing is homogeneous and simple, it is not split into two, three, four, or five, but is an undivided whole. . . . The art of prescribing medicines consists in extracting and not in compounding, it consists in the discovery of that which is concealed in things, and not in compounding various things and piecing them together. What trousers are the best? Whole ones. Those which are mended and patched are the worst. . . . Nature conferred potency upon the arcana and composed them in the proper way. Therefore learn in such a way as to understand and know them, and not in such a

Triticum.　Aqua hordei.　Sauich hordei.　Hordeum.　Sauich Tritici.　Amylum.　Frumentum.

Fig. 54. Various Grains

way as to understand yourself in the end but not nature. Nature is the physician, not you. From her you must learn, not from yourself; she compounds the remedies, not you. See to it that you find out where nature has her pharmacies, where her virtues have been written down, and in what boxes they are stored.   *I/8, 84–85*

Everything external in nature points to something internal; for nature is both inside man and outside man. An example. . . . Herbs are gathered together in an apothecary's shop and can be bought there, and in one shop more numerous and varied herbs can be found than in another; similarly there is in the world a natural order of apothecary's shops, for all the fields and meadows, all the mountains and hills are such shops. Nature has given us all of them, from which to fill our own shops. All nature is like one single apothecary's shop, covered only with the roof of heaven; and only One Being works the pestle as far as the world extends. But man has such a shop only in part, not wholly; he possesses something, not everything. For nature's apothecary's shop is greater than man's.   *I/11, 195*

A good remedy was worth as much a thousand years ago as it is now, and a bad remedy was then as worthless as it is now. For although it is as old as the good one, and has come down to us in the same way, it is no better for that reason. . . . The tares among the corn are as old as the corn, nevertheless, they cannot be used instead of the corn. In my opinion, the world should awaken to this fact, and because the good surpasses the bad in worth, we should abandon the bad, and should not be reluctant or complacent when we are confronted with the task of rejecting the bad.   *I/10, 59*

Although our forefathers, if they were reborn, would have been surprised and taken aback by our remedies, this should

1/1, 173

be our least concern. However, we do not reject their remedies, but are careful to preserve what is good in them.

We have experience, but it is not complete; we know that the curative herbs of nature have a cooling effect, but we do not know when they can also be warming. We know that one day they are efficacious and another day not, that they help one man and not another, that they are sometimes use-

ful and sometimes not. Sometimes we despair, and then they help; and many a time when we place hopes in them, they leave us in the lurch; often when we think that something is sure, it is futile, but often it actually is sure; for we do not have them in our power. And what we do not have in our power can at any time deceive us.

1/4, 540

All the remedies are on earth, but we lack the men to gather them. They are ready

Fig. 55. Physician and Apothecary

to be harvested, but the reapers have not come. But one day the reapers of the right remedies shall come, and undeterred by empty sophistry we will cleanse the lepers and make the blind seeing. For this virtue is concealed in the earth, and it grows everywhere. But the presumption of the sophists prevents the mysteries of nature and their great miracles from

1/9, 78

coming to light.

Nature is so careful and exact in her creations that they cannot be used without great skill; for she does not produce anything that is perfect in itself. Man must bring everything to perfection. This work of bringing things to their perfection is called "alchemy." And he is an alchemist who carries what nature grows for the use of man to its destined end. But within this art distinctions must again be made: if someone takes a sheepskin and uses it untanned as a coat, how crude and clumsy it is in comparison with the work of a furrier or clothmaker! If a man fails to perfect a thing that nature has given him, he is guilty of even greater crudeness and clumsiness, especially when man's health, body, and life are at stake. For this reason more diligence should be spent on alchemy, in order to obtain still greater results. Artisans have explored nature and its properties in order to learn to imitate her in all things, and to bring out the highest that is in her. Only in medicine has this been neglected, and therefore it has remained the crudest and clumsiest of all the arts.

I/8, 180

God created iron but not that which is to be made of it. . . . He enjoined fire, and Vulcan, who is the lord of fire, to do the rest. . . . From this it follows that iron must be cleansed of its dross before it can be forged. This process is alchemy; its founder is the smith Vulcan. What is accomplished by fire is alchemy—whether in the furnace or in the kitchen stove. And he who governs fire is Vulcan, even if he be a cook or a man who tends the stove. The same is true of medicine. It too was created by God, but not in its finished state, but still concealed in dross. To release the remedy from the dross is the task of Vulcan. And what is true of iron is true of the remedy. What the eyes perceive in herbs or stones or trees is not yet a remedy; the eyes see only the dross. But inside, under the dross, there the remedy lies hidden. First it must be cleansed from the dross, then it is there. This is alchemy, and this is the office of Vulcan; he is the apothecary and chemist of the medicine.

I/11, 186–88

God enjoined the physician to fight against the transience

of things. This transience also characterizes the Great World in which God himself practises medicine. The physician, by following the instructions of the Great Physician, must act against accidents that befall things. For the Great Physician created the ore but did not carry it to its perfect state; He has charged the miners with the task of refining it. In the same way He enjoined the physician to purify man's body . . . from which purification man emerges as indestructible as gold. . . . This is an action which—like that performed by fire on gold—frees man from the impurities that he himself does not know. And it is like such fire that the medicine should act.

Fig. 56. Physician with Urine Flask

1/7, 273

Quicksilver manifests itself in three forms. In the first it is still unborn; in the second it is as it is in itself; in the third it appears such as it has been prepared by the alchemist's art. As for the first, you should know that you must take it with the ore . . . and refine it, according to the rules. As for the second, its body must be separated from the ore and purified by fire. It achieves its third form when it has gone through fire and is like a molten metal. Upon these three forms of manifestation of *mercurius*, or quicksilver, is based the cure of the French disease.

1/7, 113

The practice of medicine is a work of art. And because it is a work of art it must prove its master. But how each part

Fig. 57. Broadside on
Syphilis

is to be judged can be seen only from the work as a whole. It is the art that imparts its wisdom to the work. For through this wisdom the art creates the work. *I/11, 128*

Is not a mystery of nature concealed even in poison? . . . What has God created that He did not bless with some great gift for the benefit of man? Why then should poison be rejected and despised, if we consider not the poison but its curative virtue? . . . And who has composed the prescriptions of nature? Was it not God? . . . In His hand there abides all wisdom, and He alone knows what He put into each *mysterium*. Why then should I be surprised and why should I let myself be frightened? Should I, because one part of a remedy contains poison, also include the other part in my contempt? Each thing should be used for its proper purpose, and we should use it without fear, for God Himself is the true physician and the true medicine. . . . He who despises poison does not know what is hidden in it; for the arcanum that is contained in the poison is so blessed that the poison can neither detract from it nor harm it. *I/11, 136–37*

In all things there is a poison, and there is nothing without a poison. It depends only upon the dose whether a poison is poison or not. . . . I separate that which does not belong to the arcanum from that which is effective as the arcanum, and I prescribe it in the right dose . . . then the recipe is correctly made. . . . That which redounds to the benefit of man is not poison; only that which is not of service to him, but which injures him, is poison.

When a medicine is found in accordance with the star, when hot is applied against hot, and cold against cold, all this accords with the arcanum. For in administering medicine we must always set entity against entity, so that each becomes in a sense the wife or husband of the other.

Every cure should proceed from the power of the heart; for only thereby can all diseases be expelled. Therefore, and take good note of this, it is particularly absurd to act in opposition to the heart. The heart wants to dispel the diseases, then why do you drive them toward the heart? . . . After all, the curative power must come from the heart, and the disease must be driven into the remotest corner. . . . Every medicine should act outward from the heart, and not in the direction of the heart. It starts from the heart and is made to work by the heart's own power.

Blessed and thrice blessed is the physician who recognizes the medicines in their living action, who knows how to obtain them, and who knows that they are not dead. For there are many medicines in the world which have already died, and others die continually. Therefore the physician is right to complain and speak of it. For heaven renews itself, new times come, and the time of certain plants is gone. Each new time brings death in its train, the death of the past. But heaven will renew that which is to serve the future. Thus, new virtues will one day flow into the occult remedies of medicine.

A physician should know how to judge the age of people, as well as the age of illnesses and medicines, and the age of the world. For today it is easier to cure than it was a thousand years ago. And two thousand years ago it was more difficult, and still more difficult three thousand years ago. The farther back we go in time, the more difficult was the task.

I/11, 138–41

I/8, 107

I/7, 241–43

I/4, 448

Therefore one should never neglect to take age into account, whether it be the age of time, of the world, of the man, or of the disease. *1/4, 502*

Medicine is an art that will survive until the Last Judgment. And even if all physicians died out, medicine would abide eternally, and new physicians would arise continually. Consider that there is Someone who instructs them always anew. He who has created the art of medicine also deserves praise for having created the physician. *1/7, 93*

Fig. 58

III

MAN AND WORKS

Fig. 59. Alchemistic Oven

Believe in the works, not in the words;
words are an empty shell, but the
works show you the master.   I/8, 89

WHAT man can give an account of or explain how he learned to till the soil, to raise vines, or to make cheese? No one unless he can point to his teacher, and the teacher will in turn point to his teacher, and so on and on, until we come to the first teacher. And to whom can he point? To no one except to Him who created man; for He also gave him his knowledge. What would men do if they had not been ordained to work? The commandment was: "In the sweat of thy face shalt thou eat bread.". . . God said: "Let it be!" And there was everything, but not "art," nor the light of nature. But when Adam was driven out of Paradise, God created the light of nature for him by ordering him to gain sustenance through the toil of his

101

Fig. 60. Adam and Eve Driven from Paradise

hands, and He also created the light of Eve when He said: "In sorrow thou shalt bring forth children." Thus the creatures that had hitherto been like unto angels became earthly and mortal. And Eve was taught to raise her children, and thus cradles and nursing came into being. The word was sufficient to create man; it was also sufficient to create the light that man needed . . . when he was driven out of Paradise. For only then did "the inner man," "the man of the second creation," come into being.

We received all the members of our body at the first crea-

I/8, 290–92

102

tion, after all other things had been created. But the knowledge that man needs was not yet in Adam but was given him only when he was expelled from Paradise. Then he received "knowledge" through the angel; but not all knowledge. For he and his children must learn one thing after another in the light of nature, in order to bring to light that which lies hidden in all things. For although man was created whole as regards his body, he was not so created as regards his "art." All the arts have been given him, but not in an immediately recognizable form; he must discover them by learning. . . . Just as the herbs in the garden must be sown and planted, and do not grow unless this has been done, whatever we sow is but earth, as it were, that we give to the earth and again extract from it. The same is true of the "art" that is engraved and planted in us. He who taught it to me received it from the light of nature, and I have received it just as he has; it must be engraved in all of us. Yet it happens that many herbs grow without having been sown, and these are often the best. There are also many important species that are better than those that are sown. Such is the power of the earth, and such is the light of nature; they do not rest. Therefore, give heed to your inner garden . . . and also to yourself that you may learn that which no one can teach you, and which will amaze everyone.

I/8, 290–92

Man should study in three schools. . . . He should send the elemental or material body to the elemental school, the sidereal or ethereal body to the sidereal school, and the eternal or luminous body to the school of eternity. For three lights burn in man, and accordingly three doctrines are prescribed to him. Only all three together make man perfect. Although the first two lights shine but dimly in comparison with the brilliant third light, they too are lights of the world, and man must walk his earthly path in their radiance.

I/12, 197–98

Fig. 61. Lecture

Everything that man does and has to do, he should do by the light of nature. For the light of nature is nothing other than reason itself.

1/1, 306

Only he is the enemy of nature who fancies himself wiser than nature, although she is the greatest school for all of us.

1/9, 216

You should not only know your way about grass and hay, you should not only rummage in cases and boxes—this is the way of the earth and of transience; you should also approach

104

things from the standpoint of eternity, yet with the resources of mortal man. If we are given the ability to learn from God —as has been amply demonstrated—we also have the ability to learn from nature.

I/12, 188

To learn and to do nothing is little. To learn and to do is great and whole.

I/7, 76

One man is heavy in the limbs, another on the contrary is tender and delicate; which of the two should be praised and which censured? Neither; for both have stomachs and hearts, red blood and red flesh, bones, marrow, and hair; their brains are developed, but they are still lacking in intelligence. . . . Therefore you should not judge people according to their stature, but honour them all equally. What is in you is in all. Each has what you also have within you; and the poor grows the same plants in his garden as the rich. In man, the ability to practise all crafts and arts is innate, but not all these arts have been brought to the light of day. . . . Those which are to become manifest in him must first be awakened. What can be learned for men is not properly learning, because everything is prefigured even in the child; it must only be awakened and summoned forth in him. . . . The child is still an uncertain being, and he receives his form according to the potentialities that you awaken in him. If you awaken his ability to make shoes, he will be a shoemaker; if you awaken the stonecutter in him, he will be a stonecutter; and if you summon forth the scholar in him, he will be a scholar. And this can be so because all potentialities are inherent in him; what you awaken in him comes forth from him; the rest remains unawakened, absorbed in sleep.

I/13, 298–99

We are born to be awake, not to be asleep!

I/9, 256

Therefore, man, learn and learn, question and question, and do not be ashamed of it; for only thus can you earn a name that will resound in all countries and never be forgotten.

I/13, 377

We desire to explore the same things as our forefathers desired to explore. However, we should not blindly accept everything they taught, but only that knowledge which is

Fig. 62. The Astrologer

needed in our own time. For what is gone is gone, and the new time confronts us with new tasks! Although the ancients left behind many things that we can and should love, these things have not come down to us in such a way that from now there is no need to learn anything more than what we have received from them; on the contrary, we should improve on all these things, we should go further in our explorations and study new things. This lesson and this commandment to learn are valid until the end of days. *I/12, 169*

Much must be lopped from a tree, from its limbs and branches, before it stands right and beautiful and without a flaw. . . . How many books were written before at last a few immortal ones came into being; these are the fruitful boughs that grace the tree. A student must learn, and write a great deal in vain, before he can master the alphabet; should we for this reason ascribe value to the badly written letters and keep looking at them? No, only the last and best, which he has written correctly and well understood! *II/1, 77*

Just as flowers cannot bloom before May and the corn cannot be ripe before the harvest time and wine cannot be pressed before autumn, so the time for learning cannot be curtailed. Learning is our very life, from youth to old age, indeed, up to the brink of death; no one lives for ten hours without learning. *I/8, 214*

He who is guided by the ways of nature becomes well versed in the two branches of philosophy, that of heaven and that of the earth. He is blessed with such great knowledge that neither life nor death, neither health nor illness is hidden from him. *I/8, 373*

Fig. 63. Scholars

Fig. 64. The Physician in His Study: portrait of the Spanish physician Luis Lobera de Avila

1/7, 336

Not will alone, only will and deed make for perfect achievement.

1/7, 264–65

All things on earth have been given into the hands of man. And they are given into his hands in order that he may bring them to the highest development, just as the earth does with all that it brings forth. But this highest should be for man the lowest—a beginning; it is a seed which he is beholden to shape into something greater.

Nothing created is beyond man's fathoming. And everything has been created to the end that man may not remain idle, but walk in the path of God, that is to say, in His works and not in vice, not in fornication, not in gambling and not in drinking, not in robbing, not in the acquisition of goods, nor in the accumulation of treasures for the worms. To the end that he may experience God's spirit, His light, and His angelic ways in all things which are of divine nature. It is more blessed to write about nymphs than about the ecclesiastical hierarchy, more blessed to write about the origin of the giants than about court etiquette, more blessed to praise Melusina than cavalry and artillery, and more blessed to speak of miners under the earth than of tournaments and chivalry. For in the former the spirit deals in divine works, while in the latter it is busied in worldly things, to please the world in vanity and impurity. *I/14, 116–17*

Behold the herbs! Their virtues are invisible and yet they can be detected. Behold the beasts which can neither speak nor explain anything, and yet nothing is so hidden in them that man cannot learn of it. Thus there is no thing on earth or in the sea, in chaos or in the firmament, that does not become manifest at the appointed time. It is God's will that nothing remain unknown to man as he walks in the light of nature; for all things belonging to nature exist for the sake of man. And since they have been created for his sake, and since it is he who needs them, he must explore everything that lies in nature. *I/12, 148–49*

It is not God's will that His secrets should be visible; it is His will that they become manifest and knowable through the works of man who has been created in order to make them visible. Thus Christ, whom no one recognized as the second person of the Trinity, was considered by everyone a man, because what He actually was remained invisible. . . . For God is the revealer of that which is hidden in all things. . . . And it is no different with man. No one sees what is hidden in him, but only what his works reveal. Therefore man should work continually to discover what God has given him. . . . We too should make manifest that which

109

1/12, 59–60
He has put in us, to the end that the unbelievers may see what God can achieve through man.

God has planted many marvellous secrets in man, so that they lie in him like seeds in the earth. And just as the seeds burgeon from the earth in spring, so the flowers and fruits that God has put in men will come to light at the appointed time. God is pleased with all the fruits of the earth that ripen at their appointed time, He is pleased also with the fruits of

Fig. 65. The Garden of Health

man when they grow ripe for harvest; for He is glad when His creatures retain nothing in themselves, when everything grows and unfolds from them, and when they praise God, their Creator, through their works. The earth brings forth all things and holds back nothing, not even the least thing; all the more should man help the gifts that God has sown in him to prosper and thus become a saint, a hymn in his praise. For it is the saints who embody and make manifest what God has put into them. Man should always keep this in mind, he should not fall asleep, but in daily effort should

1/12, 227
strive for his summer lest it be always winter round him.

Christ charged us with a task which must guide us all, which we must forever strive to perform. His commandments and teachings apply not only to the eternal light but also to the light of nature. He enjoined us: "Seek, and ye shall find." It is our task to seek art, for without seeking it we shall never learn the secrets of the world. Who can boast that a roast squab flies into his mouth? Or that a grapevine runs after him? You must go to it yourself. We can seek in various ways: . . . but the seeking that is needed here concerns the occult things. When the goal of the seeking is hidden, the manner of seeking is also occult; and because knowledge is inherent in the art, he who seeks the art also finds knowledge in it.

I/12, 150–51

All things are given into the hands of man though he make no effort to obtain them; they grow without his help. The ore takes its shape without human aid, and the flowers likewise. But if he wants to use or enjoy them, he must expend labour upon them. For although iron is iron, it is not of itself a plowshare or a carpenter's ax. Although corn means bread, it is not ready to be consumed as bread. So is it with all products; God has given them to us that through them we may preserve ourselves, and He has also given us the arts that we need to this end. Therefore we must be versed not only in all the plants of nature, but also in the art with which God has endowed us for the purpose of preparing them. In this practice we must withstand the test, and being natural bodies, we must during our stay on earth be guided by the light of nature. Let us not be idlers or dreamers, but always at work, both physically and spiritually, so that no part of us remains inactive. Such work in the sweat of our brow may even drive away the devil and his pack, for where man is at work none of them can abide.

I/12, 241

God makes a house; man too can build one. God has hands and feet in His word, man has them in his limbs. One man can cure another by means of a remedy, which he must set to work by means of his body; God does this by one word. . . . A man walks on his feet, the spirit walks without feet. . . . God wills the earth to grow trees, pears, and other fruits, and creatures of all kinds. . . . Similarly He wills that

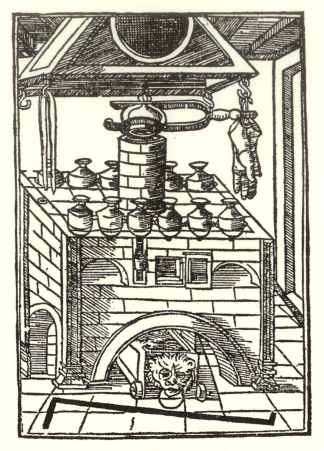

Fig. 66. Alchemistic Oven

all the arts—music, the crafts, the sciences, and doctrines of theology—which He created, and which rest in the "firmament," should become real. . . . And this must be done by man, just as the pears are brought to maturity by the tree. For the "firmament" needs an agent through which to work, and this agent is man and man alone. Man has been so created that through him the miracles of nature are made visible and given form.

I/12, 56–57

The herbs were created like the trees and the stars; they were not with God at the beginning of time, that is to say, before the creation of heaven and earth. None of them was with the spirit of God; He created them one after another. Thus He made the stars, the planets, the earth, water, fire, air, the mountains, the metals, the herbs, and so on. And as He created them, they were born; then they became tangible and visible, and out of nothing they became substance, for our own use. But God never lets anything stand empty, but fills everything; would not a stone, for example, be empty if no virtues were inherent in it? And what would man be if no soul dwelt within him? It is the soul that fills him. What would a cow be if it did not give milk? The milk is the "virtue" that fills it. . . . Man has a soul, and by it he and all men should live: in fulness and not in barrenness!

Fig. 67. Astronomers and Celestial Globe

. . . What good would the earth be if it did not bear fruit? The fruit is its fulness. And what good would the fruit be if it were hollow? None at all! Therefore, God created nothing empty, but filled all things. Anyone who wanted to build a house that had no purpose would be a fool; and the same is true in this case.

God's hand cast the stars in the orbit of the firmament,

I/14, 215–16

113

and thus determined their course; the pace and circle of each star . . . now high, now low, for all stars without distinction. If one is high the other is low, if one is in exaltation the other is in declination, to the end that one yield to the other, that each serve the purpose for which God created it, and that everything be fulfilled. . . . No star can be idle; no star stands still, all exercise daily, to awaken nature and

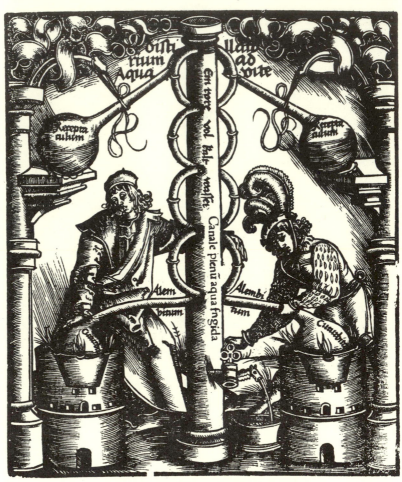

Fig. 68. Preparation of the Elixir of Life
(*"forma furni ad distillandum
aquam vitae"*)

drive her to her daily work. And just as the stars have no
rest, so also do the things of nature work without respite.   *I/13, 147–48*

Winter means the rest of all things in nature, for after the
production of their fruits they should rest. Yet this is no real
rest, for they continue to labour and labour and prepare for
a new summer, for a new birth, and for a new bestowal of
their fruit. Thus nothing is idle in nature, all things are at
work from hour to hour, from day to day, from night to night.
Only man rests at night and does not work on the Sabbath
because of the commandment. But the day of rest was not
ordained for the spirit, which must not stand still and idle;
it is established only for the rest of the body, as of the beasts
of the field, and for whatever pertains to it. The spirit must
always be at work; neither sleep nor Sabbath can make it
still and quiet. The same goes for all creatures; even though
the body rests, their spirit never stands still and continues to
work each day.   *I/13, 148*

Happiness does not consist in laziness, or sensual pleasure,
or riches, or chattering, or gluttony. In labour and in sweat
must each man use the gifts that God conferred upon him
on earth, either as a peasant in the fields, as a workman in
the smithy, in the mines, on the seas, in medicine, or as one
who proclaims the word of God.   *II/1, 253–54*

Fig. 69. Books

The proper way resides in
work and action, in doing and
producing; the perverse man
does nothing, but talks a great
deal. We must not judge a man
by his words, but by his heart.
The heart speaks through words
only when they are confirmed
by deeds.   *I/9, 223*

All things that we use on earth, let us use them for good
and not for evil. And never for more or for anything other
than the purpose for which they exist. We should add nothing and take away nothing, spoil nothing, better nothing.   *II/1, 90*

If you are called to write a book, you will not fail to do so,

Fig. 70. Vintage

even if it is delayed for sixty or seventy years, or even longer. If you carry it within you and turn it over in your mind, you need not rush at it at once. It will not always remain within, it will have to come out, like a child from the womb of its mother. For only what is born in this way is fertile and good, and then it never comes too late. . . . Have patience and do not see a fig in every thistle. Wait: the hour will strike, then everything will come forth from you. . . . What must be born of you, and what is in you, that comes out, and you know not how or whence it comes, or whither it strives to go. And in the end you find it in that which you have never *II/1, 79–80* learned or seen.

By their heavenly fruits, that is to say, by their works, men are known. In them it becomes manifest whether man walks in the path of God or not, whether he is a son of nature or of God, a son of the "old" or of the "new" birth—of the birth for blessedness or for unblessedness—whether he belongs to the righteous or the unrighteous, the elect or the non-elect. Such knowledge is needed, and very much needed. For if we go wrong in the beginning, we shall err still more in the middle, and most of all in the end. *I/12, 388*

When the things we need are ripe for harvest, the season we need sends their harvester and their wagoner, that each thing may be brought to light at its appointed hour. *I/9, 285*

Anyone who imagines that all fruits ripen at the same time as the strawberries knows nothing about grapes. *I/10, 14*

Hope is one of the loftiest emotions we can experience; we must trust in our art and hope that it will not fail. For wherever we lack hope, our fruits will also be lacking. Only he who can do something hopes; he who can do nothing has no hope, but only doubts. And he who knows something and hopes does not go astray, nor does he doubt. He awaits the hour that will teach him what is the will of God. *I/7, 369*

It is not of ourselves that we have wisdom and the arts, but through a mediator. He is the invisible spirit which gives us art in the same way as the fields give us fruit. . . . Thus God's spirit bestows His gifts in accordance with His orders: to one, the invention of the alphabet, to another, of the forge, to a third, of the lyre, and so to each the invention of something that is needed on earth. But once the things have been invented, we can also learn them of ourselves. . . . Everything we invent has its origin in the spirit. Therefore, let us not concern ourselves with how things have come to us, but trust that everything is done at God's command. . . . Everyone must understand that no bird could fly unless God had so ordained. *I/9, 340-42*

We must not brood over things of divine nature, but recognize them only in their works; for these are the signs of the Master who lives in heaven. As the house is the sign of its master and confirms him to be a carpenter, as the pot is the sign of its potter, so the works are signs of their Master and bear witness that He is God Himself.

1/14, 240

Every believer should be a philosopher . . . in order to

Fig. 71. Chemical Dissolution of Bodies

know what is of benefit to him, to his life and his health. . . . He should know what he eats and drinks, what he wears and what he does; and to what use he can put these things for the prolongation of his life. . . . If he eats what is useful to his health and avoids what may shorten his life, that is the proper way to fast. For all our actions should be directed toward a long life. Therefore he should also study all causalities that he may know what God created out of nothingness; the firmament that he may understand its effects; the earth that he may see what grows in it; the sea and the air that he may recognize his Creator in all things. Only a cripple in knowledge can believe that God created His creation without unfolding it. Rich is he who knows God by His works, who draws from them his faith in Him, and who does not pass them by like a man who is colour-blind. For God wills that man know Him completely and not only half and without clarity.

I/13, 247–48

Pray, seek, knock at the gates in the name of God, then everything you need will be given you in excess; for in His name and through Him all things happen. And work diligently to be perfect in your craft, for God has made it perfect to the end that your works may praise, honour, and celebrate Him.

I/10, 23

Fig. 72. *Illuminatio:* alchemistic-symbolic illustration of the psychic rebirth

Fig. 73. Cosmic Harmony

I/8, 343

Everything that is within can be
known by what is without.

It is not God's will that all He has created for the benefit
of man and has given him as his own should remain hidden.
. . . And even if He did conceal some things, He left nothing unmarked, but provided all things with outward, visible
marks, with special traits—just as a man who has buried a
treasure marks the spot in order that he may find it again.

I/11, 393

We men discover everything that lies hidden in the mountains by external signs and correspondences, and thus also
do we find all the properties of herbs and everything that is
in the stones. There is nothing in the depths of the seas,
nothing on the heights of the firmament, that man is unable
to discover. No mountain, no cliff, is so vast as to hide or con-

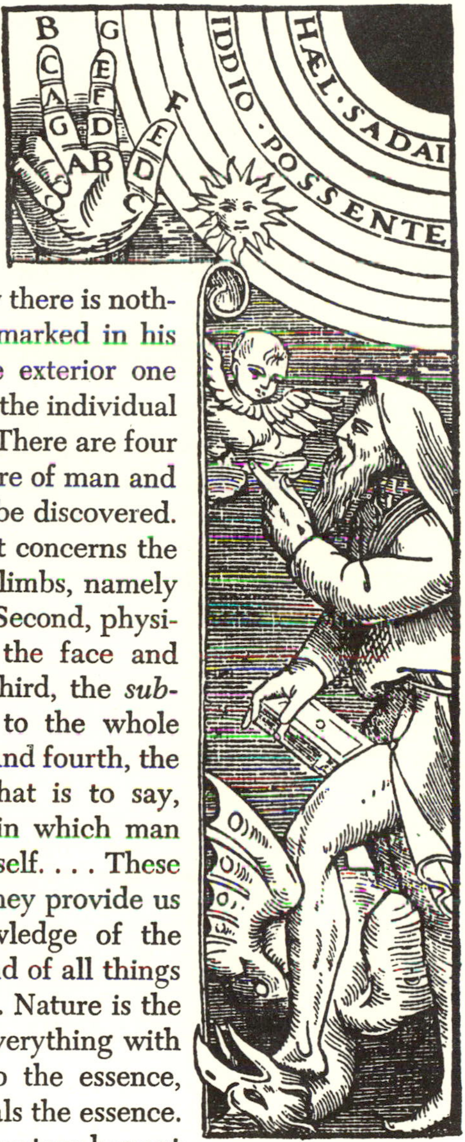

ceal what is in it from the eyes of man; it is revealed to him by corresponding signs. . . . For each fruit is a sign, and through it we discover what is contained in that from which it stems. Similarly there is nothing in man that is not marked in his exterior, so that by the exterior one may discover what is in the individual who bears the sign. . . . There are four ways by which the nature of man and of all living things can be discovered. . . . First, chiromancy; it concerns the extreme parts of man's limbs, namely the hands and feet. . . . Second, physiognomics; it concerns the face and the whole head. . . . Third, the *substantina*, which refers to the whole shape of the body. . . . And fourth, the customs and usages, that is to say, manners and gestures in which man appears and shows himself. . . . These four belong together; they provide us with a complete knowledge of the hidden, inward man, and of all things that grow in nature. . . . Nature is the sculptor: she endows everything with the form which is also the essence, and thus the form reveals the essence.

There is nothing that nature has not signed in such a way that man may discover its essence. . . . The stars have their orbits by which they are known. The same is true of man. As you can see, each herb is given the form that befits

I/12, 174–77

Fig. 74. Man and the Annual Cycle

121

its nature; similarly, man is endowed with a form corresponding to his inner nature. And just as the form shows what a given herb is, so the human shape is a sign which indicates what a given man is. This does not refer to the name, sex, or similar characteristics, but to the qualities inherent in the man. The art of signs teaches us to give each man his true name in accordance with his innate nature. A wolf must not be called a sheep, a dove must not be called a fox; each being should be given the name that belongs to its essence. . . . Since nothing is so secret or hidden that it cannot be revealed, everything depends on the discovery of those things which manifest the hidden. . . . The nature of each man's soul accords with the design of his lineaments and arteries. The same is true of the face, which is shaped and formed according to the content of his mind and soul, and the same is again true of the proportions of the human body. For the sculptor of Nature is so artful that he does not mould the soul to fit the form, but the form to fit the soul; in other words, the shape of a man is formed in accordance with the manner of his heart. . . . Artists who make sculptures proceed no differently. . . . And the more accomplished an artist would be, the more necessary it is that he master the

Lactuca.   Scariola.   Apium, Thachon.   Eruca; & Nasturtium.   Ocimum.   Portulaca.

Fig. 75. Herbs

art of signs. . . . No artist can paint or carve, no one can produce an accomplished work, without such knowledge. . . . Only he who has some knowledge of this can be a

1/12, 91–93 finished artist.

Behold the *Satyrion* root, is it not formed like the male privy parts? No one can deny this. Accordingly magic discovered it and revealed that it can restore a man's virility and passion. And then we have the thistle; do not its leaves prickle like needles? Thanks to this sign, the art of magic discovered that there is no better herb against internal prickling. The *Siegwurz* root is wrapped in an envelope like armour; and this is a magic sign showing that like armour it gives protection against weapons. And the *Syderica* bears the image and form of a snake on each of its leaves, and thus, according to magic, it gives protection against any kind of poisoning. The chicory stands under a special influence of the sun; this is seen in its leaves, which always bend toward the sun as though they wanted to show it gratitude. Hence it is most effective while the sun is shining, while the sun is in the sky. As soon as the sun sets, the power of chicory dwindles. Why, do you think, does its root assume the shape of a bird after seven years? What has the art of magic to say about this? If you know the answer, keep silent and say nothing the scoffers; if you do not know it, try to find out; investigate, and do not be ashamed to ask questions. *I/13, 377*

When a carpenter builds a house, it first lives in him as an idea; and the house is built according to this idea. Therefore, from the form of the house, one can make inferences about the carpenter's ideas and images. What nature has in mind . . . no one can know until it has acquired form and shape. . . . Now note well that virtue forms the shape of a man, just as the carpenter's ideas become visible in his house; and a man's body takes shape in accordance with the nature of his soul. . . . Nature acts no differently. She gives man an outward appearance that is in keeping with his inner constitution. . . . And each man's soul can be recognized, just as the carpenter can be known by his house. *I/12, 177–78*

Through the art of chiromancy and the art of physiognomics . . . it is possible to tell by the shape, form, and colour, and nothing more, the qualities and virtues of each

herb and root; these are their signs. And for this we need no
other test or long study. For God has carefully differentiated
all His creation from the beginning, and has never given to
different things the same shape and form.

I/13, 376

Physiognomics is the art of discovering what is within
and hidden in man. . . . It tells us in what relation his
heart stands to God and his neighbour, what eyes are those

of a rogue and what eyes
are not, which tongue is
cunning and which is not,
which ears are open to evil
and which to good. By it
we know a man's tempera-
ment and his attitude
toward God and his fellow
men. . . . For his conduct
toward God, his ways of
acting, hearing, and see-
ing, all these are signs by
which his heart can be
known. That which fills
the heart overflows in the
mouth; and what a man's
heart desires, that is what
his ears hear, and his eyes

Fig. 76. Physiognomics

seek after. The physiognomics of the heavens provides us
with exactly similar insights. . . . For it is written: by their
fruits ye shall know them!

I/12, 343

If we want to make a statement about a man's nature on
the basis of his physiognomy, we must take everything into
account; it is in his distress that a man is tested, for then his
nature is revealed. For *in extremis*, things reveal their nature and become visible; then we can say: he is an upright
man, a steadfast man, a faithful man, he manifests his inner
being. . . . One man reveals more traits of loyalty and less
of disloyalty; one man is to a large extent this, another man

that. Therefore we should keep an eye on the outward characteristics which nature gives a man by shaping him in a certain way. For nature shapes the anatomy of a pear in such a way that the pear develops into a pear tree; and she creates a medlar's anatomy, in such a way that it develops into a medlar bush; and the same is true of silver and of gold. Nature also forges man, now a gold man, now a silver man, now a fig man, now a bean man.

I/14, 183–84

There are many kinds of chiromancy; not only the chiromancy of man's hands, from which it is possible to infer and discover his inclinations and his fate, to ascertain what good or evil will befall him; there are yet other kinds of chiromancy, for example, that of herbs, of tree leaves, of wood, of rocks, of mines, or the chiromancy of landscapes, of their roads and rivers, and so on. . . . All this must be studied and well understood, and the physician should also study the lines of the herbs and the leaves, and by the application

Fig. 77. Chiromancy

of chiromancy, he should discover their efficacy and virtues. Those who work wood, such as carpenters, cabinet-makers, and the rest, must estimate the quality of wood by means of chiromancy, and discover its uses, what it is good for. Similarly, a miner should study mines with the help of chiromancy, in order to know what ores and metals a mine contains and whether they are deposited close to the surface or

1/13, 375–76

deep below it. And in the same way the cosmographer should study the chiromancy of landscapes, countries, and streams.

Customs are innate in us, and we are brought up in certain customs. Our manners and customs depend on the way in which we are brought up. By finding out whether or not these customs serve God and our fellow man, whether we observe them steadily or whether we waver like reeds in the wind, we obtain a clear picture of our nature. Therefore you can discern man's immortal part in his visible, innate, characteristic signs, and you can know him even by his appearance; for the outer reveals the inner.

1/12, 344

Fig. 78. Man and Planet

Fig. 79. The Rose

God gives us no art that does not bear in itself the necessity of its fulfilment.

I/9, 287

Human nature is different from all other animal nature. It is endowed with divine wisdom, endowed with divine arts. Therefore we are justly called gods and the children of the Supreme Being. For the light of nature is in us, and this light is God. Our mortal bodies are vehicles of the divine wisdom. Within our power there are arts that we owe to no one but God; they are given us in the hour of our conception. For this reason there is no justification for the skeptical question: "Is man able to see the future and is he able to know it?" Such doubts imply that not man, but only God, is capable of this knowledge. But since God has created the art, He is not alone to have the knowledge, it is also inherent in his art . . . and this art He has entrusted to man. Who conferred the word upon the prophets? God alone. Who taught the arts? Again God alone. And if everything comes from God, why should art be incapable of something that God is capable of? Therefore, study without respite, that the art *I/12, 120–21* may become perfect in us.

Who gives man all the arts, all the skills that he achieves? Man does not give them to himself. No more than an ass becomes a lute-player does man by himself become something he is not. Since man is more gifted than an ass, it follows that he can learn lute-playing and even more difficult things. But not from the firmament. For who is there that can play the lute? No one. But how could someone teach it if he did not know it himself? What we can do must come to us from another who can do it; for nothing can be learned from someone who knows nothing. And although we

Fig. 80. Mars and Venus

speak of heavenly songs and symphonies, they are produced neither by harps nor lutes, but are a noise in the clouds, an echo from the earth. Thus all things come from God, and *I/14, 250* God plants all things in us according to His will.

In the stars all skills are arts, all crafts are hidden, and also all wisdom, all reason, as well as foolishness and what belongs to it; for there is nothing in man that does not flow into him from the light of nature. But what is in the light of nature is subject to the influence of the stars. The stars are our *I/12, 22* school in which everything must be learned.

If there had been no Venus, music would never have been invented, and if there had been no Mars, neither would the crafts ever have been invented. Thus the stars teach us all the arts that exist on earth; and if the stars were not active in us, and if we had been compelled to discover everything in ourselves, no art would ever have come into being.   *I/12, 23*

Just as the aspect of the heavens has been constantly renewed from the days of Adam down to our own time, so new arts arise from year to year. And not the arts alone, but every new thing, all wars, all governments, and everything that our brain produces, receive their guidance from the stars now and at all times. And if all musicians died, and all craftsmen died, this master would remain . . . and would always instruct new ones.   *I/12, 23*

Not all the stars have yet completed their action and asserted their influences. Therefore, the invention of arts has not yet come to an end, and for this reason no one who has discovered something new or who undertakes to explore some unknown field should be held back. . . . Give heed to those who each day seek for something new and each day find something new, whatever it may be—whether in the arts or in the revelations of natural wisdom. For it is the heavens that are responsible for it. Thus new teachings, new arts, new orders, new diseases, new remedies succeed one another, for . . . at all times the heavens are at work. And it remains for man to decide what portion of these things he should take to himself and what he should not. . . .   *I/12, 24–25*

There are seven ways in which we become versed in the arts:

First, a spirit—let us say, an angel—may teach man certain arts. . . . Such instruction is comparable to that of a schoolmaster who merely awakens in a child that which is already in him. It is an evocation, a revelation. . . .

Secondly, a man often gives advice which proves helpful but which he himself does not understand. The light of nature is responsible for the happy outcome. For the advice that was given might have resulted not in good but in evil, because the devils never fail to instil some of their falsity into all things.

Thirdly, many arts have come to the light of day through experience. For instance: a sick man tries out an unknown remedy which he hopes will help him, and lo and behold: it

Fig. 81. The Seven Liberal Arts

is effectual. The light of nature has led him to it, and pointed out to him something which he had not noticed before.

Fourthly, many sorcerers have achieved skill in "nigromancy, necromancy, chiromancy, hydromancy"—i.e., in those false arts that concern themselves with soothsaying. . . . But these are not genuine arts as they fancy; no, it is the light of nature that confers a skill upon them under such a cloak, in order to gratify their covetousness. For thus does the light of nature play with men.

Fifthly, many arts have come to the light of day through genuine chiromancy; and the chiromancies of the hands, of herbs, or of wood have introduced the chiromancers to the art. Not without good reason was chiromancy so highly honoured by the ancients. We use it only for soothsaying, but the ancients used it as a means for learning the arts.

Sixthly, physiognomics has also led to many arts. It is the art that reveals characteristics hidden within. By means of it, we can discover the inward through the outward not only in man but also in all created things. . . .

Seventh, arts have developed on the basis of the outward form of things, that is to say, when one form is similar to another, and the similar is cured by the similar—cancer has been applied against cancer, dragon root against snake bite and so on.

But it is possible to enumerate other arts which have been given to us through the discoveries of astronomy and philosophy or through a deeper understanding of the properties of herbs and various other natural things.

I/8, 292–93

Fig. 82. The Dancers

All of us should know that art, science, and skill exist only to be conducive to joy, peace, unity, purity, respectability, to gratify our needs and help us to serve our fellow men. This is also true of music. It is the remedy of all who suffer from melancholy and fantasy, disorders that ultimately make them desperate and solitary. But music has power to hold them in human company and preserve their minds; it drives out the spirit of witches, demons, and sorcerers.

II/1, 105–6

An art is the most durable good, the best wealth, which no thief can steal, no fire, no water, destroy; and if someone took my body away, he still would not have my art, for it is hidden in me, a possession that defies seizure.

I/14, 506–7

Our life is founded not only in bread, but also in arts and words of wisdom that come from the mouth of God. We should fill ourselves with these, and look upon a full belly as mortal, but upon those other things as eternal. For all

Fig. 83. The Harpist and the Nine Muses

those who.live on those things will shine like the sun in the

1/11, 173

kingdom of God.

Although there are many names, the arts are not separated, and one kind of knowledge is not severed from an-

1/8, 147

other; for one is in all.

Know that man makes great discoveries concerning future and hidden things, which are despised and scoffed at by the ignorant who do not realize what nature can accomplish by

132

virtue of her spirit. . . . Thus, the uncertain arts are in such a state that a new generation must come, full of prophetic or sibylline spirit, which will awaken and direct the skills and arts. The arts of this kind . . . are quite old, and enjoyed great reputation among the ancient. They were kept secret and taught secretly. For the students of these arts devoted their time to inner contemplation and faith, and by such means they discovered and proved many great things. But the men of today have no longer such capacity for imagination and faith; today their minds are exclusively concerned with things that are pleasant to the flesh and the blood; only what the flesh and the blood want and desire is being studied, that alone is still being practised. . . . These arts are uncertain today because man is uncertain in himself. For he who is not certain of himself cannot be certain in his actions; a sceptic can never create anything enduring, nor can anyone who serves only the body accomplish true spiritual works.

I/12, 485

If we would know the inner nature of man by his outer nature; if we would understand his inner heaven by his outward aspect; if we would know the inner nature of trees, herbs, roots, stones by their outward aspect, we must pursue our exploration of nature on the foundation of the cabala. For the cabala opens up access to the occult, to the mysteries; it enables us to read sealed epistles and books and likewise the inner nature of men.

II/1, 102

Fig. 84. Magic Sigils

133

All of you, whose faith leads you to divine man's future, past, and present, you who see land beyond the horizon, who read sealed, hidden missives and books, who seek for buried treasures in the earth and in walls, you who teach so much wisdom, such high arts—remember that you must take unto yourselves the teachings of the cabala if you want to accomplish all this. For the cabala builds on a true foundation. Pray and it will be given you, knock and you will be heard, the gate will be opened to you. . . . Everything you desire will flow and be granted you. You will see into the greatest depth of the earth . . . and into the third heaven. You will gain greater knowledge than Solomon. . . . But only if you seek the kingdom of God above all else will this be granted you. The art of the cabala is beholden to God, it is in alliance with Him, and it is founded on the words of Christ. But if you do not follow the true doctrine of the cabala, but slip into geomancy, you will be led by that spirit which tells you *II/1,100–101* nothing but lies.

Fig. 85. The Poet and the Thinker

The interpretation of dreams is a great art. Dreams are not without meaning wherever they may come from—from fantasy, from the elements, or from another inspiration. Often one can find something supernatural in them. For the spirit is never idle. If the earth gives us an inspiration—one of her gifts—and if she confers it upon us through her spirit, then the vision has a meaning.

1/12, 259

Anyone who wants to take his dream seriously, interpret it, and be guided by it, must be endowed with "sidereal knowledge" and the light of nature, and must not engage in absurd fantasies, nor look upon his dreams from the heights of his arrogance; for in this way nothing can be done with them. Dreams must be heeded and accepted. For a great many of them come true.

1/12, 491

For the most part presentiments appear to man in so unimpressive a form that they are ignored. And yet Joseph discovered in his sleep who Mary was and by whom she was with child. And because dreams are not sufficiently heeded, no faith is put in their revelations, although they are nothing other than prophecies. . . .

Fig. 86. Mary with the Child and the Three Kings

The wise man must not neglect them, but recall that Christ too appeared in invisible form and was ridiculed. If he understands that inconspicuous things must not be ridiculed but judged with wisdom, he will also know Christ. The scoffers have no understanding, but the wise possess the knowledge that God has conferred upon them.

1/12, 104–6

The dreams which reveal the supernatural are promises and messages that God sends us directly; they are nothing but His angels, His ministering spirits, who usually appear to us when we are in a great predicament. . . . Of such apparitions we must know how they take place and how they come to us; when we are in great need, we can obtain them from God's kindness if our prayer pours in true faith from a truthful mouth and heart. Then God sends us such a messenger who appears to us in spirit, warns us, consoles us, teaches us, and brings us His good tidings.

1/14, 520–21

From time immemorial artistic insights have been revealed to artists in their sleep and in dreams, so that at all times they ardently desired them. Then their imagination could work wonders upon wonders and invoke the shades of the philosophers, who would instruct them in their art. Today this still happens again and again, but most of what transpires is forgotten. How often does a man say as he wakes in the morning, "I had a wonderful dream last night," and relate how Mercury or this or that philosopher appeared to him in person and taught him this or that art. But then the dream escapes him and he cannot remember it. However, anyone to whom this happens should not leave his room upon awakening, should speak to no one, but remain alone and sober until everything comes back to him, and he recalls his dream.

1/14, 520

Fig. 87. The Dreamer

Fig. 88. The Great Sage: portrait of
Hermes Trismegistus

> Magic is the most secret of the arts
> and the highest wisdom concerning
> the supernatural on earth. . . .   *1/14, 538*

Magic has power to experience and fathom things which
are inaccessible to human reason. For magic is a great secret
wisdom, just as reason is a great public folly. Therefore it
would be desirable and good for the doctors of theology to
know something about it and to understand what it actually
is, and cease unjustly and unfoundedly to call it witchcraft.   *1/14, 538*

After all, God has permitted magic, and this is a sign that
we may use it; it is also a sign of what we are; but we must

137

not interpret this sign as a summons to practise magic. For if a man practises false magic, he tempts God. . . . And if he tempts God, woe to his soul!

I/9, 271

All skills and arts come from God, and nothing comes from any other source . . . and therefore no one may vilify astronomy, alchemy, or medicine, or philosophy, or theology, acting, poetry, music, geomancy . . . or any other high art. Why not? What then does man invent of himself? Not even the slightest rag with which to patch his breeches. What new thing can the devil invent? Nothing on earth, nothing pure and simple; not even so much as is needed to catch and kill a louse on your head. But as soon as something is kindled in us by the light of nature, the devil pretends to be our guide and makes bold to falsify all things that God has given us, to slander them, and to make them deceptive, and thus does he spoil everything. . . . The devil makes bold to brand God's works as lies, in order to abuse Him; he seduces those who are weak in their faith and leads them astray in order to make them desert God and cultivate false arts and grievously affront Him. They spend their time in lies, and although they too brood, and inquire and explore, they nevertheless must die without finding the truth.

I/8, 208–9

A test and a proof are always required to distinguish the sacred from the profane, and to discover from what virtues the various miracles derive. A careful examination is required before one can establish whether it is the spirit of nature or the spirit of God which appears to us in such a miracle. Learn to recognize this distinction well! It is most indispensable to know what comes from *divinatio* and what from *divinitas*. These terms are alike, they derive from the same root, but not so the miracles—these spring from different sources.

I/12, 213

The Holy Scriptures call sorcerers—without distinction—all those who were versed in supernatural things and were not at the same time holy. But this matter must be given some consideration. God wills us to live simply, like the apostles, and not to brood over things and explore hidden

Fig. 89. The Magus

things which occur in a supernatural manner, because it is not His will that we misuse such knowledge to the injury of our fellow men, and thus damn our bodies and souls. For this reason we must not regard as sorcerers all those who are so called in the Holy Scriptures. If we did we should have to look upon the three Wise Men of the East as arch-sorcerers, for they were more versed in the arts and things supernatural than anyone before them or anyone living in their time. But Holy Writ speaks of them not as sorcerers but as magi; and how should we interpret this? Only to mean that they did not misuse their art and their great occult wisdom. For magic is an art which reveals its highest power and strength through faith. It is true, however, that if it is misused, it can give rise to sorcery.

I/14, 521

As God awakens the dead to new life, so the "natural saints," who are called magi, are given power over the energies and faculties of nature. For there are holy men in God who serve the beatific life; they are called saints. But there are also holy men in God who serve the forces of nature, and they are called magi. God shows His miracles through His holy men, both through those of the beatific life and through those of nature; what others are incapable of doing they can do, because it has been conferred upon them as a special gift.

1/12, 130

Fig. 90. Magic Sigils Effective against
Gout

Fig. 91. *Turba Philosophorum*
(Disputing Alchemists)

Who can be an enemy of alchemy,
since it bears no guilt? Guilty is he
who does not know it properly and
who does not apply it properly.

I/11, 186

Let it be for you a great and high mystery in the light
of nature that a thing can completely lose and forfeit its
form and shape, only to arise subsequently out of nothing
and become something whose potency and virtue is far
nobler than what it was in the beginning.

I/11, 348–49

Nothing has been created as *ultima materia*—in its final
state. Everything is at first created in its *prima materia*, its
original stuff; whereupon Vulcan comes, and by the art of
alchemy develops it into its final substance. . . . For alchemy means: to carry to its end something that has not yet
been completed. To obtain the lead from the ore and to transform it into what it is made for. . . . Accordingly, you

141

Alchimia die kunst redet.

Fig. 92. Alchimia

should understand that alchemy is nothing but the art which makes the impure into the pure through fire. . . . It can separate the useful from the useless, and transmute it into its final substance and its ultimate essence. *I/11, 188–89*

The transmutation of metals is a great mystery of nature. However laborious and difficult this task may be, whatever impediments and obstacles may lie in the way of its accomplishment, this transmutation does not go counter to nature, nor is it incompatible with the order of God, as is falsely asserted by many persons. But the base, impure five metals—that is, copper, tin, lead, iron, and quicksilver—cannot be transmuted into the nobler, pure, and perfect metals—namely, into gold and silver—without a *tinctura*, or without the philosophers' stone. *I/11, 356–57*

Since ancient times philosophy has striven to separate the good from the evil, and the pure from the impure; this is the same as saying that all things die and that only the soul lives eternal. The soul endures while the body decays, and you may recall that correspondingly a seed must rot away if it is to bear fruit. But what does it mean, to rot? It means only this—that the body decays while its essence, the good, the soul, subsists. This should be known about decaying. And once we have understood this, we possess the pearl which contains all the virtues.

Decay is the beginning of all birth. . . . It transforms shape and essence, the forces and virtues of nature. Just as the decay of all foods in the stomach transforms them and makes them into a pulp, so it hap-

I/2, 47

Fig. 93. Lion Swallowing the Sun: "the true green and golden lion," symbolic picture of the transmutation of the *prima materia*

143

pens outside the stomach. . . . Decay is the midwife of very great things! It causes many things to rot, that a noble fruit may be born; for it is the reversal, the death and destruction of the original essence of all natural things. It brings about the birth and rebirth of forms a thousand times improved. . . . And this is the highest and greatest *mysterium* of God, the deepest mystery and miracle that He has revealed to *I/11, 312–13* mortal man.

♓

The great virtues that lie hidden in nature would never have been revealed if alchemy had not uncovered them and made them visible. Take a tree, for example; a man sees it in the winter, but he does not know what it is, he does not know what it conceals within itself, until summer comes and discloses the buds, the flowers, the fruit. . . . Similarly the virtues in things remain concealed to man, unless the alchemists disclose them, as the summer reveals the nature of the tree.—And if the alchemist brings to light that which lies hidden in nature, one must know that those hidden powers are different in each thing—they are different in locusts, different in leaves, different in flowers, and different in ripe and unripe fruits. For all this is so marvellous that in form and qualities the last fruit of a tree is completely unlike the first one. . . . And each thing has not only one virtue but many, just as a flower has more than one colour, and each colour has in itself the most diverse hues; and yet they con- *I/8, 191–92* stitute a unity, one thing.

Alchemy is a necessary, indispensable art. . . . It is an art, and Vulcan is its artist. He who is a Vulcan has mastered this art; he who is not a Vulcan can make no headway in it. But to understand this art, one must above all know that God has created all things; and that He has created something out of nothing. This something is a seed, in which the purpose of its use and function is inherent from the begin-

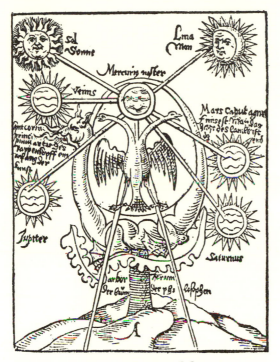

Fig. 94. *Mercurius Noster*: alchemistic-symbolic representation of quicksilver, or mercury, as one of the planets which is the source and cause of all transmutation

ning. And since all things have been created in an unfinished state, nothing is finished, but Vulcan must bring all things to their completion. Things are created and given into our hands, but not in the ultimate form that is proper to them. For example, wood grows of itself, but does not transform itself into boards or charcoal. Similarly, clay does not of itself become a pot. This is true of everything that grows in nature.

I/11, 186–87

♓

The *quinta essentia* is that which is extracted from a substance—from all plants and from everything which has life

145

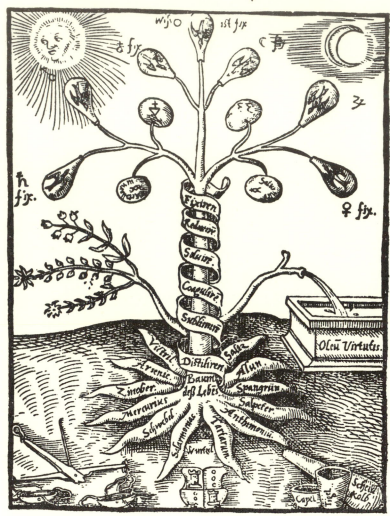

Fig. 95. The Stages of Alchemical Operations

—then freed of all impurities and all perishable parts, refined into highest purity and separated from all elements.
. . . The inherency of a thing, its nature, power, virtue, and
curative efficacy, without any . . . foreign admixture . . .
that is the *quinta essentia*. It is a spirit like the life spirit, but
with this difference that the *spiritus vitae*, the life spirit, is
imperishable, while the spirit of man is perishable. . . . The
quinta essentia being the life spirit of things, it can be extracted only from the perceptible, that is to say material,
parts, but not from the imperceptible, animated parts of
things. . . . It is endowed with extraordinary powers and
perfections, and in it is found a great purity, through which
it effects an alteration or cleansing in the body, which is
an incomparable marvel. . . . Thus the *quinta essentia* can
cleanse a man's life. . . . Therefore each disease requires

Fig. 96. The Philosophers' Stone: alchemistic-symbolic
representation

its own *quinta essentia,* although some forms of the *quinta essentia* are said to be useful in all diseases.

1/3, 118–20

Only what is incorporeal and immortal, what is endowed with eternal life, what stands above all natural things and remains unfathomable to man, can rightly be called an arcanum. . . . Like the divine curative powers, it has power to change us, to renew us, and to restore us. . . . And although the arcana are not external and although they do not constitute a symphony to the divine essence, they must be considered heavenly as compared with us mortals, for they can preserve our bodies, and by their influences achieve marvels in us that reason cannot fathom. . . . The arcanum is the entire virtue of a thing, multiplied a thousandfold. . . . Up until the present epoch, which is still young, only four arcana have come to our knowledge. . . . The first arcanum is the *prima materia,* the second the *lapis philosophorum,* the third the *mercurius vitae,* and the last the *tinctura.* . . . The *prima materia* can consume a man's old age and confer a new youth upon him—thus a young herb from a new seed grows in a new summer and a new year. . . . The second arcanum, the *lapis philosophorum,* purifies the whole body and cleanses it of all its filth by developing fresh young energies. . . . *Mercurius vitae,* the third arcanum, has a purifying action; like a halcyon, which puts on new feathers after moulting, it can remove the impurities from man— down to the nails and the skin—and make him grow anew. Thus it renovates the old body. . . . *Tinctura,* the last arcanum, is like the *rebis*—the bisexual creature—which transmutes silver and other metals into gold; it "tinges," i.e., it transforms the body, removing its harmful parts, its crudity, its incompleteness, and transforms everything into a pure, noble, and indestructible being.

1/3, 138–41

Here on earth the celestial fire is a cold, rigid, and frozen fire. And this fire is the body of gold. Therefore all we can do with it by means of our own fire is to dissolve it and make it fluid, just as the sun thaws snow and ice and makes them liquid. In other words, fire has not the power to burn fire, for gold itself is nothing but fire. In heaven it is dissolved, but on earth it is solidified. . . . God and nature do nothing in vain, or without a purpose. The place of all things indestructible is not subject to time, it has no beginning or end, it is everywhere. Those things are efficacious when all hope has been given up, and they may accomplish miraculously what is considered impossible, what looks hopeless, absurd, or even desperate.

I/14, 413–14

Ↄ(

But to write more about this mystery is forbidden and further revelation is the prerogative of the divine power. For this art is truly a gift of God. Wherefore not everyone can understand it. For this reason God bestows it upon whom He pleases, and it cannot be wrested from Him by force; for it is His will that He alone shall be honoured in it and that through it His name be praised for ever and ever.

I/14, 431

Fig. 97. Uroboros, "Serpent that Eats His Own Tail": representation of the hermetic alchemistic transmutation process and symbol of eternity, time, etc.

Fig. 98. The Astronomer

1/11, 378

Know that the philosopher has power over the stars and not the stars over him.

Astronomy is an indispensable art; it should rightly be held in high esteem, and studied earnestly and thoroughly. . . . For it teaches each man the condition and disposition of his soul, his heart, his thoughts; it teaches him whether they are false, or righteous and good, whether they are malignant or not. And it teaches how the hour of conception affects the child's fate, although it is less important than the conjuncture of the stars at the time of his birth.

1/12, 169

The astronomer should be able to find his bearings in the firmament with the help of his natural reason, in a natural way, as a philosopher or a physician finds his way among the

150

Fig. 99. Astronomy Lesson

things of nature, which derive from the elements. But he should not have a higher opinion of this art, and place more reliance in it than behooves a prisoner. The prisoner, too, has all the qualities that belong to a man, but he is prevented from unfolding them; he cannot do what he wants. The same is true of the firmament: it lies imprisoned in the hands of the Supreme Mover. What this hand intends to do with it is hidden to the astronomer. . . . For his art may be impeded, furthered, or changed by the hand of the Supreme Helmsman. *I/12, 91*

Know that there are two kinds of stars—the heavenly and the earthly, the stars of folly and the stars of wisdom. And

151

just as there are two worlds, a Little World and a Great World, and just as the little one rules over the great one, so the stars of the microcosm rule over and govern the Stars of heaven. For never forget that God has created the planets and all other stars not to rule over and govern man, but to obey Him as do all other created things.

Fig. 100. Jupiter

In the stars there dwell reason, wisdom, ruse, strife, weapons, just as they do in us men. For we originate in them; they are our parents, and from them we have received our reason, wisdom, strife, etc. We have received all these from the stars, and accordingly these same things are in the stars; with the sole difference that in us men they become material, corporeal, visible, while in the stars they are invisible, subtle, spiritual. But let no one fancy that the wisdom and reason, which we have received from heaven, come directly from God! They do not come directly from Him, but exist in us men as a reflection of the corresponding qualities of the macrocosm, the Great Creature. But the wisdom which comes to us from God Himself stands above the other and is stronger than the heavens and the stars.

The art of astronomy helps us to discover the secrets of the innate disposition of the heart and makes manifest the good and evil qualities with which nature has endowed man. For man is a child of the Great World, and his nature is rooted in it. And because the earth and the stars are characterized by different natures, and the Kingdom of God by yet another, we must discover each of these by its signs. . . . For the art of astronomy distinguishes fancy and opinion from science and knowledge. And it teaches us with what great reason all things proceed in their course. What in its essence belongs to the ways of God must be learned from God, but concerning what belongs to the mortal sphere we are instructed by the firmament, the Great Creature. *1/9, 578*

It is not true that the firmament exerts a compelling action upon man; on the contrary man himself acts upon the world more than he is influenced by it. Therefore it would only be just if one refrained from writing about the action of the firmament as is usually done. . . . For this action has in-

Fig. 101. Blood-Letting Chart

fluence only upon the emotions and upon the heathen, sensual reason. But we are Christians, and we should live like Christians. If we live like heathen, other influences are visited upon us, influences that cannot be understood on the basis of the stars. . . . Christ said that pestilence, drought, famine, and earthquakes would follow fast upon one another, and so they will—let no one forget it!—and they will not be announced in advance by the earthly planets. We must pay greater heed to the words of Christ than to those of astrology. He alone decrees the signs of the seasons and tides and fulfils the seasons of the nations.

1/11, 241

The stars are subject to the philosopher, they must follow him, and not he them. Only the man who is still animal is governed, mastered, compelled, and driven by the stars, so that he has no choice but to follow them—just as the thief cannot escape the gallows, the murderer the wheel, the fish the fisherman, the bird the snare, or the game the hunter. But the reason for all this is that such a man does not know himself and does not know how to use the energies hidden in him, nor does he know that he carries the stars within himself, that he is the microcosm, and thus carries in him the whole firmament with all its influences. Therefore he can rightly be abused as stupid and unwise, and must live in dire servitude to all that is earthly and mortal.

1/11, 378

Christ and His apostles prophesy the seasons of the nations, but the astronomer states the seasons of natural events. This is a mighty difference; take note of it and understand it aright, ye scientists and theologians! For what God prophecies takes place and nothing can prevent it from coming true. But what the astronomer predicts may or may not happen. Thus prophecy springs from one source, astronomy from another. The true knowledge of man's essence can be attained only on the basis of his eternity; it cannot be understood by any other sign.

1/12, 19

When Christ came all other wisdom died out and vanished, and since then it has been of no value. . . . Christ brought eternal wisdom into the world, and since then it has been just and proper to renounce the inferior kinds of wisdom and adhere to the higher kinds; and though I myself often write in the manner of the heathen, I am a Christian and must recognize that the inferior wisdom must yield to the greater. The wisdom of Christ is more profound than that of nature, consequently a prophet or an apostle must be held in higher esteem than an astronomer or a physician; and it is better to prophesy from God than through astronomy, it is better to cure through God than by means of herbs. The message of the prophets is without an error. The apostles have power to cure the sick and raise the dead, and likewise their works are without a flaw. Who then can doubt that astronomy and its light have paled beneath the light of Christ?—Nevertheless it is our duty to say that the sick need a physician, while few need an apostle; similarly many forecasts must be made by the astronomer and not by the prophets. Thus each has his part—the prophet, the astronomer, the apostle, and the physician. For this reason astronomy has not been abolished, nor forbidden to us Christians; we have only been commanded to use it in a Christian manner. For the Father has set us in the light of nature, and the Son in the eternal light. Therefore it is indispensable that we should know them both.   *1/12, 496-97*

ЭC

Man's wisdom is in no way subjugated, and is no one's slave; it has not renounced or surrendered its freedom. Therefore the stars must obey man and be subject to him, and not he to the stars. Even if he is a child of Saturn and if Saturn has overshadowed his birth, he can still escape Saturn's influence, he can master Saturn and become a child of the sun.   *1/11, 378*

The wise man is the man who lives by divine wisdom and is an image of Him in whose likeness he was created. The wise man rules over both bodies—the sidereal, or aerial, and the elemental, or material, body. Man must serve both, he must go the ways of each, in order to fulfil the law of the Lord and live in harmony with nature, and with the will of God and with the divine spirit. He must not prefer the mortal body and its reason to the eternal "image," nor must he reject this "image" for the sake of the animal body and find eternal salvation in the wisdom of the animal body. . . . The wise man lives after the image of God and is not guided by the ways of the world. And he who imitates the image of God will conquer the stars.

I/12, 41–42

Fig. 102. A Prophet

IV

MAN AND ETHICS

Fig. 103. The Stages of Reality

For what is a man profited if he shall gain the whole world, and lose his own soul?

1/14, 207

Even if we are born deaf and dumb, why should we remain deaf and dumb forever? It was God who has endowed us with speech, and how could children learn to speak, if He did not grant them His divine help? The word and the ear have been given us as implements with which to study God's creation in so far as He permits us to do so. What avails it a man to see if he does not know what he has seen? To what end has man been created except that he may learn to distinguish between good and evil and choose the good? If we have no knowledge of this, we know nothing of God. But who can say that a man who knows nothing is happy? A man who has knowledge will never succumb to a temptation,

159

nor has such a man ever been found to be superstitious. Where, then, does superstition pervail? Among those who know nothing. Where is vanity? Only among those who have no knowledge. And where is folly? Among those who are content with their own want of judgment and do not strive toward God's wisdom.

1/9, 339

It behooves a pious man to be wise and skilful, so that he may understand what he believes. If a fool and know-nothing has faith, his faith is dead. Works alone lead one to faith, that is to say the works of nature, her signs and marvels. And since faith is based on works, signs, and marvels, it is fitting that we philosophize as believers and not as heathen, and that we profess the Christian creed. But there are believers of different kinds; and we are convinced that he who wants to believe must also know; for only from knowledge, and because of knowledge, does faith arise. Through this knowledge, which comes from philosophy and precedes faith, a man can be either blessed or damned; damned, though he know and believe in all God's signs and marvels, if for example the fruit of his knowledge fails to mature, and dies away. For he who knows much should bear much fruit. And if he does not, he may be regarded as a liar and not a philosopher. For first comes knowledge, then faith, and then the fruit; this is the ground on which the philosopher must stand.

1/13, 246

The lover goes a long way to meet a beautiful woman; how much farther should one go to discover a beautiful art? The Queen of Sheba came from beyond the seas only to hear Solomon's wisdom. Now why did so exalted a queen pursue Solomon's wisdom? For the reason that wisdom is a gift of God and must be sought in him to whom God has given it. And similarly all art must be sought in those whom God has endowed with it.

1/11, 145

Man possesses two kinds of reason: angelic and animal. The angelic reason is eternal, and comes from God, and belongs to God; God has also given us the animal reason . . . but it is not eternal, for the body dies, and it dies with the body. No animal thing endures after death. Death is only the death of the animal part, not of the eternal part of man. . . . A beast is not a man, it is a beast; and man is not a beast, but the image of God. Man is the instrument through which God reveals His miracles; yet he is like a beast in that he is mortal.

Not the humanity in him, but the beast is mortal; man will be resurrected on the Day of Judgment and stand before God, but not so the animal, not so the beast in him. Man will be called to give an account of himself, but not so the beast. . . . Therefore, a man who is not a man of wisdom and of arts is only an abortion; he is not a man but only a beast.

There are two kinds of wisdom in this world — one eternal and one perishable. The eternal wisdom originates directly in the light of the Holy Ghost, the other wisdom directly in the light of nature. The one that comes from the light of the Holy Ghost is of only one kind—it is the just and flawless wisdom. But the one that originates in the light of nature is of two kinds: good and evil. The good wisdom is inseparable from the Eternal, the evil from Doom. . . . Is it not a high privilege of man to distinguish eternal wisdom from temporal wisdom, and to understand that the mortal is worthless when compared with the eternal?

I/13, 310–11

Fig. 104. True and False Wisdom: The fool says, "Thee, O fortune, we make into a goddess, we exalt thee to heaven." The sage says, "Trust in virtue, fortune is more transitory than the waves"

This treasure has been given man because he is the image of God, and therefore he should always strive to be worthy of this image, and distinguish a good and an evil kind of temporal wisdom, and thus discover that the good consists primarily of eternal wisdom, and only subsequently of temporal wisdom. And of this other wisdom let him retain only the good kind, and reject the evil kind. For wisdom does not command you, but you alone command yourself.

I/12, 8–9

Hands and feet in themselves do not constitute a man; the wisdom of nature and the faculties she bestows are needed to complete him. Therefore man should not turn to the carnal part of his body; for all this is animal. He should concern himself only with that part of his body which is invisible and intangible—the light of nature, the natural wisdom that God has inculcated in the stars and that passes from them to man.

I/12, 55

Natural reason and eternal wisdom belong together. Natural reason may exist without eternal wisdom, when it follows the heathen way, and is not concerned with the Eternal. But eternal reason cannot exist without natural wisdom because man must find the eternal in the natural. Therefore a man who dwells in God is endowed with both to be his guides in all things.

I/12, 29

To all of us falls one heritage—wisdom. All of us inherit of it equally. But one man makes the best of his heritage, and another does not; one buries it, lets it die, and passes over it, another draws profit from it—one more, another less. According to how we invest, use, and administer our heritage, we obtain much or little from it; and yet it belongs to all of us, and it is in all of us.

I/13, 294–95

God recognizes all talents that originate in His wisdom, each according to its own character. Much work leads to great knowledge. And all such talents partake of God's love; he to whom God reveals them has them.

I/9, 376

The light of nature says: wisdom has no other enemy than the man who is not wise. Therefore wisdom has no other enemy but lies, and thus he who teaches and writes in God has no other enemy but him who is not in God.

I/12, 284

Wisdom consists in knowing and not in imagining; a man who has wisdom understands all things and uses them with reason, his reason and wisdom are free from stupidity, free from folly, free from confusion and doubt. Let the right path, the right reason, the right mind, and the right weight and measure be the scale of all things—for it is by knowledge that all things are governed, led, and brought to their perfection.

I/11, 171

He who knows nothing loves nothing. He who can do nothing understands nothing. He who understands nothing is worthless. But he who understands also loves, notices, sees. . . . The more knowledge is inherent in a thing, the greater the love. . . . Everything lies in knowledge. From it comes every fruit. Knowledge bestows faith; for he who knows God believes in Him. He who does not know Him does not believe in Him. Everyone believes in what he knows.

I/11, 207

He who inherits God's wisdom walks on water without wetting his feet; for in the true art inherited from God, man is like an angel. But what will wet an angel? Nothing. Similarly, nothing will wet the wise man. God is powerful and He wills it that His power be revealed to men and to angels in the wisdoms and the arts. He wills it that the world and the earth be like Heaven. Not with regard to chastity, for this is a matter decided by the body, not with regard to fasting, for this too is imposed upon the body, and not in works, for these belong to the body, but in wisdom and the arts. . . . Can any man be a fool who follows the will of God? No, he cannot. Can anyone be unlearned who follows the will of God? No, he cannot. Can anyone be an ignoramus who follows His will? Certainly not. All this goes counter to the will of God; for He does not want us to be fools, uninformed, ignorant, and without understanding; He wants us to be awakened to knowledge in all the great things of His creation, which He has given us in

163

1/13, 306 order that the devil may know we belong to God and are like unto angels.

Know that nothing could pass from us to God were there not an angel in us, who takes our inner message to Heaven. Nor would anything of God come to us without such an agent, who is swifter than all our thoughts. . . . Before a thought occurs to us, it has been with God and then returned to us. What God wills, He brings about through the spirit in us, which is charged with performing His work in us . . . It is incumbent upon the soul to serve as man's angel, and upon man to make use of his angel; for the angel is nothing other than the immortal part of man.

1/12, 305

Fig. 105. The Angel

What have the angels power to do? All things. For in them is all the wisdom of God and all His art. . . . The angels are pure and clean, without sleep, in an eternal waking state. The body of man is imprisoned in sleep, therefore he must be awakened if he would attain to the wisdom of angels, that is to say, to the wisdom and the art of God. . . . For God has given His power to the herbs, put it in stones, concealed it in seeds; we should take it from them, we should seek it in them. The angels possess wisdom in themselves, but man does not. For him wisdom lies in nature, in nature he must seek it. His harvest is stored up in nature. Through nature God's power is revealed to man, through nature he enters into his Father's heritage, in wis-

1/13, 304-5 dom and in the arts.

The nature of a man's virtue is like that of his feelings. His treasure lies where his heart is. If it is with God, God is his treasure, and He attracts him. If his feelings are at-

tached to nature, it is she who attracts him. But if his attitude is dual, so is his work. For as the man is, so are his
virtues and powers. *I/12, 161*

Fidelity cannot be divided or mixed, any more than God's
truth. All this cannot be divided, just as love cannot be
divided; for fidelity and love are one thing. . . . When a
man studies only for the sake of appearances, for the sake
of outward splendour, and contents himself with mere talk,
with superficial titles, there the highest fidelity is lacking.
All such doings are unfaithful and have nothing in common
with love. *I/8, 213*

The Scripture says: *compelle intrare,* which means: com-
pel them to enter; namely, from the lie into the truth. It is
said to the end that he who boasts a sword may see to it
that the truth is taught and not the lie. For only the truth
can forestall all lies and encourage man to learn and grow
in piety and not in malice. Of his own accord man inclines
to evil, but if he is compelled to be good, the good will be
revealed to him. *I/10, 213*

We should write and assert the truth; but if we are in
doubt and do not know the causes, we should abstain from
writing. This rule should be observed not only in medicine,
but also in chronicles, in the writing of history, in all books,
and also in the interpretation of Holy Writ. . . . For otherwise lies are spread among the people, who prefer darkness
to light. . . . The Scripture says: the letter killeth, but the
spirit giveth life. . . . That is to say, the spirit which bears
nothing but the truth in itself. If a man adheres solely to the
truth in his writings, it is not mere letters that he writes; it
is the spirit that he sets down in its truth, the spirit that is
invisible in itself and that must come to us through the
written or spoken word. . . . But if a man does not write
the truth, he writes lies; and the letter that is a lie kills.
Therefore let any desirous of writing be careful to keep

1/10, 83

always to the truth, that he may kill no one. For to kill is forbidden under the penalty of forfeiting eternal life.

The promises that we give one another, let us keep them even though the ground burst open beneath our feet. It is better that we should sink into the earth than that we should lie to our fellow men. For the lie destroys our own heart. The lie makes false storekeepers, false traders, false brothers; all deceit springs from the lie. Therefore make sure that when you say yes, it should remain a yes, and not become a no.

1/14, 287

God must nourish us, no one else can do it. He acts toward us as a master toward his servants; each servant is treated according to his bent, and so does God with us. If a man would nourish himself on truth, God gives him enough of it, and that is his nourishment. God owes us our nourishment and gives it to us in the form in which we ourselves desire it. If we desire it in the form of lies, even truths become lies in us, and we live like liars. For God gives the liars their nourishment just as He gives it to the truthful. He must nourish all of us, whether we be good or evil, just as he must make provision for the sun, the earth, and all creation.

1/8, 210

It is God's will that we keep our vows and promises and that we do not waver in this but remain steadfast as a rock. For each yes is a promise, a vow. And it must be kept unbroken, whether it be good or bad. What you promise, keep! If it is good, it will be revealed as good to all men; if it is evil, men will discover where the righteous and the unrighteous stand, where the devil has his children.

1/14, 277

⊢O⊣

Our beginning is faith. It may be enclosed in our hearts like a treasure in an unused shrine, and lie there, well protected . . . and if a poor man should come to us, we should open our hearts and give him the gift that is in our heart—this gift is love. If we have drawn out the love that lies in this treasure, and if we walk in the path of love on earth, we may also look forward to the third virtue—the hope of eternity. But he who does not know how to draw love from his treasure, his hope is like empty straw.

II/1, 85–86

Speech is not of the tongue but of the heart. The tongue is merely the instrument with which one speaks. He who is dumb is dumb in his heart, not in his tongue. Therefore the words of the tongue should come from the heart, for it is the heart that holds truth, loyalty, and love. He who speaks should draw them thence, and speak from the heart, then his yes will be a yes, and his no a no. If you say yes, abide by it, even if it is evil; and if you say no, abide by it, even if it is evil. For what is in our heart is thereby revealed, and thereby you may be known. As you speak, so is your heart.

I/14, 276–77

Fig. 106. The Heart

Of ceremonies you should know that they are superfluous; for if we are to receive something from God, He looks into our hearts and not at the ceremonies. If we have received something of Him, He does not wish us to use it for ceremonies but for works. He grants us favours that we may love Him in our hearts, with all our strength and all our soul, and that we may thus help our fellow man. And if whatever He gives us serves only this purpose, all ceremonies become superfluous.

I/9, 344

He who loves much is given much. Salvation is the lot of all, but the gifts that spring from love are unequal. . . . No one may say: God, our Father, has given me more life than you; for He has given an equal share of life to all. And in the exact same measure are the goods of the earth meted out, since the earth belongs to us and to no one else. And since it is ours, we are entitled to possess it all in the same measure, and not in unequal measures. But if a greater share falls to one man than to another, and a lesser to this man than to that man, and thus there is inequality of distribution, the rich man should nevertheless refrain from asserting that he possesses more than the poor man. For if he has more, that much more should he give away, and not eat everything himself, but like the others content himself with an equal share. God metes out many things, this to one man, that to another, to each his own. But the highest good is meted out to all of us equally—and that is the enjoyment of life on this earth. Hence we should act accordingly and help one another. Those who have much should give much to those who have nothing, that they may be found generous in their gifts.

II/1, 121–22

━┼O┼━

The true faith of the jurist should rest upon mercy; and all his striving should be to the end that others be forgiven. . . . For who can say what is right, and who among us mortal men can presume to pass a judgment that will be valid before God, unless it has been inspired in him by the Holy Ghost Himself? But then he would not be taking it from a book or from his imagination or from his own head! . . . How can anyone praise himself and condemn another, since no one knows who he himself really is? Here lies the greatest error and contradiction in which the jurists are imprisoned. As long as they have been promulgating the law and sitting in judgment, no one has ever been given his right; the poor is always worsted, and the rich or quick-witted man always wins and not the slow-witted, the favoured and not the unfavoured. And all this happens by virtue of the letter. It is the letter that sends the thief to the gallows—and the judge to eternal damnation. The true religion of the jurist should be: to guide men to forgive, and

pardon one another, to turn the other cheek. For not for
nothing has God so ordained.   *II/1, 103–4*

What we have received from the Holy Ghost, whether
it be wisdom, or medicine, that serves our fellow man, and
this is true of everything else. But what is not directed
toward the love of God and the fellow man does not spring
from the Holy Ghost.   *II/1, 150*

Fig. 107. The Scholar

The heart of man is so great if it is righteous that God begrudges him nothing. But if it is not righteous and holds no goodness in it, even the Lord's Prayer is poison in such a man's mouth. Thus the Lord's Prayer, though it springs from God himself, is poison in the heart of an evil man, and his eternal death; but in the heart of a good man, it leads to life everlasting. Therefore you should know that even if the rogues did all that the saints have done, it would be poison in the eyes of God. But he who is not a rogue, he who walks in the ways of God, will be pure in heart, even if he has done nothing but eat partridges.

1/14, 343–44

Fig. 108. Parental Love

It would be an error to try to build the Kingdom of Heaven upon envy. For nothing that is founded on envy can thrive; it must have another root. If anyone were to attempt it, it would be with him as with the man who dug a moat: he dug it for another and fell into it himself. For God is the judge: He allows the moat to be dug, but He knows the hearts of men; when the moat is ready, He sets dogs on the men, and thus they fall into it. God often protects one evil man from another evil man because a greater evil might come about if one evil man killed another evil man. It is the same as with the wounded man whose wounds were swarming with flies. Someone wanted to chase them away, but he said: "No, let them remain where they are! For if you drive them away, others will come, which are hungry and which will torment me again. But these have already eaten their fill."

II/1, 184

If a war breaks out, the cause of it is that God sends a punishment upon a country in order by such a punishment to renew the world. And in proceeding against a country the enemy metes out the same measure as God in Heaven metes out against that country. As a man who acts against God far exceeds the measure of malice, so another man may come, who in acting against him also exceeds the measure; and just as the first man forgot himself in acting against God, so the second man forgets himself in acting against the first.

I/12, 280

You should practise humility first toward man, and only then toward God. He who despises men has no respect for God. The Scripture says: You should live in accord with your companions as long as you walk with them on earth, so that no one may hold a grudge against you in the next world. For in the hereafter there is a pit and a hangman whom you shall not be able to escape; you will be forced into the pit and you will pay dearly for your sins!

All of you here on earth, turn away from vanity and pride, and practise humility, and confess your sins; for

II/1, 204–5

Fig. 109. The Planet Saturn as Ruler of the Year Brings Ruin and Disease

all of us are sinners. If a man confess his sins to his fellow man, and his fellow man to him, everyone confesses to be a sinner. Therefore we should also pardon and forgive one another, so that we may be blessed. And you, holders of power, if you do not confess your overweening pride toward your subjects, you will never be pardoned. If you do not, here on earth, obtain forgiveness from those to whom you are indebted, how can you expect ever to escape the pit after this life? . . . And similarly you who are masters in

Fig. 110. The Penitent

all lands . . . and who have measured with false measures. . . . Confess your sins! For this God will give full
credit to your hearts, and will grant you his pardon. *II/1, 214–15*

He who knows no repentance and no suffering can offer
no resistance to the devil. When great sins weigh upon
us . . . we should cry out to God from the bottom of our
hearts. If from the depths of our souls we call out earnestly
to Him, He will direct His eyes toward us and remit all
our sins. But if we are not steadfast in our hearts, He will

not forgive us any sin.
Who can oppose Him?
Therefore let our hearts
be alert by night and
day, without respite,
from one mass to the
other, and never aban-
don hope, but remain
steadfast, and let us
think of God's great
mercy and of the salva-
tion that lies in him. *II/1, 214*

Fig. 111. Banquet with Music

There is no greater
evil than to yield to
temptation in things which concern the body and life of man.
For Christ has ordered us to entreat Him in prayer that we
may not be led into temptation. To be unknowing and un-
clear about oneself is to meet temptation half way and to injure body and soul. When we act, let us act from full insight;
if we live in folly and stupidity we find no favour in God's
eyes, and nothing will excuse us. Therefore pray that you be
not led into temptation! *I/8, 305*

Take the good until you find something better, and in
search for something better do not let the good slip away
from you or die out. If you disregard it despite its worth,
and pursue something better, what you had escapes you; but
if you remain attached to what is good, you will always
have it if nothing better follows. *I/8, 307*

One thing is as good as another; the carbuncle is no better than the tuff stone, the fir is valued no less than the cypress; this is revealed in the light of nature. He who sets gold above silver does so out of greed; for silver like gold has been endowed with excellence. Therefore such actions do not spring from the wisdom of nature, but from mortal reason.

I/9, 90

＋○＋

He who commits adultery or leads a life of fornication has been condemned by God, whatever he may be, whether learned or not, whether of the clerical or secular estate. The Lord is no respecter of persons. In this we should follow God and set equal store by everyone—without regard for his position in life—and help, advise, and give to all in equal measure. If we observe this rule, we walk in the footsteps of the Lord. . . . For such is His will—despise no one, favour no one!

Remember that we should not call our brother a fool; for we ourselves do not know what we are. God alone can judge and know.

II/1, 123

What is the meaning of the Kingdom of Heaven? It is this: that we should forgive one another—then God will forgive us too; that we should love one another—then God

Fig. 112. The Suppliants

will love us too. . . . What is more blessed than this? And if it is in this that we find our happiness on earth, then the Kingdom of Heaven is with us.

II/1, 246

We sin in a twofold way—against God and against our fellow man. And therefore forgiveness is twofold: we forgive our fellow man, just as we wish to obtain forgiveness from God. In other words, if we forgive our enemies and

Fig. 113. The Jeweller

debtors, God forgives us, however we may have transgressed against Him and whatever sins we may have committed. Therefore we must first of all forgive one another. For the beginning is with us, the end with God.

II/1, 202–3

If you are a peasant and have many fields, many possessions, and you have full enjoyment of them—what is enjoyment? After all, you cannot eat everything by yourself! Give one part to your servants and another to those in need. Amass no treasures; the worms, flies, and moths will devour them in any event. Sufficient unto the day is the evil thereof —and the care and the misery. This in itself is not a cross; but the very next day may bring you a cross. Therefore let us be free of care and give of our own free will what exceeds our pressing need. . . . Blessed are those who die in the Lord! These are the poor who have sought no pleasure on earth.

II/1, 243

If the purpose of your labour is not wealth, but if you confine yourself to daily bread, you are blessed and you will be happy. Then you will not steal, for stealing is done for the sake of riches, and in order to eat one's bread in idleness; you will kill no one, for the purpose of killing is to gain another man's possession or for an insignificant wage to help another to gain them; nor will you bear false witness, for this is done in order to circumvent God. But how blessed you will be and how happy if you are not burdened with any guilt! If you have understood the blessed life that is achieved by confining yourself to the needs of the day, you have properly understood those three commandments of God.

II/1, 246

The wealth that properly belongs to the happy rich man consists not in treasures, which the moths devour, but in his children who stand round his table like the branches of an olive tree, which stand out in a circle round its trunk. This is the divine wealth of the blessed man, it is his share along with his work. The wealth consisting in such work and such children finds favour in the eyes of God and He delights in it. But the children of the idler will stand round his table as the thorns round a thistle.

II/1, 256–57

If you are a knight, of what use to you are your golden necklaces and your golden spurs and bridles? If you want to be a knight and a champion of blessedness, then be a knight through your generosity and not through the shedding of blood.

II/1, 167

There are not many rich people endowed by nature with blessed generosity. How many begrudge the poor even food. Such people, choking with vulgarity, cruelty, and avarice, and utterly lacking in understanding, should be taught generosity. For those who have no generosity will be eternally damned, and nothing will help them. On the Day of Judgment they will be told: "You did not feed me when I was hungry, you did not give me to drink when I was thirsty, and you did not clothe me when I was naked."

Therefore may blessed generosity be praised, that they may gain understanding and learn how to give—these stupid, arrogant, proud men, who imagine that there is no God and they themselves are the masters of heaven and earth.   *II/1, 155–56*

Not in riches does our happiness consist, but in our natural needs. For in our needs there is also love; love does not pursue riches, riches defraud the fellow man. But this is against God, and the blessed life becomes worm-eaten. If the patient gives you, physician, what you need and nothing more, then you are both blessed. If you give him health, which is his need, and nothing more, then you are both blessed. If you are a potter, then your fellow men who need your work support you by paying you a wage. Let them give you as much as you need, but no riches; riches would bring you only damnation, but poverty will bring you blessedness. For our kingdom is not of this world, but of the life everlasting.

Fig. 114. The Beggar   *II/1, 242*

Without the rich, nothing can be accomplished in behalf of the poor; the rich are bound to the poor as by a chain. . . . You, rich men, learn to know this chain, for if you ever break one link of it, you will not only be breaking the chain, but you yourselves will be cast aside like the broken link. Why do you make yourselves free from the poor and deny them your help? Just as by taking a few links from a chain, you would be making it too short, so without the poor, your path will be too short to lead to Heaven, and you will never attain to the goal that lies at the end of the chain. Know, therefore, that all your diseases on earth lie in one single hospital, whether you be rich or poor; and that is the hospital of God. This you must understand well, and consider that death and disease spare you as little as they do the poor. Examine yourselves and know that all of you need the hospital equally, and that all of you, lords and princes, as you are assembled, must lie in this hospital, and die or else recover.

1/7, 376

Blessed and thrice blessed is the man to whom God gives the grace of poverty. . . . Therefore the most blessed is he who loves poverty. It rids him of many fetters, frees him from the prison of hell. It does not lead him to practise usury, to steal, to murder, and so on. But he who loves riches sits on a shaky limb; a little breeze comes—and it enters his head to steal, to practise usury, to drive hard bargains, and other such evil practices, all of which serve him only to acquire the riches of the devil and not those of God. Therefore let the doctrine of the blessed life be taught not to those who love riches, for they will not find pleasure in it, but only to those who delight in poverty, in the community of the poor, in a just life, so that no one may surpass his fellow man in the satisfaction of his needs, but that each may suffer with the other, and help him, and rejoice and weep with him. For to be merry with the merry and to grieve with the aggrieved is fair and just.

11/1, 83–84

Become poor, indeed, and become poor as a beggar, then the pope will desert you, and the emperor will desert you, and henceforth you will be considered only a fool. But then you will have peace, and your folly will be great wisdom in the eyes of God. But if you are not ready to assume voluntary poverty, you walk away in sadness, like the disciple whom Christ commanded to sell his house, his land, and all his belongings, and to follow Him.

11/1, 83

Fig. 115. The Light of
the Heart
178

V

MAN AND SPIRIT

Fig. 116. The Creator Blesses the Globe

The Holy Ghost kindles
the light of nature. . . .

IT is nature that teaches all things, and what she herself
cannot teach, she receives of the Holy Ghost, who instructs her. For the Holy Ghost and nature are one,
that is to say: each day nature shines as a light from the
Holy Ghost and learns from him, and thus this light reaches
man, as in a dream.

I/13, 325

Everything that comes from the light of nature must be
learned from the light of nature, excepting only the image of

181

God, which is learned from the spirit that the Lord has given to man. The spirit instructs man in the knowledge of supernatural and eternal things, and after the separation of matter from spirit, it returns to the Lord. For it is given to man only as a teacher, to enlighten him in things eternal.

1/12, 20

There are two schools for man. The school of the earth teaches earthly things and has its schoolmaster from nature, in nature; indeed, it is nature herself. It inculcates knowledge of itself, that is to say, of those things which are in it. Then there is the other school, that from above. There, the teacher is our Father in Heaven. He from whom we are. . . . He teaches us in the reborn body, and not in the old body, and in this reborn man, He teaches heavenly wisdom. . . . From this school are the apostles, prophets, and those who study God, and their works and fruits are their witnesses.

1/12, 316–17

What is there in us, mortals, that has not come to us from God? He who teaches us the eternal also teaches us the perishable; for both spring from God.

1/11, 130

There are many who deem man and his power to be the highest good. There are men who consider the emperor to be the highest good, or hold the highest good to be their fellow men who do them a good turn, give them gifts, or help them. But in this they are mistaken. For is there not Someone above the emperor, Someone who is more righteous than the emperor? Is there not Someone who gives to the man, who in turn gives you what you need? Is not this Someone more? We may rise as high as we can, in search of the highest good, but all this remains within the earthly sphere: that which is eternal is above all this.

II/1, 113

If we are to follow our God, and not He us, we must do everything ourselves, for He does nothing. It is entirely up to us whether or not we do a thing. Of what benefit is ruling to a man who uses the power he has over others only for purposes of arrogance and pride, for the sake of his own pleasure and not to serve others? For the power which only castigates and afflicts others, and which in itself can do nothing but feast and revel, and blow trumpets, is not divine. But if he who has the power is just in himself, the power must so subjugate him that he is sadder than those under him. For power comes from God, and He bears the human burdens that derive from it.

II/1, 190

There is a tree from which many and diverse things are sucked and drawn, and everything is one tree . . . a tree that bears only one fruit, to be sure, but a fruit of many tastes. This tree is the Holy Ghost himself, it is also His only fruit. This fruit is apportioned in many ways, that is to say, the tree bears very diverse fruit. For when the manna fell from heaven and the people ate of it, each ate what he wanted, and it had the taste he desired. It is the same with this fruit: he who eats of the tree of the Holy Ghost tastes just what he would like to suck and eat from it. It follows that to each is given the spirit he desires: to one the spirit of wisdom, to another the spirit of science, to a third the spirit of faith, to a fourth the spirit of healing, to a fifth the spirit of power, to a sixth the spirit of prophecy, to a seventh the spirit of tongues. Thus God gives diverse things through the Holy Ghost; and not just one craft, but many hundreds of crafts, that man may know how marvellous is that spirit from which all things come.

II/1, 143–44

Each craft is twofold: on the one hand there is the knowledge that we learn from men, on the other hand the knowledge that we learn from the Holy Ghost. The making of glass is not an art for him who has learned it from someone else. But he who was the first to invent it of himself deserves to be praised as an artist, for in him we feel the action of the Holy Ghost. . . . But in him who can do only what he has learned from others, the presence of the Holy Ghost cannot be felt. . . . Man can do none of all this by his own strength; all his wisdom, his reason, and everything that is in him cannot discover the new, let alone fully develop its properties. Those who learned from the first teachers learned directly from others, but they too lived by the Holy Ghost. For the Holy Ghost put it into those men, and it has thus come down from the first to the most recent men. . . . And thus the

II/1, 144–45   spirit of God triumphs on earth among men.

Fig. 117. God the Father and the Pilgrim

Since God . . . is not an inhabitant of this earth but has His throne and His Kingdom in Heaven, it is necessary that there be someone on earth to govern mankind and guide it and show it the way through the straits of life. There is no angel, no spirit on earth, to lead men; to man alone this task has fallen. Therefore, it is not surprising that many false paths are entered upon, and it is of great importance that man should recognize his shepherd, and know who he is, lest a wolf be taken for a shepherd and mislead man by donning sheep's clothing, while concealing the devil within him. . . . For each of the two paths—the narrow one through life and the broad one in heaven—has its own shepherd, and each of these shepherds reveals and shows us his way. But it is so hard to distinguish between the two that it is almost impossible to tell the one from the other. . . . God has given man shepherds to lead him and show him the way in study and work. But the shepherds cannot of themselves gain such leadership and guidance, but only when inspired by God. . . . For man must be guided in a divine, and not in a human manner. Therefore God himself ordained and appointed man's shepherds, and taught and instructed them as to what to teach and tell the people, in order that not their will but only the will of God be obeyed.   *II/1, 264*

One of the greatest gifts that God bestows upon us is to provide us always with holy men who lead us and teach us and guide us in things eternal, in the blessed life. He has enlightened them through the Holy Ghost that they may speak marvellously of His Kingdom with a great and fiery tongue, in a language that can be understood by the many. This is the true task of the pious teachers on earth, who take their instruction from the Holy Ghost and who speak and lead. . . . But not only are they deeply enlightened by the Holy Ghost and speak important words, a marvel to all men; they also possess a mighty power on earth, which God has bestowed on them. . . . Therein they are like their master: they purify the lepers when nature no longer has power to do so, and this they do with one miracle-working sentence: "You are pure." And it comes to pass. For the great truth is such that all the forces of nature are silent and yield in the face of its power; with one single word it can resurrect the dead.   *II/1, 91–92*

It is impossible for a man to know how a nation should be governed unless he has received the grace of the Holy Ghost, that is to say unless he has eaten of the tree of the Holy Ghost. Who except God can correctly gauge the hearts of men? He who wants to govern must look into the hearts of men and act accordingly. If he does not look into their hearts, his rule is beset with errors and difficulties, and harms his country. But he whose government is inspired by the Holy Ghost governs for the good of all, even if he is severe, hard, rude, and coarse. The Holy Ghost helps him to know the hearts of his subjects. And then he can also be gentle, kind, gracious, and merciful toward them, and rejoice their hearts. If they are evil or sinful, they should be treated with kindness rather than severity; a disobedient and sinful man must be seized by the authorities with a view to correction by hard or lenient punishment. If the authority upon which power is conferred does not pluck from the tree whose fruit is the Holy Ghost—as the bees suck honey from flowers—then its rule will in time become harmful and burdensome, and will never end happily. But this is true not only of government authorities, but also of fathers and mothers, masters, lords, and all those whose function is to instruct and to lead people. Let all of them equally take their wisdom, reason, judgment from the tree; for only thus can they learn how to wean others from evil and excess. The tree teaches how people should be governed and led: it is not a common tree, created only for the pleasure of the belly and the eyes, but is the fountainhead and reservoir of the blessed life. He who applies the power and wisdom that he has received from this tree is just in his authority and just in his wisdom; his authority and wisdom endure forever and *II/1, 148–49* abide with him forever. For no part of them is perishable.

Any attempt to establish injunctions for all eternity is folly. For what can man build on earth that will be eternal? He is not even certain whether the work he has done in the morning will still be standing at nightfall! In all things do as time commands; time draws you and you must follow. God teaches you to go whither time leads. Customs change and pass away, and to cling to them is folly. And it is folly to suppose that all things are eternal. All things are the product of time, and no one can raise himself above time; everyone is subject to time. Next to God, it is the emperor who commands. What command can he decree that will apply eternally? None. Commandments that must be observed eternally are decreed by God, and the emperor must only see to it that they are fulfilled. And if he does this, his own commandments will also be observed, provided they spring from the divine commandments. And if even the emperor can is-

Fig. 118. King and Knight

șue no orders to his successors, what can the common **man** expect to do? Time rules man, but does not rule God. Therefore His commandments are eternally true, but not those of man.

I/14, 260–61

Man should lead his fellow men, but not on the basis of his own strength. For man cannot sit on God's throne and rule, but must govern, teach, and instruct through God. Only thus can he lead rightly!—Man is like a sheep, and sheep have a fold. It must stand on a rock. And if the sheep are people, and the fold is the church, the rock on which the church stands must be a man whom God has chosen for this

187

Fig. 119. Hermit Pursued by the Devil

purpose. But before a man can be entrusted with a herd, he must first be tested to determine whether he will not be like a wolf set over sheep. For if he is a wolf, he cannot be a rock for God to build on. It follows that no one is capable of truly knowing the rock of the sheepfold except him to whom it belongs, namely, its builder. And this builder is God, and He Himself set the rock. Know therefore that the rock upon which the sheepfold of man is built cannot have been established by a man, and that no man has ever undertaken to create a rock. But, whether they were bad or good, they always placed the burden on the rock which God had given them . . . and here they have always let the matter rest, entrusting themselves to the rock and believing in him whom God sent. And while God Himself from the beginning of time has given men their guides and has never relinquished his authority, but retained it in his own discretion, men have nevertheless, from pride, established successors and leaders of their own. But never has anything resulting from this had any strength—as is obvious to everyone. And if other opinions have been offered on this score, let it only be a sign that they emanated from guides appointed by Satan.

II/1, 266–67

God's enemy is the devil, Satan and Beelzebub. For the truth cannot be without adversaries. God is the supreme truth and the devil the supreme lie. Only the devil cannot appear before God, he cannot confront Him, and the sight of God is forbidden him. But man, who was created as God's vicar on earth, can be led astray and assailed by the devil. For while the devil cannot appear before God's face, he can appear to man. . . . Upon man the same power is bestowed, as was once bestowed upon the devil when he was still in heaven and had not yet been driven out. Then he was free to be presumptuous or not. But he was presumptuous, and therefore God rejected him. Man too can be presumptuous or not, therein he is like the devil when the devil was still an angel. And what befell the devil will also befall the men who are like him. Therefore we should be like the angels and not like the devil; for to this end we were born and sent into the world.

1/13, 296–97

Fig. 120. Angel Captured by Devil

To what end does man live on earth, if not to become versed in the works of God and to learn how all things have their source in Him. Now, the devil along with his infernal host is against God and the followers of God, and like a roaring lion he sets traps for each of us, each man in his own way, as has been sufficiently demonstrated. When he meets the merchant, he assumes the form of a merchant; but to the merchant God too is a merchant, only one is from God and the other from the devil. Similarly, the devil is a king to the king, a prophet to the prophet, an apostle to the apostle, a physician to the physician, a warrior to the warrior, a knight to the knight, and so on. And likewise, God is a king to the king, a prophet to the prophet, and so on. . . . Therefore must each man get wisdom and know what is of God and what of the devil, what is divine government, and who are God's prophets, but also who are the devil's. For it seems to me quite especially useful that a merchant should recognize the devil, and also that everyone else should know how the devil speaks to the merchant, the physician, the prophet, by what snares he entraps and catches each of them. *I/12, 410–11*

Let us give to God that which is God's, and to the devil that which is the devil's. To this end we must know which things are of God and which are of Satan, and distinguish among deeds, and classify them aright. *I/12, 369*

Although a man has been given a title by the people, and is called prophet, apostle, or doctor, his office is not thereby fulfilled. Many believe that it is God above who determines the acts and the choices of men on earth, but this is error. . . . Though many may claim to speak the word of God, it is not given to everyone: not to everyone is the reward granted, not to everyone is the door opened. *II/1, 219*

When God created man, He gave him his heart; in paradise He gave him knowledge of good and evil, and taught him not to do unto others what he would not have done unto himself. For such is the law, and such is the heart we received from the hand of God when He created us. Now, the heart is a rock on which man stands and shall stand, in so far as God did not appoint him to any special office or did not designate him as one of the elect, that is to say, in so far as He does not build on this man as on a rock. As you know, God made a seed issue from Abraham and blessed this seed, and promised it greatness. . . . And He gave to mankind a few chosen men, marvellously endowed with virtues and wisdom, and with reason and judgment far exceeding all others. It also pleased God to choose one part of the people and to bless it, and to let the rest be heathen. Nevertheless these others—namely the heathen—were not damned, much less were they driven out of Heaven. . . . For it was not needful that . . . God give them someone to teach and lead them . . . provided only that they stand on the foundation which God had given them, that is to say, on their hearts. . . . God has taught them what is good and what is evil, so that they may know of themselves what they should

191

Fig. 121. The Spirit

and what they should not do. This knowledge, then, is the
rock upon which they shall stand. II/1, 274–75

The spirit bloweth where it listeth; not in everything, not
in many things, but where it pleases. Many persuade themselves that they themselves are the spirit, but it is with them
above all that the spirit has never been. II/1, 78

Just as a man cannot exist without divine strength, so he
cannot live without the light of nature. For only these two
together make a man complete. . . . Everything springs
from these two; they are both in man, without them man is
nothing. But they themselves can perfectly well subsist without man. And as regards man, he is nothing by himself, and
what he fancies himself to be has no worth. His true essence
must dwell in him like a guest without whom he is nothing
and can accomplish nothing. . . . The purpose for which a
man is chosen, whether it be this or that, remains concealed
to the blood and flesh; for only in divine strength and the
light of nature does free will exist. Their spirit operates
where they will, and theirs is the free will! I/12, 231–32

Christ enjoins us to explore the nature of things! . . .
And if someone should ask, Who teaches you thus?, let me
ask you, Who taught the grass and the leaves to grow?
Christ exhorted men to take heed and learn from the example of his gentle and humble heart. From Christ flows
the spring of truth, and that which does not come from Him
is but seduction. The devil knows a thousand tricks, and he
has at his command many false signs and miracles. He gives
us no respite, he is like a roaring lion who is always at our
heels, to brand us and Christ as liars. I/11, 130

Although God has created great and marvellous things,
of which we men can gain knowledge in many ways, and
although He gave us great power to use them in diverse
ways and manners, it is most important to remember here—
and this holds for all of our actions—that we must never use
them in any shape or form except when we need them. For
consider this: woman is created that she may give birth to
children, yet not in disgrace, but only in honour and respect.

Similarly many great things were created that they might be revealed to man through religion, one abetting the other. But never otherwise than in the path of the Lord . . . although all things can be employed for good as well as for

II/1, 89   evil purposes.

It pleases God that we should achieve knowledge of His works, and that we should not with sound eyes grope in the darkness as though totally blind. It is His will that we use our eyes for the purpose for which they were given us—for gaining knowledge of Christ and His Word. For if you have eyes, it is your cross; if you have hands and feet, it is your cross, and if you are sound and well, it is your cross. Bear your cross! But at the same time follow Christ and do not in-

I/14, 35   dulge in games and pleasures. Then you will be blessed.

It must be established once and for all that our body is not ours but God's, that it is made not for us but for God, not for our own but for God's benefit. And since this is the nature of man's body, it must come entirely from God, that is from Him to whom it belongs. Therefore, whatever man has springs from God—life, sickness, wisdom, eyesight, hear-

I/13, 329   ing, reason.

The body harbours the eternal as a host harbours a guest. But there is an additional grace of God, which maintains body and soul—life. . . . Life is a gift which may be compared to a house that a lord gives to a man without owing it

I/1, 276   to him, but only that he may dwell and stay therein.

Our mortal body has no strength, for all the strength that we need and that is our due we must draw from faith.

What raises us above our mortal nature is faith; through

I/9, 261   faith we become like the spirit.

Although on earth we walk in flesh, nevertheless our faith in the Creator of all things is so great that no one can express it, and that it can be taken away from no one, except from him who rejects it of his own accord.   *I/9, 264*

Just as simply and easily as we can take a mustard seed in our hands and cast it into the sea, because it has no weight at all, so simply and easily do we cast mighty mountains into the sea by our faith.   *I/9, 260*

To die for the faith is bliss; but to die for the articles of faith is a death that springs from false faith.   *I/9, 282*

Let man not be surprised that God is with him, and that he can perform miracles on earth by virtue of His power, for man is of divine nature. "All of you are gods and sons of the Most High," says Holy Writ. . . . And it is displeasing to God that the saints of His heavenly body be despised by the earthly body; that the earthly make mockery of the heavenly.

God created everything that is in heaven

Fig. 122. Head of Christ

I/12, 328

and earth, from which grows all that man needs: his food, his drink, his remedies, his clothing, heat and cold, enough to content us each and all. But all these are resources of the heathen kind, created for the heathen, who suck at them like bees; they do not help man to gain the blessed and only life, but solely the temporal life. For this life is perishable. But that which serves the eternal and blessed life cannot . . . enter into us without Christ: from God the Father it comes to us through Christ.   *II/1, 139*

From Holy Scripture comes the beginning and guidance

of all philosophy and natural science, and it must be taken into account before anything else; without this fundament all philosophy would be expounded and applied in vain. Consequently, if a philosopher is not born out of theology, he has no cornerstone upon which to build his philosophy. For truth springs from religion, and cannot be discovered without its help.

I/12, 32

He who would be blessed on earth must found his teachings, his dominion, and his order upon Christ as his cornerstone. It is Christ from whom everything must be drawn. No doctrine avails unless it comes from Heaven, no commandment avails unless it comes from Heaven, no art avails unless it comes from Heaven. And the same is true of all the rest.

II/1, 85

Fig. 123. Baptism

Men are baptised in the name of the Father and the Son and the Holy Ghost, and therefore they should know that they must live in God, that is to say, in the ways taught by Him in Whose name they were baptised, and that they must not forsake these teachings, but live in the most perfect faith in the Son of God and follow His words and teachings. Only then does the reason that was given us by virtue of baptism enter into us. But once reason is in us, the innocence of childhood no longer protects us, we are no longer counted among the simple, but considered as beings endowed with reason, and we must make operative in us the force of baptism, that is to say, we must know of Christ and we must have faith in Him, love Him, and follow Him—a task from which simpletons and children are dispensed. . . . Consequently baptism enjoins on us, when it confers reason upon us, repentance and faith—to know both and to understand both, lest, through want of reason, we bring eternal death upon us. *II/1, 329–30*

Baptism is the hallmark of the Christian, just as his master's livery is the hallmark of the servant, or an ensign is the mark of a general, captain, or party. . . . It is also a kind of passport; let no one insult or attack its owner. It is like the priest's frock: let no one strike him who wears it. . . . And just like one who wears his master's colours but serves him ill, or like a false priest, so is a Christian who does not fulfil the virtues of his baptism, as revealed by the sign. . . . For baptism is eternal and grants no surcease, it is continuous, and unlike a colour which is intended to represent its master only for a time, it is destined to remain forever and ever, and never to pass away. . . . It is a dedication, which the devil cannot take away, a dedication to blessedness. . . . Consequently it is the highest order and the highest priesthood, and all others are false and vain. In it let us put our strength, our virtue, and our being, that we may not be breakers of our vow before the Lord our God. *II/1, 319–20*

It is the soul that bears man's burdens and joys. It has reason, foresight, and wisdom as adjuncts. These three are intended to rule over the body and to lead it, lest the soul's yoke prove too burdensome. But over them the spirit has been appointed, and the spirit governs reason as well as wisdom and foresight. Thence arises the order of life, and thus do all things spring from the light of the spirit. *I/1, 301–2*

The seat and home of the soul is in the heart, in the centre

Von der Seel.

Fig. 124. The Soul: Anima

of the man; it is the heart that nourishes the spirits which know of good and evil. It dwells within man in the place where life is, against which death fights. . . . But if the whole heart is to be filled with love of God, all opposition to God must withdraw from the soul, and that which is not divine must go, to the end that it may be all pure, untainted by any other thing, separated from all the rest, perfectly clean and pure itself.   *1/12, 299*

The soul is born in this way: when the child is conceived in the womb—that is to say, born into its seed—a word from God enters into this carnal conception, which gives the flesh its soul. Thus the soul—take good note of this—becomes the centre of man, in whom now both good and evil impulses dwell. The body is the house of the soul, but the soul is the house of the good and evil spirits which dwell in man. An example: A king sits in the middle of his council and has many councillors; some are good, some are evil. Thus he receives good and evil advice. But these advisers are in some sense in himself, they are of his own spirit. And so he is free to choose whether he wants to do what the ones or what the others advise. He is free to follow those whom he wants to follow. So is it with the spirit which stands above the soul like a king in man, amidst the council of the natural order.   *1/12, 298*

It is just and correct to call the soul a spirit, and to call the spirit God's angel in man. For both of them have come from the mouth of God and we have received them from His hand. Thus the spirit with all its powers is born of God, and thus the body of the world is provided with as many powers as man needs. And if these powers—the natural and the heavenly—are exercised in accordance with the will of God, each soul encloses them in itself, and they remain therein for all eternity. Both powers bring their wisdom, their reason, from the place whence they themselves come, and each has the nature of its creator; the divine power they bring with them from God, and the natural from nature. In the soul these are transformed into works, just as a king translates advice into deeds.   *1/12, 300*

The spirit is not the soul, but—if it were possible—the spirit would be the soul of the soul, just as the soul is the spirit of the body. For the spirit of man is not the body, and not the soul, but a third thing in man. When man's body rests in the earth, when he is relieved of labour and immersed in sleep until his awakening, when the soul has gone thither, where every debt is repaid—down to the last farthing—then the spirit dwells in the place to which God assigns it: with Him, with the soul, with the body, or in the dwelling of man. . . . For the spirit contains man's judgment of the soul, of the body, and of everything else.

I/14, 301

In God let us see nothing other than truth and justice. They are the essence of God; and these we must see in Him, to the end that we may know ourselves, and understand that we are nothing in so far as we are not like God and are not perfect like our Father in Heaven. For we too are gods—because we are His children!

No one is excepted, no one lives outside the province of God; I may be subject to my master, my master may be subject to me, I may be under him outside my own province, and he may be under me outside his province. Consequently everyone is in some way dependent upon the other, and in such love each is subject to the other.

I/8, 265

Fig. 125. The Lamp of
Eternal Light

VI

MAN AND FATE

Fig. 126. Souls Weighed in the Balance

God has given us the eternal body
to the end that we mortal men on
earth may become immortal.   *II/1, 249*

WHAT then is happiness but compliance with the order of nature through knowledge of nature? What
is unhappiness but opposition to the order of nature? If nature takes its proper course, we are happy, if nature follows the wrong course, we are unhappy. . . . He
who walks in light is not unhappy, nor is he who walks in
darkness unhappy. Both are right. Both do well, each in his
own way. He who does not fall complies with the order. But
he who falls has transgressed against it.   *I/8, 110–11*

Fig. 127. Wheel of Fortune: an angel turning the sphere of heaven

Diligence and care frighten misfortune away; lack of care and diligence invite misfortune. . . . If this is so, who has the right to speak of the wheel of fortune? It goes up, and it goes down. He who rises has only himself to thank, and the same can be said of him who goes down. . . . How can a man who has reached the lowest point in the circle of fortune say: "Misfortune has cast me down?" Since he himself is responsible? . . . Thus, in the end, man himself bears responsibility and guilt for his fate whether it has brought him fortune or misfortune. A man who goes about his task in the proper way, who has intrinsic worth, who is capable and knows what he is doing and displays diligence and care in performing his work, moves ahead. But a man who does not move ahead has no right to complain! For he is worth less than the other; and for

1/14, 199–20 this he can blame only himself and no one else.

What right has the lazy man to maintain that he has no luck, since he does nothing and never stirs from the corner of his chimney, and fancies that there is such

LA ROUE DE FORTUNE.

1/14, 198–99 Fig. 128. The Course of the World

a thing as luck which will come to him of itself and for which he need only wait? If luck were a messenger travelling across the land, it would be best to wait for it at the door. But there is no such messenger, and luck is nothing other than ability, knowledge, and skill. These are the things that help a man to get what he needs on earth. He who has not these things will never get anywhere.

Luck is a wheel; heaven keeps it in constant motion with all its signs and stars, which

204

mingle with one another in their course, or proceed or follow one another, thus forming good and bad signs. We for our part walk on earth, and our course therefore runs in a direction opposed to that of the heavenly wheel. And according to the manner in which these two circles meet will a man meet with fortune or misfortune.

I/10, 144

The sun shines upon all of us equally with its luck. The summer comes to all of us equally with its luck, and so does the stormy winter. But while the sun looks at all of us equally, we look at it unequally. God has redeemed all of us, the one as much as the other; but one does not look at Him in the same way as the other. He loves us all, without regard for person; but our love for Him is unequal. . . . When a father

Fig. 129. Wheel of Fortune

has ten children, all of them inherit equally, and the father remembers one as much as the others. He who fails to keep his inheritance cannot blame luck, but only himself.

I/14, 191

It is God who makes you fly, with or without wings. He induces your imaginings, opinions, judgments. . . . And when you have decided that you have flown as far as the third heaven, you have not even lifted yourself above the grass on the field, and you have not yet accomplished anything. You have suppressed and destroyed the fruit that was supposed to grow out of you, and now the fruit, along with you, has become worthless for it has not prospered.

II/1, 79

We sometimes say that it depends only upon our free will to do a thing or not to do it. But this is not true. We can do nothing unless God has so ordained. He who does evil must have received the power to do it from God, otherwise he could not have done it; he who does good must have received the power to do it from God, otherwise he could not have done it. How can a man do what he wants if he cannot so much as make a single hair white or black? "I may stab someone or not stab him, I may steal or not steal, I may commit adultery or not"—who is justified in speaking thus? No one.

II/1, 71

God gives us life, strength, and power; and once we have it, we can use it to serve God or the devil, our fellow men or ourselves.—But who is justified in supposing that for this reason his will is free, as long as the hangman stands behind him, and the judge is ready to pass sentence upon him?

II/1, 72–73

God destroys what is displeasing to Him, and what man cannot change by his own efforts God changes, because He does not desert his children.

I/9, 886

𝒱𝓏

How can a man say, "I am certain," when he is so far from any certainty? The truth is rather that he knows nothing—he does not know the hour of his death, nor any hour of his life and his health. . . . For he has been created without foreknowledge. . . . Whatever God may undertake, He has in the devil an adversary who can ruin everything and frustrate His intentions. How then can anyone know with certainty what may happen tomorrow? Even if a man were an angel of God, he would not know! . . . How much more uncertain must we be, poor mortals on earth! . . . As long as the world stands, all things will be uncertain. For a mixture of certainty and uncertainty does not yet produce certainty. Only divine things are certain, but not earthly things. And if the two meet, each makes the other confused and uncertain. But if the perishable part is eliminated, there arises complete certainty, such as is not otherwise possible.

I/12, 392–94

Man is capable of knowing nothing with regard to the soul, nor can he encompass its affliction and complaint, nor what will become of it on the Day of Judgment, nor what great torments it will then have to suffer. And because man knows nothing of all this, let him shun human doctrines, not turn to them. For man does not understand himself. . . . We ourselves know nothing at all, and can only judge perishable things.

II/1, 273

We hope . . . that everything will be for the best; but if we were certain of this, we should have nothing left to hope for. It has doubtless been sufficiently demonstrated that here on earth our fate is uncertain. We do not know what lies in store for us, and we do not even know what we ourselves are, whether we are good or evil, and we do not know what our fate will be in the hereafter. Our uncertainty about ourselves is at the base of the uncertainty of all things . . . only God knows us. We who would attain certainty must wait until the day of resurrection; then everyone will be endowed with certain knowledge.

I/12, 395

If at a certain moment everything seems good, beautiful, pure, and full of bliss . . . this does not mean that we have anything different from a treasure of gold and pearls, which lies in a box, and which a thief can despoil, so that nothing is left to the owner. For the thief spares no one, and takes no heed of debit or credit, piety or sinfulness; all that concerns him is to seize his loot and be off. And even if the whole world depended upon one thing, God holds it of no account, and does not take it into His reckoning. Thus our life is an uncertain treasure, which we must protect and preserve well in all our actions.

I/9, 89–90

Take an hourglass and let it run; once the sand has begun to flow, you know at what moment it will run out. It is the same with all creation! Nature too knows the boundaries of its course. According to her own appointed term, she confers upon each of its creatures its proper life span, so that its energies are consumed during the time that elapses between the moment of its birth and its predestined end.

I/1, 206

To every existing thing God has allotted a time to grow in, lest it ripen prematurely. Much happens before it yields fruit: first come the sprouting buds, then the shoots, then the flowers, and then the fruits. But all are exposed to many accidents, many kinds of danger, before they don their husks and are harvested. It is the same with man: he has his goal in death, and death is the harvester of the human fruit; death is the vintner of man's vineyard, the fruit picker of his orchard, and so on. Birth is man's spring; then his buds grow on

Fig. 130. Hourglass: with skull as symbol of death

his branches. And then come his shoots, and then his flowers, and finally his fruits. Should then the fruit of man—that is to say, what man produces—be cut off when it is still a burgeon or a shoot? Man thinks, to be sure, that he is something, and because he bears more fruit than a nut tree, he fancies that there are fruits in him at all times. But this is not so. Let man see to it that his fruits be not at all external, like those of the trees in the garden, and let him not waste and squander his time. If he disregards this truth and attempts to grind the wheat before it has been threshed, his whole life will be folly and lies. For before the appointed time God gives no fruit; everything must come in due time. . . . And as in everything else, time must complete its cycle; whether a thing ripens sooner or later depends on God. *II/1, 78–79*

The heavens manifest their influence at the appointed time, and reveal the powers that are inherent in things. For powers and virtues are subject to it. *I/8, 108*

The stars have grown out of their heavens and there they stand as though they would fly like birds through the air, in their God-given order and orbit. . . . And as they came into being at the beginning of time, so will they remain for ever and ever. The trees and fruits of the earth pass away and grow anew, but the stars will pass away only once—at the end of the world—never to return. Everything that is encompassed by the other elements is destroyed by death, corroded by rust, devoured by the moths. Only the celestial element of the stars subsists, even though their fruits come and go. *I/13, 132*

Fig. 131. Death the Reaper

If we knew the predestination of Heaven, we should also know the fate of man. Only God knows his predestination, that is to say, his end. *I/1, 207*

The life span of man is short as compared to all other creation; gold and silver will survive until the fire at the end of the world, and the same is true of stone and salt. But man does not endure so long, he has the shortest term. He does not know the hour appointed for his end; every day he may hear the voice saying: get thee hence! For the power that assails man ignores the rest of creation. *I/4, 493–94*

To each thing a term of existence is given, whether it be for good or evil purposes. The saints too have their term after which they must cease to lead their lives on earth, and

Fig. 132. *Danse macabre*

the sinners too have their term. For each thing God has set a term, which no saint can exceed, however pious, righteous or useful to his people he may be, and whether he likes it or not. When the hour has struck, all this is disregarded. . . . Death itself does not know the hour at which it will attack or kill. But it strives diligently and eagerly, so that it may not overlook the apointed minute, but prove obedient to its master in heaven.

I/9, 98–99

No man has the power to reawaken that which has died a natural death and which nature has killed at the predestined time; only by God can it be done, or by another at God's order. Nor can man restore what nature has consumed. Only what he himself has broken can he repair, and then again break it. More man cannot do by his own strength. If he were to presume further, he would trespass the power of God, and still his efforts would be in vain. . . . What dies naturally has reached its appointed term, therein lies God's will and order; even if death occurs through accident or illness, no reawakening is possible. Therefore, there is no defence against fate and against the predestined end.

Fig. 133. Sundial

I/11, 343–44

No man can know for whom the sun is shining, no man is privileged to take for himself what only God can give him. For everything lies in the hands of God and He gives to whom He desires to give. Any opposition on the part of man is futile. The hour in which you will die is foreordained—regardless of your strength, your power, and your helpers. For everything you have built for yourself will sink with you into the grave, and you will have deceived only yourself and others.

I/10, 592

Consider with what vigour nature strives against death. She resorts to heaven and earth and all their powers and virtues to help her. So also the soul must fight the devil with all her might; and she calls for God's help with all her heart, out of her very depths, with all her strength, only to resist the devil. Nature too is full of anxiety; she has recourse to everything that God has given her in order to repel death; she tries to drive out harsh, bitter death, who fights against her; dreadful death, whom our eyes cannot see, nor our hands clutch. But nature sees, touches, and

Fig. 134. The Hand of Fate

211

1/9, 95–96

knows him. Therefore she summons all the powers of heaven and earth to resist the terrible one.

What is death? . . . He is one who takes our life in many ways. . . . Therefore let us be awake and keep a vigilant eye; for he leads us to judgment, to give an account of our lives from the beginning to the end. He is the bailiff, the executioner, the summoner to the judgment of God. And what does this summons mean? . . . Nothing but this: the

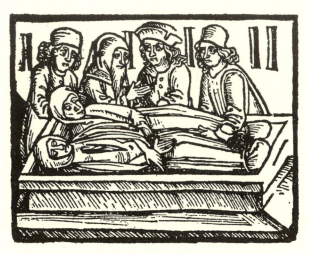

Fig. 135. Entombment

journey to God's judgment, at the appointed hour and on the appointed day, on the day of wrath, when heaven and earth will quake and rise, when the trumpets will awaken him who has been summoned. It is death who brings us the awakening and thus, we might say, returns to us what he has taken from us. . . . Earth is man's prison. We men on earth all die in sin and therefore we must go to prison and there remain until judgment, just as any other prisoner must wait. When we are summoned, body and soul separate, the spirit goes to the Lord and the body to earth. Indeed, the earth is not a prison for the spirit, but only for the body. Thus each stays in its place, and one day they both come together again.

What happens then is concealed from all men; it is known only to Him who has created body and soul.

I/9, 99–100

What transcends the animal is what constitutes man. For man has a father, who is eternal. For this father let him live and not for the beast in him. . . . God has so created man that he lives in animality, yet animality is not the true home of man.

I/13, 323–24

The spirit that is bound to the flesh is indeed called a spirit, but it is subject to death, in contradistinction to that

Fig. 136. The Journey Through Death: symbolic representation of a phase of the process of transmutation

spirit which God has given us and which is immortal. The spirit that springs from nature guides the natural reason, but the spirit of God guides divine knowledge. The two spirits leave man at the moment of death, but the first dies, while the other remains alive.

I/12, 279

A man's death is nothing but the end of his daily work, an expiration of air, the consummation of his own balsamic curative power, the extinction of the rational light of nature, and a great separation of the three—body, soul, and spirit —a return to the womb. The earthly and natural man is of the earth, and the earth is his mother, to which he must return and lose therein his earthly and natural flesh, that he may be born a second time on the Day of Judgment in a new, heavenly, and transfigured body.

I/11, 333–34

The death of all things in nature is nothing other than a reversal and change of the powers and virtues, a transcendence of good and evil, an eradication and destruction of the first nature and a birth of the second and new nature. For know that many things which are good in life and bear great power and virtue in themselves, later have but little or no power and virtue when they have died or been killed, but are dull and powerless. Similarly, there are many things which are evil in life, but which in dying or after they have *1/11, 332–33* died manifest manifold power and virtue.

Only that is gold which has been cleansed of all dross, which through fire has been brought back to its native state, to lead, which has gone through pure antimony, that is to say, has been brought to efflorescence in antimony and has been properly prepared and transformed. And just as this procedure amounts to a testing of gold, so it may serve as a parable for the testing of the resurrected body. For this body too will have to cast off all dross of earthly life, and then it will have to go through an even more difficult test by fire; it will have to go through a melting, a preparation and elaboration comparable to the stage of pure antimony, it will have to suffer a transformation in *aqua fortis*

Fig. 137. Resurrection from Death. (The caption reads: "After my many and several sufferings and great martyrdom—I am resurrected—clarified—and free of all flaw.") An alchemistic-symbolic representation of "purified gold," the end-stage of the process of transmutation

that will make it quite clear and pure. This does not mean that the impure becomes pure, and that the putrefied and murky part becomes clean. For the impure always remains impure, dirt remains dirt; but the pearl concealed in it is taken out, and it is this pearl that is transfigured. For the

Fig. 138. Toward the Celestial Spheres: Beatrice leads Dante through the sphere of the moon to the firmament of fixed stars, which is surrounded by the eighth and last celestial sphere, the Empyrean, or Heaven of Pure Light. In the center of the circles is the earth with the planets revolving around it

pearl itself has never been impure, it has only lain hidden in the darkness.

II/1, 310–11

The supreme good is so constituted that neither gold nor silver nor any other thing that derives from the elements stands above it. Nothing can be the supreme good except that which is immortal, eternal, and imperishable, and stands above all of us. Therefore it is an error to suppose that a perishable thing can be equal in value to the supreme good. Only he who masters mortality is the master, and it is the righteous who masters it in the end. . . . What fills our bellies is a valuable possession; and what quenches our thirst or makes us merry or gives us joy is likewise a valuable possession. But a far more valuable possession is that which gives us life, and still more, that which confers eternity upon us. . . . What avail us the garden, the vineyard, the cornfield which exist for the sake of the belly? They leave us and we leave them. . . . For the highest good that life and earth have given us leaves us when we die, and deserts us in anguish and pain. Therefore our truly supreme good can only be that which leads us from death to resurrection, into *II/1, 111–12*   eternal life.

We cannot by our eyes recognize the supreme good. Nor can we gauge it or know it by means of our tongues. There is nothing in the body that can reveal the supreme good; for only the spirit from heaven can do this. . . . It is the soul in us which strives for the supreme good, not the body. . . . And he who does not have the light of the soul in him regards gluttony, drinking, and so on as the supreme good. But these are only pleasures of the body; and if a man dies, that which he has deemed to be the supreme good dies with *II/1, 112*   him.

The summer is the supreme good for the bees, it gives them a pleasant occupation, wax and honey. Pillage and rapine are the supreme good for the wolf, that is to say, sheep and goats are his supreme good, for that is how he is made. For the beasts of the air, on the land, in the water, the supreme good is their favoured element. . . . Thus water is the supreme good for the fishes, grass for the cows, and air for the birds. But with man it is different. His supreme good is not of this earth. He must continue his search after he leaves this earth, and can hope for more after this life than the animals, because he must rise to the High- *II/1, 115*   est.

Man has two bodies: one from the earth, the other from the stars, and thus they are easily distinguishable. The elemental, material body goes to the grave along with its essence; the sidereal, subtle body dissolves gradually and goes back to its source, but the spirit of God in us, which is like His image, returns to Him whose image it is. Thus each part dies in that medium from which it has been created, and finds rest accordingly.

I/12, 18

Man has a body which does not spring from matter and consequently is not subject to any physician; for it was breathed into man by God, and like every breath, is intangible to our hands, and invisible to our eyes. . . . According to Holy Writ we shall be resurrected in the flesh on the Day of Judgment and called to account for our misdeeds. But

Fig. 139. Dying Man

the body that has sinned is a body invisible to our eyes; hence we may assume that this same body must rise again with us. For we shall not give an account of the health and sicknesses of our visible bodies . . . but of the things that proceed from the heart, because only these actually concern man, and they belong to a body which does not consist of matter, but comes from the breath of God. But since one day, clothed in the flesh, we shall see our Lord and Saviour, it follows that the body which derives from the *limbus,* and is material, will also be present at that moment. Who can be ignorant of this transfiguration, which is accomplished through the mouth of God, and by virtue of which both bodies will be present? For we shall rise again in the flesh, and we only know one flesh, not two; two bodies, and one flesh, namely that which is on earth. . . . The flesh made out of earth is nature, and is subject to her measure and her justice. But the evil that arises from the flesh does not come from material nature, but springs from the intangible, ethereal body; it is this body which exceeds the measures of nature. . . . Consequently man has a second, immaterial body; it is the ethereal body, which Adam and Eve acquired in Paradise through eating the apple; it was only by acquiring this body that man became completely human, with knowledge of good and evil. Because he has this body, man can eat more than is required by nature, and drink more than he needs to quench his thirst. God in His benevolence has set before our eyes the things that we desire—good wines, fair women, good food, good money. And this is the test: whether we keep ourselves under strict control, or whether we break and exceed the measure of nature. For the two bodies are wedded, and both—that from God's breath and that from the earth—are united as in marriage. To exceed the measure is therefore an evil and adulterous deed, an act of infringing on all obligations, because the intangible body vowed that it would not overburden the natural body, and would not drive it beyond its measure. But if this vow is not kept—what is it but a violation of the marriage, which is subject *I/9, 117–19* to God by the highest oath?

The first separation, with which we must begin, starts with man: he is called a microcosm—that is to say, the Little World. For his sake, the macrocosm—the Great World—was created, and it is man who establishes separations within the macrocosm. But the final separation of the microcosm, man, takes place in death. For in death the two bodies of man separate from each other—the divine from the earthly, that is to say, the eternal from the elemental body—and the first soars up to Heaven like an angel, but the other drops down to earth like lead.

Our earthly body is infertile and worthless. It is made fertile by God in order that another body may spring from it—the body which will be resurrected. . . . But this resurrection is not effected in the flesh in which we live in this world. For this flesh originates in the earth and does not belong to heaven. Nor can the earthly body be transfigured for it is consumed and destroyed in the ultimate fire. On the Day of Judgment, how-

I/2, 361

Fig. 140. The Soul Goes to Heaven: the seven angels with the six keys, standing for the six works of charity, with which they open heaven and receive the soul into heaven

ever, the other creature arises from us, the creature which is born of the other Adam and of God.

II/1, 304

As for the flesh, understand that it is of two kinds: the flesh from Adam and the flesh that does not spring from Adam. The flesh from Adam is a crude flesh, for it is earthen and it is nothing but ordinary flesh that can be touched and bound like wood or stone. But the other flesh, which does not spring from Adam, is an ethereal body and can neither be tied or grasped, for it is not made of earth. Now, the flesh from Adam is the man from Adam, that is to say, mortal man; he is crude like the earth, which is solid, so that a man cannot go through walls or partitions, unless he makes a hole for himself through which he may slip. For nothing yields to him. But to the flesh which does not spring from Adam, every wall yields; this means that such flesh can do without doors or holes, and pass through walls and partitions without breaking anything.

I/14, 120

In the blessed life nourishment is not sought on the earth, after the manner of the beasts, but taken from eternity, as the angels are fed on eternity. For a beast devours like a beast, and man, too, in so far as he is a beast, finds his food in the earth. But he ought not to be like a beast; his essence stems from the eternal and he should therefore feed on things eternal. For he was created not beast but man, in the image and likeness of God. The beast, however, is subject to man in water, on land, and in the air. And precisely because man is master of the beast, he ought not to make his eternal salvation depend upon power, but use the beast that is subject to him as nourishment for his worm-like body, as long as he dwells on earth and stays in the body which is master of the beast. This body is not the same body as that which feeds on the tree that grows from the root of God, our Father. For this body of man is an eternal body, in the image of God, like Him and therefore im-

Fig. 141. Poverty, Disease, Lust, Death

220

mortal. Man was created immortal and brought to Paradise where no death was. Only after he was driven out of Paradise was he subject to death. Then he lost part of his essence; that is to say, he remained like the image of God, but not like His essence. This was taken from him by death.

II/1, 134–35

He who hears and learns much on earth, will also be learned when he is resurrected. He who knows nothing will be inferior. For in the house of God there are many mansions, and to each his mansion will be allotted according to his learning. To be sure, we are all learned, but not equally; we are all wise, but not equally; we are all skilful, but not equally. He who explores himself goes farthest; for the exploration of things and the gathering of knowledge lead to God and dispel the vices of the world. Such men shun worldliness, subservience to princes, courtly manners, polite gestures; they learn tongues, which also contain lies and curses. The miraculous works of God bear witness to the light of man, and are not concerned with vain talk. Subservience to men—what is it but a worthless shadow? Neither wage nor reward accrue to man from such subservience. He dies, and in death he is nothing but dirt. What can man make of himself by his own strength? He must learn more

Fig. 142. Resurrection:
The Rule of Christ

than obedience, he must let obedience be, and love his neighbour. Then obedience will grow of itself, as flowers and fruits grow from a good tree.

1/14, 117

It is a naïve philosophy that puts all blessedness and eternity in the elements of our earth, and it is a foolish opinion that looks on man as the noblest of creatures, since there are more worlds than ours alone. . . . But doubt will be impossible in the end, when all things are gathered together in their eternal aspects. For in the end much will be discovered and manifested in diverse ways; and I am speaking not only of those things which contain an eternal part within themselves, but also of those which have borne, nourished, and preserved something in which an eternal part is inherent. For eternity manifests itself both in those who rule and govern, and in those who are only the servants of those who rule. And it is contrary to true philosophy to affirm that the little flowers do not partake of eternity; although they wither away, they will nevertheless appear in the assembly of all the generations. And nothing has been created in the *mysterium magnum*, in God's great marvellous world, that will not also be represented in eternity.

1/13, 409–10

When the end of the world draws near, all things will be revealed, from the lowest to the highest, from the first to the last—what each thing is, and why it existed and passed away, from what causes, and what its meaning was. And everything that is in the world will be disclosed and come to light. Then it will become manifest that many who are known as highly learned have no knowledge of these things. Then the true scholars and the vain chatterers will be recognized—those who wrote truthfully and those who traded in lies, those who stood on firm ground and those who stood on no ground at all; and to each will be meted

Fig. 143. St. John with the Seven-Headed
Dragon on Patmos

out according to his diligence, his earnest labours, and
his truth. And in that place, not everyone will be or remain
a master, or even a physician. For then the tares will be
separated from the wheat, and the chaff from the grain. . . .
Then blessed will be those men whose reason will reveal
itself. For the hearts of all men will be opened to the light
of day; and whatever offences they may have perpetrated
will be written on their foreheads.   *I/14, 150–51*

As men who descend from Adam we are nothing but dust
and ashes, there is nothing among us but strife and dissension, misery and wretchedness, and this life of ours is
full of wrath, sorrow, and lamentation, hatred and conflict.
Why then should we continue to seek in our bodies what
cannot be found in them, and ascribe to our bodies faculties

they do not possess? Would it not be better to consider that all things can be mastered by patience? For only when the mortal body has died and passed away can we begin to seek the immortal body in which we would wish to live. There we shall accomplish everything that the philosopher bade us. And this means: let us direct our thoughts toward Paradise, where a new life begins, where another fruit, another *1/12, 347–48* office, another order, another master and father await us.

Man is God's most beloved creature, more beloved than the angels; this is proved by the Lord's death, which he dies for man and not for Lucifer. If God intercedes for man, it is because He has greater joy in the recovery of one lost sheep than in the recovery of ninety-nine others that did not stray from the fold. The difference between man and the angels is that we are the sheep of God, while Lucifer was not a sheep; that we were found, while Lucifer was not. God interceded for man because man bears eternity in himself; He died for the human race lest man in his short time on earth bring eternal doom upon himself, lest his flesh seduce him to lewdness. Lest man suffer such a fate, He died on the cross and gained joy everlasting for those whose spirit feels repentance and sorrow for the sins of the *1/12, 294* flesh.

Although Christ had to give up His life, He did not lose the battle, but won it. He was resurrected from death and ascended to Heaven; for He was not here on earth that He should die of disease . . . or on a pillow or cushion, but that He might suffer from the death of the cross. . . . Indeed to fight and to struggle means to live. He who is slain and remains on the battlefield has won the victory. He who remains alive cannot be victorious, because he has never been smitten. Only he who has been smitten carries off the victory. He alone has stood his ground. . . . Only the defeated can be victorious. The undefeated escapes; but *II/1, 293* what honour has he, of what victory can he boast?

What is as mighty and so powerful and so marvellous in its action as lightning? Since Christ foretold that his second

224

Fig. 144. Ascension of Christ

coming would be as lightning fallen from Heaven, it is needful that we know the nature of lightning. For it strikes hard and heavy, and is so wondrous in nature that man can hardly conceive of it. . . . To him who considers this, let the lightning serve as a warning to commit no sin, or *I/13, 191–92* turn aside from the path of God.

Consider that here on earth there is no joy without sweat, anguish, and suffering. But when we leave this world, we enter into the eternal body, and in it we shall find rest and *II/1, 260* joy—joy upon joy, eternity upon eternity.

As each day brings its own cares and burdens, so is each man burdened with his cross. Under the cross we will enter in the Kingdom of Heaven; indeed, the cross itself *II/1, 195* is of Heaven.

Nothing will subsist of the world, neither the elements nor the firmament, nor anything that is in them, but one day the prophecy will come true: the world will be consumed by fire, and the fire will consume the water, as well as the stones and all metals. . . . And there is nothing that will be able to defend itself or to resist the fire. Thus everything will return to the state in which it was once, as is said in the Holy Scripture: "The spirit of God brooded over the waters" . . . Then nothing perishable will exist, *I/12, 322* for everything will be like unto the spirit of God.

Fig. 145. The Eye of
Consciousness

VII

GOD, THE ETERNAL LIGHT

Fig. 146. God the Father Blesses the Globe

I<small>F MAN</small> had not been created, who would have known of God's wisdom? Of his power and glory? No one, not even the angels in Heaven would have known. But in the act of creation His wisdom came to the light of day, and likewise His power and glory—and the being and nature of God were made manifest.

I/13, 330

If you attempted to explore the mathematics of Heaven, you would find nothing that could be measured. For Heaven has no beginning and no end, and no one knows the middle.

The mortal body ought to hold this heavenly mathematics in high esteem, and thereby achieve a more profound insight. . . . It has been demonstrated that where there is no beginning and no end, there is no art. But where no number has value . . . and where nothing is first and nothing is last, who can be a mathematician? Where everything has no beginning and no end, no art can be applied, and no distinction can be made! How can man guided by the light of nature find his way in Heaven? Though he may stand in the light of eternity, he can only know that he does not know the beginning and the end of things. . . . Our striving to form ideas about all things has been instilled in us only that we may consider God and not the creatures. But if God could be encompassed, all the rest could also be encompassed; but this is impossible. . . .

1/12, 402

There is one single number that should determine our life on earth, and this number is One. Let us not count further. It is true that the godhead is Three, but the Three is again comprised in the One. And because God transforms Himself into the One, we men on earth must also strive for the One, devote ourselves to the One and live in it. In this number is rest and peace, and in no other. What goes beyond it is unrest and conflict, struggle of one against another. For if a calculator sets down a number and counts further than one, who can say at what number he will stop? But this question is the difficulty that gnaws at us and worries us. How much more pleasant and better it would be if we always walked in the path of the One.

1/10, 581

Fig. 147. The Eye of God

Even if we had in
our hands all the arcana
and elixirs of the Great and
the Little World, but not Thee, O
Lord, all this would be nothing! Close
to Thee, in Thee, and with Thee alone is the
eternal life and the light. In our bodies,
after the great death, when it is as
though renewed by the divine fire,
the light will be translucent,
and only then will it truly
shine. God grant that
this may be soon!
. Amen. Amen.
Amen.*

* "De limbo aeterno," Salzburg MS.

Fig. 148. Apocalypse: John before the Throne

KEY TO SOURCES

GLOSSARY

BIBLIOGRAPHY

INDEXES

KEY TO SOURCES

The reference numbers in the text relate to the part, volume, and page numbers in the Sudhoff-Matthiessen edition where the preceding passage may be found. The following summary of the Sudhoff-Matthiessen edition, based on the tables of contents of the volumes, provides the Paracelsian title of each source.

Sudhoff, Karl, and Matthiessen, Wilhelm, eds. *Paracelsus. Sämtliche Werke.*

Part I: Medizinische, naturwissenschaftliche und philosophische Schriften. vols. 6–9, Munich: O. W. Barth, 1922–25; vols. 1–5, 10–14, Munich, Berlin: R. Oldenbourg, 1928–33.

Volume 1. Earliest Works, c. 1520

Volume 2. Works Written in Southwestern Germany, 1525–26

Volume 3. 1526 and First Months of 1527

Volume 4. Lectures in Basel, Summer 1527

Volume 7. Works on Syphilis and Others Written in Nuremberg, 1529

Volume 8. Works Written in the Upper Palatinate, Regensburg, Bavaria, and Swabia, 1530

Volume 12. *Astronomia Magna*

Volume 13. *Writings of Uncertain Date*

Volume 14. Philosophia Magna. Spuria

Part II: Die theologischen und religionsphilosophischen
Schriften. vol. 1, Munich: O. W. Barth, 1923.

Volume 1

GLOSSARY

A

ALCHEMY. The medieval precursor of chemistry. Its object was the artificial production of gold, of the philosophers' stone, of the elixir of life. The procedures of medieval alchemy were often religious in character. They represented a kind of religious ritual intended to symbolize the belief that man was eternally and immutably integrated in a hierarchically organized cosmic order; the transmutation of the lesser metals served as a tangible illustration of a profound inner experience. This was considered not merely as a chemical process, but also as a mystical process, of which the alchemist himself, in his role of mediator, was a part, and in which he strove to release his own divine "spark of light," imprisoned in his material body. In the view of the alchemists, this result could be achieved only *deo concedente*—that is to say, only with the help of God's grace. The pursuits of the alchemists can be classified as follows:

(1) The art of the transmutation of metals—chrysopoeia.

(2) The manufacture of arcana (secret remedies), particularly of *elixir vitae* (elixir of life) and *aurum potabile* (potable gold)—pharmacopoeia. For Paracelsus alchemy was largely the art of preparing therapeutically effective medicines.

(3) The magical production of the homunculus or "son of wisdom" or the *lapis philosophorum* (philosophers' stone) —philosophical alchemy.

ANATOMY. A structure in its organic totality or the original form which underlies each individual form. (Cf.

PLANET.) Paracelsus was not much concerned with "anatomy" in the modern sense.

ANIMA. The soul. In Paracelsus this term is largely identified with the "sidereal body." But he also uses it to designate everything similar to the breath, all refined, volatile matter (the term has always been used in this sense in alchemy), as well as the specifically effective part of a medicine, its essence. (Cf. SULPHUR.)

ANTIMONY. The element, used as an occult alchemistic remedy; the name also designates symbolically a specific stage in the process of transmutation (see p. 214). "Just as antimony purifies gold and leaves no slag in it, in the same form and shape it purifies the human body" (Paracelsus, quoted by Sticker). This "purification" refers specifically to diseases, and symbolically to the soul.

APOCALYPTIC BEAST. The seven-headed dragon mentioned in the Revelation of St. John (ch. 12-13) as the embodiment of evil. (Cf. BABYLON, and fig. 143.)

AQUA FORTIS. "Strong water": nitric acid which was used to separate gold and silver and also in alchemical manipulations.

ARCANUM (plural: arcana). Paracelsus calls arcana all so-called "secret medicines," whose efficacy is manifested in the secret virtues inherent in the various herbs, minerals, metals, etc. They are discovered by a special science, and obtained through special manipulations. (Cf. also QUINTA ESSENTIA.)

ART. Paracelsus uses this word to designate skill in any profession, but more particularly in therapeutics and alchemy; in other words, the term is not confined, as it is in modern usage, to music, literature, and the fine arts.

ARTS, UNCERTAIN. Paracelsus calls geomancy, pyromancy, hydromancy, chiromancy (q.v.), etc., *artes incertae* (uncertain arts), because in his view knowledge of these "arts" does not come to man directly from God's spirit but from his human imagination; therefore man can misuse them and be deceived and led astray by them.

ASCENDANT. The sign of the zodiac or the star which rises on the horizon at the moment of a man's birth. But Paracelsus also uses this term in a cosmic and mystical sense, to denote man's relation and connexion with the whole of creation, to symbolize the "rising" of nascent man as one who will complete and carry on the marvellous work of creation.

ASPECT. The relative position of the stars, which according to ancient doctrines may result in a generally favourable or unfavourable situation for a given individual.

ASTRAL BODY. The sidereal body in man. (Cf. ASTRUM, BODY.)

ASTRONOMY. In Paracelsus' day, astronomy and what we call "astrology" were not yet distinguished from one another, and he uses this term for both. He consistently rejects astronomy as an art of prophecy or magical interpretation of the future, and considers it only as a method for arriving at an understanding of the all-embracing unity and harmony of creation, indispensable for any true knowledge of the natural processes. Paracelsus' conception of astronomy might be designated as a kind of cosmosophy. Man is placed at the centre of the cosmos and is related to it from every point of view; on the other hand, Paracelsus insists that man is the image of God and enjoys an inner freedom that is granted him by God. This suffices to show that for Paracelsus man was free from determination by astral influence. Thus Paracelsus' view of astronomy has little in common with astrology, fortune-telling, magic, etc. In the Paracelsian system, astronomy is the science which "deals with the comparison between the microcosm and the macrocosm, in order to elucidate the physiological nature of the first, and to grant an insight into the rational active principle of both" (quoted in Kayser). It is in this sense that astronomy constitutes the "second pillar" of the

247

Paracelsian system (philosophy, alchemy, and ethics being the other three), and Paracelsus wanted every physician to master it as an indispensable foundation for medicine.

ASTRUM. The impression engraved in man at the hour of his birth by the external heaven, which inside man's body forms a separate "heaven" and which constitutes this man's specific character.

AURUM POTABILE. Fluid gold, the quintessence of gold. Gold is the highest of all elixirs (cf. ELIXIR). On the one hand it can transmute all metals into gold, on the other hand it is a rejuvenating elixir of life. "This gold elixir transforms each thing, in which it is incorporated, into its own likeness, and . . . it also purifies and preserves the human body. . . . Its power as an arcanum surpasses that of any poison" (quoted in Sticker).

AZOTH. In several of the sixteenth-century portraits of Paracelsus, the pommel of the sword upon which his hand rests bears the inscription "Azoth." From the poem printed under the picture shown in fig. 1, we may gather that Azoth was the name of a secret medicine, a kind of *elixir vitae*, an infallible remedy, an *alexipharmakon* (counter poison). According to an old tradition, these miraculous virtues were inherent in a white powder that Paracelsus always carried with him in a case inside the pommel of his sword. It was allegedly for this reason that he never put aside his sword, even at night.—Azoth is also the secret name of Mercurius, which was extracted from certain ores, a universal medicine that comprised the virtues of all the others. Hence it is also a name for the philosophers' stone. It is a *spiritus animatus*, an animated spirit. It occurs in writings as early as those of the mysterious philosopher "Mary the Jewess" of Zosimos in the fourth, of Olympiodorus in the fifth, and of Jâbir ibn Hayyan, an Arab alchemist, in the tenth century. (It is also interpreted as standing for alpha and omega, i.e., Zeus or Theos.)

248

B

BABYLON. "Babylon the Great, the Mother of Harlots" of the Revelation of St. John (ch. 17), the ravening beast, the epitome of evil, which was identical with Tiamat, the Babylonian primal mother. (Cf. APOCALYPTIC BEAST.)

BALSAM. The life-preserving principle in all living beings; a remedy that can be extracted by alchemistic methods. It originally referred to the fluid which preserved mummies from decay. It has a functional significance similar to that of Yliaster (q.v.).

BODY. Paracelsus distinguishes three kinds of body:
(1) The elemental body, which is physical and animal, and to which the lower instincts belong.
(2) The sidereal body, i.e., the astral body, which is volatile and animated, which cannot be perceived by our senses, and to which the higher instincts belong.
(3) The illumined body, the imperishable, essential kernel of man, the "spark of God," which is also called the resurrected flesh.
The first two bodies are mortal, only the third is immortal. According to Paracelsus, each body returns to its source after death. The elemental body becomes water and earth, the sidereal is slowly dispersed in air; the illumined body rises to God. Paracelsus ascribed materiality to the first two bodies, although he says that the sidereal body is "as subtle as the light of the sun." Flesh and blood form the "elemental" body; feeling, thought, and mind the "sidereal" body of man. Characteristically, Paracelsus ascribes a bodily quality even to the spirit and the soul, even though it is an invisible and intangible quality. In each body are inherent the instincts corresponding to its nature: "luxury, lewdness, etc.," in the elemental body, "feeling, art, wisdom," in the sidereal body, and the striving for the knowledge of God in the eternal body.

C

CABALA. Tradition; the term designates the Jewish Neo-platonism of the Middle Ages, which originated in Gnosticism and the apocalyptic writings of the first century A.D. and comprises two basic works: *Sepher Yezirah* ("The Book of Creation") and *Zohar* ("The Splendour of Light"). The first dates from the ninth century; the second was composed by Moses de Leon in the thirteenth century.

CHIROMANCY. Not only the art of reading the lines of the hand, but more generally the art of inferring the inner constitution of any object from its outward characteristics.

COMPOSITIO HUMANA. For Paracelsus, man is composed of the four elements which also make up all the rest of creation. Each of these elements is based upon three substances, namely mercury, sulphur, and salt, which form the flesh and blood of the elemental body and, as faculties of the sidereal body, develop into "feeling, wisdom, and art." Here as elsewhere the fundament is expressed by the mysterious number 7 ($= 4 + 3$). (Cf. PLANET.) But the *compositio humana* is in addition conceived as a compound of *limus terrae* and *limus coelorum;* moreover, one part of it is perishable and another eternal, since it belongs simultaneously to the realm of nature and the realm of God.

CONCORDANCE. The basis for the various "correspondences" assumed by Paracelsus, particularly those between microcosm and macrocosm.

CONSTELLATION. The position of the stars at a specific moment; in a broader sense, a specific conjuncture of diverse factors, obtaining at a given moment. Paracelsus often denotes by this term a force (sympathy) that establishes relations between things, and thus causes certain situations in man's inwardness to affect the constellations and, conversely, causes the constellations to influence developments in the "lower sphere," which includes the sphere of man's life.

COSMOGRAPHER. A student of the theory of the cosmos.

CURE. Paracelsus admits three forms of cure—by the application of medical remedies, by uttering the "efficacious word," and by divine miracle. To effect either of the first two, the physician is required to know not only all the specific remedies, but also the great interconnexions between man, cosmos, and God; without this knowledge, he cannot know the arcana nor apply them correctly. For instance, a sick person cannot be cured at the time arbitrarily chosen by the physician, but only at a time appropriate to his nature and destination. The cure also depends upon the physician's personal nature and attitude, which must be in concordance with the disease and the patient. Therapeutic practice, as conceived of by Paracelsus, must always emphasize the patient's total personality.

D

DISEASE. Any disturbance in the equilibrium of forces (which are organized in pairs of opposites) which results in the dissolution of the natural order of any entity, including the soul. A disease can arise in any separate sphere (in the elemental or the sidereal body) or as a result of a disturbance in the relation between them; it can be produced by natural causes (then it is predestined) or be decreed by God as a punishment or trial. Paracelsus tried to ascertain a rational basis for the origin of some of the mental and nervous diseases.

DIVINATIO. Prediction, prophecy.

DIVINATOR. Interpreter and diviner of the future. Paracelsus contrasts this concept with the revealed knowledge that comes from God.

DIVINING RODS. Forked rods for the discovery of water, hidden treasures, and minerals.

DIVINITAS. Divinity.

E

ELEMENTAL LIGHT. The vital manifestations of man, which spring from the sphere of instinct and which also characterize animals. Partly coincides with the "light of nature" (q.v.).

ELEMENTS. According to the ancient conception, the four elements are earth, water, air, and fire; the former two are considered cold and heavy, more akin to matter, the latter two warm and volatile, more akin to the realm of the soul. According to Paracelsus, water and earth form the "elemental body," fire and air the "sidereal body" (q.v.). Paracelsus conceives of them not in the modern sense, as chemical substances, but as the four fundamental forms of matter, which are potentially and sometimes invisibly contained in all perceptible things, even if they no longer manifest themselves outwardly in their typical original form. According to Paracelsus, there are four higher (spiritual) and four lower (physical) elements; the latter are the so-called *matrices*, "mothers," while the higher are the *patres*, "fathers," corresponding to the lower. Therefore all beings have four fathers and four mothers. (Cf. the Gnostic "Ogdoad," a group of eight divine beings or eight aeons.)

ELIXIR. The secret remedy for the prolongation of life, which has always been the ardently-yearned-for goal of the various magical and alchemical manipulations. Paracelsus also uses this term in the meaning of *essentia* (q.v.). As elixir of life it confers immortality upon man, and in a symbolic sense is identical with the panacea which releases man from his *prima materia* and leads him to the fulfilment of his personality.

ENS (plural: *entia*). An existent, an entity, a definite physical, psychic, or spiritual thing. The *entia* are influences, principles, and hence causes and "birth-givers" of bodily disturbances and illnesses. Paracelsus distinguishes five such *entia* (cf. pp. 75 ff.).

ESSENTIA. Essence, as opposed to "poison"—the active good principle in things, which is often designated also as *virtus*, "virtue, power."

ETHER. Paracelsus almost always uses this term to designate the air; thus it belongs to the lower sphere.

EXTRACTIVA. The means by which the essences of things are extracted.

F

FIRMAMENTAL EXTRACT. Extract of the astral components of man; similar to the elixir of life.

FLESH OF ADAM. Identical with the sinful animal body; contrasted with the illumined body, the "subtle flesh that is not of Adam."

FRENCH DISEASE. See SYPHILIS.

G

GEMS. Precious stones, sometimes also colored fossils.

GEOMANCY. A kind of divination based on the observation of either a heap of earth or little stones thrown on a table, or of crevices, mountain chains, and in general of the configuration of the earth's surface.

H

HEAVEN, HEAVENS. Paracelsus uses this term in the sense common today and also to denote "the stars," and the "upper sphere," which is opposed to the "lower sphere," that is, the earth. (Cf. THE STARS.)

HOMO MAXIMUS. The macrocosm (q.v.), conceived as the principle of man.

HYDROMANCY. Divination by means of water, based on the observation of whirlpools, springs, lakes, or smooth, brilliant surfaces of water.

I

IMAGE. Primarily the image of God, in the likeness of which man was formed; but Paracelsus also uses this term in the broader sense of "prototype."

IMAGINATION. Paracelsus identifies this faculty with "the stars" or the "firmament" in man; that is to say, fantasy results from the action of the astrological heaven, which forms in us the "astral man," i.e., the true, inner, or higher and "right" man, the "sidereal body," and the faculties inherent in it.

IMPRESSIO. Impression or imprint. By this term Paracelsus primarily means the character and constitution-forming action of "the stars" (cf. THE STARS, SIDEREAL BODY). *Impressio deltica* denotes a magical influence obtained by means of the imagination.

INCARNATIVA. A medical remedy intended to further the healing of wounds; it was supposed to make the flesh grow.

INCUBUS. An evil spirit that descends upon sleeping persons; a kind of nightmare or demon that attacks women at night. According to Paracelsus, such demons are created by the power of the imagination. (Cf. SUCCUBUS, WOMAN.)

INFLUENCE. Primarily, planetary influence.

L

LAPIS PHILOSOPHORUM. The philosophers' stone. In chemistry and alchemy, this term denotes gold in a special sense, or its supreme and definitive form, or else the substance which transmutes metals into gold; it also denotes the panacea. In the symbolic sense, however, the philosophers' stone stands for the highest wisdom, the final goal of the process of man's initiation, enabling him to bring his personality to the highest possible fulfilment, and often it means the perfect man himself. Paracelsus uses the term in the sense employed by hermetic philosophy, hence chiefly as a symbol for man's highest degree of wisdom. In the hermetic philosophy, if a man discovered or produced the "stone," it accomplished his "second birth," the birth of the pure, dross-free body, the "second Adam," or, as symbolized in the alchemistic procedure, the release of the "pearl" from the darkness in which it lay hidden, the freeing of the divine spark from its "dungeon." (There are parallel doctrines in Gnosticism and Manichaeism.)

LEAD. Not merely the metal, but also an alchemistic symbol for dark, heavy, lustreless primal matter. This matter is at the beginning of both the process of spiritual maturation and the alchemical transmutation into gold. *Aurum philosophorum est plumbum,* "the philosophers' gold is lead," we read in *Pandora,* an alchemistic work published by Hieronymus Reusner (Basel, 1582, and again in 1588). In the doctrine of correspondences, lead corresponds to the planet Saturn.

LIGHT OF NATURE. Intuitive knowledge gained by the experience of nature and implicit in all beings at their birth, in contrast to the knowledge given by revelation. It is one of Paracelsus' basic concepts. In a cosmological sense, it is a secret radiation of nature and makes possible the discovery of natural mysteries. In an anthropological sense, it is man's active intelligence (Paracelsus also calls it "reason"), a kind of knowledge guided by intuition and developed by experience. The light of nature belongs to the sphere of creation and operates only within it; it originates in the spirit of God. As Paracelsus says, "the light of nature was kindled by the Holy Ghost." But although the natural light is inseparably bound to the Holy Ghost, it constitutes an independent source of knowledge.

LIMBUS. Formless and quality-less matter, endowed with primal life, the sole mother of everything earthly, the "chaos" of the alchemists, which contained as in a reservoir all things, in a potential state (cf. Kayser). It also constitutes the primal matter in the *compositio humana,* and consists of the *limus coelorum* and the *limus terrae* (q.v.). (Cf. PRIMA MATERIA.)

LIMUS COELORUM. The basic heavenly substance, which in addition to *limus terrae* forms the other, eternal part of the *compositio humana,* or human compound.

LIMUS TERRAE. The primal stuff of the earth, the clay out of which God created all tangible things. Often identical with *limbus* (q.v.).

M

MACROCOSM. The totality of creation as opposed to the microcosm, or man. Also designated as "the Great Creature" or "the Great World," in its cosmogonic sense it denotes the primal man (the Gnostic Adam or the Hindu Purusha).

MAGIC. Paracelsus distinguishes two kinds of magic—good magic, which is consistent with Christian religion and applies occult natural knowledge for purposes beneficent to the sick and favourable for the exploration of nature; and bad magic, which is heathen sorcery used for evil purposes. For therapeutic purposes Paracelsus used, among other things, seals, amulets, and incantations, which at that time formed part of the equipment of the occult sciences.—The word "magic" derives from Old Persian *magus,* "priest" or "priest-scientist." The three Magi who travelled from the East, in the New Testament, were Chaldean astrologers. For Paracelsus, magic is above all a method for gaining insight into occult heavenly and earthly things; not, however, on the basis of or by means of sorcery but by way of intuitive knowledge, which is obtained by the grace of God and by concentrated contemplation and which reveals the great hidden interrelationships between God, the world, and man. This art was still alive for the "magical man" of that time, but must be rediscovered today if we are to understand it.

MAGNALIA. All medical remedies and works to which Paracelsus attributes a special efficacy owing to the divine power inherent in them he called *magnalia Dei,* and he extends this notion to include the whole of creation, all "marvellous works of God."

MANIFEST. See REVEAL.

MATRIX. Primal womb, primal mother, the still formless receptacle of form.

MATTER. Paracelsus uses this term to designate all kinds of matter within the cosmos, from the coarse and tangible to the refined and intangible.

MEDICINA ADEPTA. Supernatural therapy, occult medicine, that medicine which rests upon the knowledge of the interrelations between heaven and man and deals with those diseases which are caused by a disturbance of this interrelationship, or by "heaven." (A number of mental diseases as well as epidemics belong to this category.)

MEDICINE. Paracelsus uses the same German term—*Arznei* —to designate the science of medicine, therapeutics, and medication.

MELUSINA. A legendary, magic being, whose name Paracelsus also uses to designate an arcanum. He conceives of it as a psychic force whose seat is a watery part of the blood, or as a kind of *anima vegetativa* (vegetative soul).

MERCURY. One of the three basic substances of man. Because of its vivacity and volatility, mercury, or quicksilver, serves often as the alchemistic symbol for the "psychic substance," or "ethereal body," and is usually mentioned in association with sulphur and sal (qq.v.). (See fig. 94 and fig. 121.) This metal is used as (1) *argentum vivum*, quicksilver (chemical sense), and (2) *anima mundi, spiritus vitae,* the soul of matter, the spirit of life (philosophical sense). It is symbolized by the Dragon, the Snake, etc.

MICROCOSM. Man, who as the image and son of the macrocosm contains all of its essential parts in miniature. According to the theories prevalent at Paracelsus' time, there was a correspondence between the parts of the human

257

body and man's psychic properties on the one hand and the various parts of the cosmos on the other. (Cf. THE STARS, CONCORDANCE.) Paracelsus conceives of the microcosm and macrocosm as independent entities.

MYSTERIUM MAGNUM. The Great Mystery. Paracelsus also uses this term to designate the whole of creation.

N

NECROMANCY. The art of conjuring the spirits of the dead and of wresting predictions from them; a kind of medieval spiritism.

P

PHILOSOPHY. Knowledge of all natural processes and their profound essence. It corresponds to the modern term "natural sciences." See also SAPIENTIA.

PHYSIOGNOMICS. The art of discovering the character of a person from his facial features and skull structure.

PLANET. In accordance with the old tradition, Paracelsus numbers among the planets not only Venus, Mars, Mercury, Jupiter, and Saturn but also the sun and the moon. The planets thus total seven, a number which has been regarded from time immemorial as one of the most significant symbols within the cosmos (see fig. 62 and fig. 94). In accordance with his cosmological theories, Paracelsus sees close reciprocal association between planets, metals, and medical remedies and draws far-reaching medical inferences from this association. The planets are also in man, they are his "anatomy." In keeping with his theory of the organic unity of the microcosm and macrocosm, Paracelsus believed that there was an inner, invisible connexion between the cosmic situation of each period (this includes the positions of the planets) and the course of human history—for instance, the outbreak of wars, the emergence of new arts, inventions, etc.

PLANTS. Primarily, all herbs and vegetation. But Paracelsus uses this expression in a broader sense to denote everything that has capacity for growth and development, that is to say, all living beings.

PRAESAGIUM. Forecast, divination, omen. In Paracelsus' own words: "*Praesagium* is a thing by which one shows something that is not this thing" (quoted in Sudhoff-Matthiessen). Such a statement, in contrast to statements based on the correspondences, can be made on the basis of any heterogeneous things.

PREDESTINATION. The course of destiny as predetermined by God or by nature. Paracelsus assumes that everything created has an inherent and hidden term, a kind of "inner clock."

PRIMA MATERIA. The still undifferentiated primal substance; in a cosmogonic sense, chaos; in an alchemistic and symbolic sense, everything that is in or has returned to its original state, as well as the unconscious initial state of the soul before it has attained fulfilment, that is to say, "before the removal of its dross."

PROGNOSTICATION. Interpretation of the future, prognosis, advance knowledge. In Paracelsus' own words: "To prognosticate is to state a thing about the invisible on the basis of the visible" (quoted in Sudhoff-Matthiessen).

Q

QUINTA ESSENTIA. Each of the four elements contains a fifth—which is the quintessence, an ethereal substance of particular subtlety that constitutes the "virtue," or active principle, of each being. The quintessence is the vehicle of the special curative power of herbs, metals, stones, etc.; to extract it was the primary object of pharmaceutical alchemy. In a philosophical sense, the quintessence is a kind of life principle and hence related to the Yliaster (q.v.). In therapeutics Paracelsus was using the quintessences as "specifica."

R

REBIS. The hermaphrodite, or bisexual being; in its unity, that is to say, by combining the two antitheses, the male and the female principle, it represents, in accordance with an old alchemistic idea, the highest and most desirable degree of the process of transmutation—totality.

REVEAL, MANIFEST. Paracelsus uses these verbs and their derivatives primarily to designate the potential ability of all created things to bring to light their prefigured immanent "final form." Everything created is fulfilled by being raised from its potential state to its actual state. (Cf. LIGHT OF NATURE.)

S

SAL. Salt, one of the three basic substances composing matter and man. In a chemical sense, Paracelsus also uses this term to designate everything that is earthly, material, that can never be entirely consumed, but is turned into ashes. Symbolically it also designates the material and physical part of man. Usually occurs in association with mercury (the spirit) and sulphur (the soul) (qq.v.).

SAPIENTIA. Wisdom. In most cases Paracelsus uses this term in the same meaning as *scientia* (science) and philosophy; all three designate both knowledge obtained by experience and the treasure of wisdom that lies hidden in all beings.

SATURN. The planet; the term is also used, however, as a symbol for "lead," or primal matter, the "original" matter from which the "final" matter is obtained. Saturn is the star of the melancholic, of the inhibited and socially hindered, but also of a dark primal wisdom (cf. p. 155 and fig. 109).

SATYRION. An orchis root, once regarded as an aphrodisiac because of its similarity to testicles.

SCIENTIA. See SAPIENTIA.

SEED. A kind of vital sap, a quintessence of all parts of man, in contradistinction to "sperm." In many cases the sperm serves to transmit it. "Seed" also means everything that exists only potentially, not actually.

SENSIBLE (INSENSIBLE). Perceptible (or not perceptible) by the senses.

SEPARATIO. Division, separation. *Separatio elementorum* is a process that separates the pure from the impure, the light from the heavy, alcohol from wine, the refined from the crude, etc. It is an alchemistic operation and denotes the process by which individual things are detached from the chaotic primal mass in which they were potentially contained, or by which they are put back in their primal state. As an alchemistic symbol, the term designates any clarifying differentiation or separation of things that have been improperly mixed, hence also of soul and body after death. Paracelsus calls *separatio* the primal division of the pre-existing chaos into primal force and primal matter, which upon emerging from their original unity became perceptible and tangible material creation; it is God's will that makes operative the *separatio* as a factor in the process of begetting. "Primal force, primal matter, and *separatio*—or the primal law—cannot be encompassed by our human understanding; all three together constitute the *mysterium magnum*" (quoted by Kayser).

SIBYLLINE. Oracular. The sibyls were oracular virgins, priestesses of Apollo, who uttered their prophecies in a state of wild ecstasy. The *Sibylline Books*, a collection of prophecies in verse, were allegedly the work of the Cumaean Sibyl.

SIDEREAL BODY. The same as "astral body." A part of the human body, consisting of fire and air, which receives the impressions of "the stars," and is responsible for the body's vital motions. Called also the "ethereal body," it is contrasted with the elemental body and, according to Paracelsus, forms a kind of psychic body which is, however, as mortal as the other. (Cf. BODY.)

SIDEREAL KNOWLEDGE. The knowledge obtained through the sidereal body, or the *astrum;* above all, knowledge concerning the occult cosmic and natural relationships.

SIEGWURZ. German name of a bulbous herb (*Allium victorialis*), to which virtues of all kinds were ascribed (see p. 123).

SIGNATURE. External characteristics corresponding to inner qualities, which serve as signs, by which everything internal and invisible can be discovered. The idea of the "signature" underlies the Paracelsian doctrine that the similar can be cured by the similar; the higher a creature in the order of creation, the more difficult it is to discover its inwardness, the less unambiguously, thinks Paracelsus, does its inner nature manifest itself in the outward form. Most hidden of all is the essential core in man, whereas in plants, for example, it is often obviously expressed in their form and colour.

SOPHISTS. All pseudo-scientists who lead their public astray by many ingenious words, and especially physicians who deceive their patients.

SOPHISTRY. In line with the foregoing, all idle, fallacious, and scientifically misleading verbiage.

SPERM. Paracelsus distinguishes "sperm" from "seed": the sperm is the tangible material component of the germinating fluid; it does not include the spirit and the essence, the active forces of the seed (q.v.).

SPHERE (LOWER, UPPER). Paracelsus calls the earthly realm the "lower sphere" and the realm of the firmament the "upper sphere." All of man's "animal" qualities and instincts, all his elemental parts, belong to the lower sphere; all his psychic qualities and "higher instincts" are part of his "sidereal body" and belong to the upper sphere.

SPIRIT. The "consciousness," the essence, and the "life" of a thing (cf. also SPIRITUS); the divine spark in man.

SPIRITS. Paracelsus means by this word "psychic forces"; these can be recognizable externally and can manifest themselves as distinct and clearly defined forces or actions, or can be projected into others as human beings. In the language of modern depth psychology, such forces might best be designated by the terms "dissociated parts of the ego" or "psychic partial personalities," which can be encountered in descriptions of certain mental diseases and neuroses.

SPIRITUS. Spirit, aerial spirit. In Paracelsus, the fiery spirit, the spark that God breathed into man, and that constitutes the immortal essence of each creature. In the phrase *spiritus arcanus* or *spiritus arcanorum*, he uses this term to designate the permanent and immanent "radiating" energy of an occult remedy. (Cf. SPIRITUS VITAE.)

SPIRITUS VITAE. The spirit of life, mercury, Yliaster—like *spiritus arcanus* (cf. SPIRITUS), the radiating energy inherent in every living body, which is part of the general "cosmic radiation" (universal energy). It is only indirectly related to the divine spiritual part of man; everything created also possesses the light of nature, which also comes from God or the Holy Ghost.

STARS, THE. The totality of the firmament as well as its influence on the bodily constitution and soul of man (on the "inner stars," which are in interaction with the cosmic constellation). The term is often used in the same sense as "heaven," "heavens," and "firmament." (Cf. SIDEREAL BODY, IMAGINATION, ASTRUM.)

STARS, INNER. See THE STARS, SIDEREAL BODY.

STARS, OUTER. See THE STARS.

SUBSTANCE. Paracelsus uses this term sometimes in a chemical sense, to designate the three main substances which are also the "fundaments" of man, i.e., mercury, sulphur, and salt. (Cf. MERCURY, SULPHUR, SAL.)

SUCCUBUS. The nocturnal demon that haunts males (cf. INCUBUS).

SULPHUR. One of the human components. Chemically, anything that can be consumed by fire; symbolically, related to the soul. Sulphur usually occurs in association with mercury (the spirit) and salt (the body).

SYDERICA. Probably vervain or vulnery herb (*Sideris, Sideritis*) with its starlike flower (see p. 123).

SYPHILIS. *Morbus gallicus,* "French disease," the venereal disease today called syphilis; in the late Middle Ages, also called "plague of lewdness." It was allegedly brought from America by Spanish soldiers toward the end of the fifteenth century, whereupon it spread suddenly and with unprecedented rapidity throughout Europe. Each nation called it by the name of another suspected of having exported it. At one time it was called the Spanish disease, then the Neapolitan disease (because the army of Charles VIII, king of France, was suddenly afflicted with it in the course of the Neapolitan campaign), but most often the French disease. Paracelsus, however, was not the first to use mercury as a remedy against syphilis; mercury was until recently considered the most effective cure. Paracelsus believed that this disease was caused by succubi, "demons which are begotten through fornication in brothels." He took an extraordinary interest in syphilis and its treatment, as evidenced by a number of his writings.

T

THEORICA. In alchemy, philosophical preparation, meditation, and interpretation; in medicine, the analysis and explanation of the disease.

THYMIAN. An herb with a two-lipped calyx, also called common caraway.

TINCTURE. Dye; all fluids that can bring about a transmutation; also fluid occult remedies. (Cf. TINGEING.)

TINGEING. Dyeing; an alchemistic process which stands symbolically for external change, the ennobling of outward form. Alchemistically, used for "changing the colour of, transforming." The red tincture was used to dye the base metals the colour of gold, and also as a panacea.

TRANSMUTATION. Not only an external but also a substantial change in contradistinction to "tingeing." In the medieval view, the elements could gradually be changed into one another, and the various metals transmuted.

TUFF. A kind of volcanic, porous stone; tufaceous limestone.

U

ULTIMA MATERIA. Matter raised to its definitive state; cosmogonically, world matter raised to its final form; in an alchemistic and symbolic sense, the spiritually matured personality.

V

VULCAN. Roman god of fire and subterranean forges. The name is used by Paracelsus to symbolize the transforming power in man (often identical with Archeus); he expresses the transforming power of fire, through which things are freed of dross and matured. This power extends from the primitive transformation of food in man's digestive tract to the subtlest symbolic forms of psychic metamorphosis.

W

WILD CHICORY. An herb with bright blue blossoms.

WOMAN. Paracelsus accepts the medieval dogma according to which woman is the "second creature," her place in the hierarchical order being below that of man, after whom she was created. She exists primarily "for his sake," as the matrix or womb of the human race. This defines and fulfils her important and honourable task on earth. But in this sense woman is also the vehicle of physical matter, of darkness, and according to Paracelsus, she is responsible for the development of all diseases. For before the creation of woman, when Adam was still innocent and walked in the pure spirit of God, there were no diseases; they came into the world only through the original sin, hence through woman. Paracelsus assigns a subordinate role to woman as an earthly creature. But at the same time he considers her completely equal to man as a human being, and her soul has a share in immortality. For in her, too, the "image of God" is engraved, in her too dwells the immortal illumined body, which returns to the Creator after the death of the elemental and the sidereal body. Thus, whereas Paracelsus does not assign to woman a spiritually creative task, he does assign to her an ethical task. (See pp. 24 ff.)

Y

YLIASTER (var.: Yliastrum, Ilyaster, Iliastes, Iliadus). A word probably composed of *hyle* (matter) and *astrum* (the stars), that is to say, of two components of the basic substance of the cosmos, or *prima materia;* Paracelsus uses this term to mean "chaos" or the mystical concept of primal man, or *homo maximus.* Yliaster is also a spiritual vital force.

BIBLIOGRAPHY

I. Editions of Paracelsus *

Der grossen Wundartzney Das Erst Buch, Des ergründten und bewerten, bayder Artzney Doctors Paracelsi . . . Getruckt und vollendet . . . durch Heynrich Stayner. Augsburg: Heynrich Stayner, 1537.

Opus chyrurgicum. Wund- und Artzney-Buch . . . durch Herrn Adam von Bodenstein. Franckfurt a. M.: S. Feyrabend und S. Hüter, 1565.

Pyrophilia vexationumque liber D. Phil. Theophrasti Paracelsi . . . Per Doctorem Adamum a Bodenstein. Basileae: per Petrum Pernam [1568].

Metamorphosis Doctoris Theophrasti von Hohenheim . . . Durch Doctor Adamen von Bodenstein. [Basel, 1572].

Doctoris Aureoli Paracelsi Labyrintus und Irrgang der vermeinten Artzet . . . Durch D. Adam von Bodenstein. Basel: durch Samuel Apiarium, 1574.

Aureoli Theophrasti Paracelsi Eremitae, Philosophi summi Operum Latine redditorum. Basileae: ex officina Petri Pernae [1575].

Onomasticon, eigne auszlegung etlicher seiner Wörter u. preparirungen, zusammengebracht durch Adamen von Bodenstein. Basel: Peter Perna, 1575.

Kleine Wundartzney Theophrasti von Hohenheim . . . Drey Bücher begreiffendt. Basel: bey Peter Perna [1579].

Theophrasti Paracelsi Libri V. De Vita longa, brevi et sana . . . nunc vero opera et studio Gerardi Dornei Commentariis illustrati. Francofurti: Elias Rab, 1583.

Erster [–Zehender] Theil Der Bücher und Schrifften . . . Philippi Theophrasti Bombast von Hohenheim, Paracelsi genannt.

* Sixteenth- and seventeenth-century editions are listed chronologically.

267

Durch Johannem Huserum. Basel: Conrad Waldkirch, 1589–91. 10 vols.

Aureoli Philippi Theophrasti Bombasts von Hohenheim Paracelsi . . . Philosophi und Medici Opera Bücher und Schrifften . . . durch Joannem Huserum. Strassburg: in verlegung Lazari Zetzners [1603].

Aureoli Philippi Theophrasti Bombasts von Hohenheim Paracelsi . . . Philosophi und Medici Opera Bücher und Schrifften. Strassburg: in verlegung Lazari Zetzners, 1616–18.

Chirurgische Bücher und Schrifften . . . Philippi Theophrasti Bombast von Hohenheim, Paracelsi genandt . . . Durch Johannem Huserum. Strassburg: in verlegung Lazari Zetzners, 1618.

Philosophia Mystica, Darinn begriffen Eilff unterschidene Theologico-Philosophische doch teutsche Tractätlein, zum theil auss Theophrasti Paracelsi, zum theil auch M. Valentin Weigelii. Newstadt bey Lucas Jennis [1618].

. . .

Four treatises of Theophrastus von Hohenheim, called Paracelsus. Translated from the original German, with introductory essays by C. Lilian Temkin, George Rosen, Gregory Zilboorg, and Henry E. Sigerist; edited, with a preface, by Henry E. Sigerist. Baltimore: The Johns Hopkins University Press, 1941. (Publications of the Institute of the History of Medicine, The Johns Hopkins University, 2d ser.: Texts and Documents, vol. I.)

Der gefangene Glanz. Aus den Werken des Paracelsus zur 4. Jahrhundertfeier seines Todes. Selected, with an introduction, by Lothar Schreyer. Freiburg: Caritas, 1940; new edn., 1948.

Paracelsus. Die Geheimnisse. Lesebuch aus seinen Schriften. Edited by Will-Erich Peuckert. Leipzig: Dieterich, 1941.

——. *Die Kärntner Schriften. Ausgabe des Landes Kärnten.* Edited by Kurt Goldammer with the collaboration of Johann Daniel Achelis et al. Klagenfurt, 1955.

——. *Leben und Lebensweisheit in Selbstzeugnissen.* Selected, with an introduction, by Karl Bittel. Leipzig: Reclam, [1944]; 2nd edn., 1950.

———. *Sämtliche Werke. Nach der 10 bändigen Huserschen Gesamtausgabe (1589–1591) zum erstenmal in neuzeitliches Deutsch übersetzt . . . von Bernhard Aschner.* Jena: G. Fischer, 1926–32. 4 vols.

———. *Sämtliche Werke. I. Abteilung. Medizinische, naturwissenschaftliche und philosophische Schriften.* Edited by Karl Sudhoff. Vols. VI–IX, Munich: O. W. Barth, 1922–25; I–V, X–XIV, Munich, Berlin: R. Oldenbourg, 1928–33.*

———. ———. *II. Abteilung. Die theologischen und religionsphilosophischen Schriften.* Edited by Karl Sudhoff and Wilhelm Matthiessen. Vol. I. Munich: O. W. Barth, 1923.*

———. ———. ———. ———. Vol. IV: *Auslegung des Psalters Davids. Teil I. Kommentar zu den Psalmen 75 (76) bis 102 (103).* Edited by Kurt Goldammer. Wiesbaden: Franz Steiner, 1955.

———. *Sämtliche Werke in zeitgemässer kurzer Auswahl.* Edited by J. Strebel. St. Gallen: Zollikofer & Co., 1944–49. 8 vols.

———. *Sozialethische und sozialpolitische Schriften. Aus dem theologisch-religionsphilosophischen Werk . . .* selected and edited, with an introduction and notes, by Kurt Goldammer. Tübingen: Mohr, 1952.

Paracelsus: seine Weltschau in Worten des Werkes. Edited by Erwin Jaeckle. Zurich: Atlantis-Verlag, [1942].

Paracelsus. Volumen Medicinae Paramirum. Translated from the original German, with a preface, by Kurt Friedrich Leidecker. Baltimore: The Johns Hopkins Press, 1949. (Institute of the History of Medicine, The Johns Hopkins University, Supplements to the *Bulletin,* no. 11.)

———. *Von der Bergsucht und anderen Bergkrankheiten.* Edited by Franz Koelsch. Berlin: J. Springer, 1925. (Schriften aus den Gesamtgebiet der Gewerbehygiene, new series, no. 12.)

Schriften Theophrasts von Hohenheim, genannt Paracelsus. Edited by Hans Kayser. Leipzig: Insel-Verlag, 1921.

Theophrastus Paracelsus, das Buch Paragranum. Edited by Franz Strunz. Jena: E. Diederichs, 1903.

* See summary in Key to Sources, pp. 235ff., above. Publication of the II. Abt. resumed only in 1955, with Vol. IV, under different editorship.

Volumen Paramirum und Opus Paramirum. Edited by Franz Strunz. Jena: E. Diederichs, 1904.

Von der rechten Heilkunst; ein Paracelsus-Lesebuch. Edited by Ludwig Englert. Stuttgart: Hippokrates-Verlag, 1939.

II. BIOGRAPHICAL AND CRITICAL WORKS

ABERLE, KARL. *Grabdenkmal, Schädel und Abbildungen des Theophrastus Paracelsus.* Salzburg, 1891.

ACHELIS, JOHANN DANIEL. "Über die Syphilisschriften Theophrasts von Hohenheim. I. Die Pathologie der Syphilis. Mit einem Anhang: Zur Frage der Echtheit des dritten Buches der Grossen Wundarznei," *Sitzungsberichte der Heidelberger Akademie der Wissenschaften. Mathematisch-naturwissenschaftliche Klasse,* 1938, 9. Abhandlung.

——. "Die Überwindung der Alchemie in der paracelsischen Medizin," ibid., 1942, 3. Abhandlung.

Acta Paracelsica. [Periodical published by the Paracelsus Society.] Munich: Verlag der Paracelsus-Gesellschaft, 1930–32. Heft i–v (no more published).

ALLENDY, RENÉ-FÉLIX. *Paracelse, le médicin maudit.* 5th edn., Paris: Gallimard, [1937].

ARTELT, WALTER. "Paracelsus im Urteil der Medizinhistorik," *Fortschritte der Medizin* (Berlin), L (Oct. 28, 1932), 929-39.

ATZROTT, ERNST HERRMANN GEORG. "Bombastus Philippus Aureolus Theophrastus von Hohenheim, gen. Paracelsus . . . Ein mittelalterliches Forscher- und Wanderleben," *Hippokrates* (Stuttgart, Leipzig), Jahrg. 7, Heft 14 (May 21, 1936), 388-93.

BAYON, HENRY PETER. "Paracelsus; Personality, Doctrines and His Alleged Influence in the Reform of Medicine," *Proceedings of the Royal Society of Medicine* (London), XXXV (Nov., 1941), 69-76.

BETSCHART, ILDEFONS. *Theophrastus Paracelsus; der Mensch an der Zeitenwende.* 2nd edn., Einsiedeln and Cologne: Benziger & Co., [1942].

BIRCHLER, LINUS, with FRITZ GEORG ADOLF MEDICUS and HANS

FISCHER. *Beiträge zur Charakteristik von Theophrastus Paracelsus.* Basel: B. Schwabe & Co., 1936.

———. "Das Erbgut des Paracelsus," *Gesundheit und Wohlfahrt* (Zurich), Jahrg. 20 (1940), Heft 3/5, 125–30.

BITTEL, KARL. *Paracelsusdokumentation, Referatblätter zum Leben u. Werk d. Theophrastus v. Hohenheim, Blatt A44* "Para und Paracelsus." Stuttgart: Paracelsus-Museum, 1943.

BLASER, ROBERT-HENRI. *Neue Erkenntnisse zur Basler Zeit des Paracelsus.* Einsiedeln, 1953. (*Nova Acta Paracelsica*, Supplementum I, to vol. VI.)

———. "Paracelse et sa conception de la nature," *Travaux d'Humanisme et Renaissance* (Geneva), III (1950).

BROWNING, ROBERT. *Paracelsus.* [Dramatic poem.] London: E. Wilson, 1835.

BRUNN, WALTER A. L. VON. *Paracelsus und seine Schwindsuchtslehre.* Leipzig, 1941. (Praktische Tuberkulose-Bücherei, 26.)

DAMUR, CARL. "Paracelsus." *Neue Schweizer Rundschau* (Zurich), Jahrg. 9 (Oct., 1941), Heft 6, 333–43.

DARMSTAEDTER, ERNST. *Arznei und Alchemie, Paracelsus-Studien.* Leipzig, 1931. (Studien zur Geschichte der Medizin, 20.)

———. "Paracelsus und das Aurum potabile," *Alchemistische Blätter* (Berlin), 1927.

———. "Paracelsus, De natura rerum," *Janus: Archives internationales pour l'histoire de la médecine et la géographie médicale* (Leiden), XXXVII (1933), 1–18, 48–62, 109–15, 323–24.

DIEPGEN, PAUL. "Paracelsus. 1493–1541." *Die grossen Deutschen: Neue deutsche Biographie.* Edited by Willy Andreas and Wilhelm von Scholz. Berlin: Propyläen-Verlag, [1935]. (Vol. I, 520–31.)

———. *Hippokrates oder Paracelsus?* Stuttgart, Leipzig: Hippokrates Verlag, 1937. (Kleine Hippokrates-Bücherei, IX.)

EIS, GERHARD. "Späte Paracelsus-Exzerpte aus unbekannten Handschriften," *Centaurus* (Copenhagen), IV (1955), 148–62.

ENGLERT, LUDWIG. *Paracelsus, Mensch und Arzt.* Berlin: W. Limpert, 1941.

FISCHER, HANS. "Die kosmologische Anthropologie des Paracelsus als Grundlage seiner Medizin," *Verhandlungen der Naturforschenden Gesellschaft in Basel*, LII (1941), 85–136.

FRANCÉ, ANNIE. *Die Tragoedie des Paracelsus*. Stuttgart, Heilbronn: W. Seifert, 1924.

GALDSTON, IAGO. "The Psychiatry of Paracelsus," *Bulletin of the History of Medicine* (Baltimore), XXIV (1950), 205–18.

GEILINGER, MAX. *Das Spiel vom Paracelsus*. [In three acts.] Zurich: Rascher, 1938.

GOLDAMMER, KURT. "Die bischöflichen Lehrer des Paracelsus," *Sudhoffs Archiv für Geschichte der Medizin* (Wiesbaden), XXXVII (1953), 234–45.

——. "Neues zur Lebensgeschichte und Persönlichkeit des Theophrastus Paracelsus. I. War Paracelsus Doktor der Theologie? II. Die Ehelosigkeit des Paracelsus," *Theologische Zeitschrift herausgegeben von der Theolog. Fakultät der Univ. Basel*, III (1947), 191–221.

——. *Paracelsus. Natur und Offenbarung*. Hannover: Oppermann, 1953. (*Heilkunde und Geisteswelt*, edited by Johannes Steudel, vol. V.)

GUNDOLF, FRIEDRICH. *Paracelsus*. Berlin: G. Bondi, 1927.

HAERING, THEODOR. "Cusanus—Paracelsus—Böhme. Ein Beitrag zur geistigen Ahnenforschung unserer Tage," *Zeitschrift für deutsche Kulturphilosophie* (Tübingen), II (1935), 1–25.

HÄMMERLI-SCHINDLER, THEODOR. "Paracelsus zum 400jährigen Todestag," *Praxis; Schweizerische Rundschau für Medizin* (Bern), XXX:39 (Sept. 25, 1941), 640–43.

HARTMANN, FRANZ. *Grundriss der Lehren des Theophrastus Paracelsus*. Leipzig: W. Friedrich, 1898.

HARTMANN, R. JULIUS. *Theophrast von Hohenheim*. Stuttgart and Berlin: Cotta, 1904.

HOOYKAAS, REIJER. "Die chemische Verbindung bei Paracelsus," *Sudhoffs Archiv für Geschichte der Medizin und der Naturwissenschaften* (Leipzig), XXXII (1939), 166–75.

HULT, OLOF T. "Om Paracelsus i äldre och nyare forskning," *Lychnos* (Uppsala), I (1936), 183–207.

JAEGER, FRITZ. *Theophrastus Paracelsus 1493–1541*, Salzburg:

Mora, 1941. (Illustrated book with articles by various contributors.)

JUNG, CARL GUSTAV. *Paracelsica*. Zurich, Leipzig: Rascher, 1942.

KOCHER, PAUL H. "Paracelsan Medicine in England; the First Thirty Years, ca. 1570–1600," *Journal of the History of Medicine and Allied Sciences* (New York), II:4 (autumn, 1947), 451–80.

KOLBENHEYER, ERWIN GUIDO. *Das dritte Reich des Paracelsus*. Munich: Georg Müller, 1925.

——. *Das Gestirn des Paracelsus*. Munich: Georg Müller, 1921.

——. *Die Kindheit des Paracelsus*. Munich: Georg Müller, 1917.

KOYRÉ, ALEXANDRE. "Paracelse," *Revue d'histoire et de philosophie religieuses* (Strasbourg), III:1–2 (1933), 46–75, 145–63.

LEJEUNE, FRITZ. *Theophrastus von Hohenheim. Paracelsus*. Berlin: H. Hillger, 1941.

LESSING, MICHAEL BENEDICT. *Paracelsus, sein Leben und Denken*. Berlin: G. Reimer, 1839.

LINDROTH, STEN. "Hiärne, Block och Paracelsus. En redogörelse för Paracelsusstriden 1708–1709," *Lychnos; Lärdomshistoriska samfundets årsbok* (Uppsala), 1941 [191]–229.

——. *Paracelsismen i Sverige till 1600–talets mitt*. Uppsala: Almqvist & Wiksells, 1943. (Lychnos-bibliotek, 7.)

LOCHER, HANS. *Theophrastus Paracelsus Bombastus von Hohenheim, der Luther der Medicin und unser grösster Schweizerarzt*. Zurich: Meyer & Zeller, 1851.

MARX, HELLMUT. "Die Gestalt des Paracelsus," *Klinische Wochenschrift*, XX:37–38 (Sept., 1941).

MATTHIESSEN, WILHELM. *Die Form des religiösen Verhaltens bei Theophrast von Hohenheim, genannt Paracelsus*. Düsseldorf, 1917. (Doctoral dissertation, University of Bonn.)

——. "Theophrast von Hohenheim, genannt Paracelsus, Zehn theologische Abhandlungen," *Archiv für Reformationsgeschichte* (Leipzig), Jahrg. XIV (1917), no. 53, 1–48; no. 54, [81]–122; Jahrg. XV (1918), no. 57/58, 1–29; no. 59/60, [125]–156.

MEDICUS, FRITZ. "The Scientific Significance of Paracelsus," *Bulle-*

tin of the History of Medicine (Baltimore), IV (1936), 353–66.

MILT, BERNHARD. "Conrad Gesner und Paracelsus," *Schweizerische Medizinische Wochenschrift. 59. Jahrgang des Correspondenz-Blattes für Schweizer Ärzte* (Basel), no. 18 (May 4, 1929), 486–88; no. 19 (May 11, 1929), 506–9.

——. "Paracelsus und Zürich," *Vierteljahresschrift der Naturforschenden Gesellschaft in Zürich*, Jahrg. 86 (1941), 321–54.

MURPHY, K. "Marvellous Paracelsus," *Irish Journal of Medical Science* (Dublin), December, 1941, 635–40.

NENNINGER, J. E. "Zur Entwicklung des Arzneischatzes im Zeitalter des Paracelsus," *Ciba-Zeitschrift* (Basel), special issue, June 18, 1942: *Die Arznei und ihre Zubereitung*, pp. 44–51.

NETZHAMMER, P. RAYMUND. *Theophrastus Paracelsus*. Einsiedeln: Benziger & Co., 1900.

Nova Acta Paracelsica. Jahrbuch der Schweizerischen Paracelsus-Gesellschaft. I–V (1944–48), Basel: Birkhäuser; VI– (1952–), Einsiedeln. Published by the Swiss Paracelsus Society in irregular sequence.

OOSTERHUIS, R. A. B. *Paracelsus en Hahnemann, een renaissance der geneeskunst*. Leiden, 1937. (Doctoral dissertation.)

PACHTER, HENRY M. *Paracelsus; Magic into Science*. New York: Henry Schuman, 1951. (The Life of Science Library, XX.) (German edition: *Paracelsus; Das Urbild des Doktor Faustus*. Zurich: Büchergilde Gutenberg, 1955.)

PEUCKERT, WILL-ERICH. *Pansophie; ein Versuch zur Geschichte der weissen und schwarzen Magie*. Stuttgart: W. Kohlhammer, 1936.

PETERNELL, P. *Der König der Ärzte. Ein Paracelsus-Roman*. Salzburg: Berglandbuch, 1941.

RECLAM, ERNST HEINRICH. *Die Gestalt des Paracelsus in der Dichtung: Studien zu Kolbenheyers Trilogie*. Leipzig: Reclam-Druck, 1938.

ROSEN, GEORGE. "Some Recent European Publications Dealing with Paracelsus," *Journal of the History of Medicine and Allied Sciences* (New York), II:4 (autumn, 1947), 537–48.

SARTORIUS VON WALTERSHAUSEN, BODO, FREIHERR. *Paracelsus am Eingang der deutschen Bildungsgeschichte.* Leipzig: F. Meiner, 1935.

SCHLEGEL, EMIL. *Paracelsus in seiner Bedeutung für unsere Zeit.* Munich: O. Gmelin [1907].

SCHMALTZ, DIETER. *Pflanzliche Arzneimittel bei Theophrastus von Hohenheim, genannt Paracelsus.* Stuttgart: Hippokrates-Verlag, Marquardt u. Cie., 1941.

SCHROETER, JOACHIM. "Chemisches und Mineralogisches bei Paracelsus," *Neue Zürcher Zeitung,* Dec. 7 and 8, 1941.

———. "Die Stellung des Paracelsus in der Mineralogie des 16. Jahrhunderts," *Schweizerische mineralogische und petrographische Mitteilungen* (Zurich), XXI (1941), 313–31.

SCHWARBER, KARL. Die Paracelsus-Ausstellung der Basler Universitätsbibliothek. Notice of this exhibition appeared in: *Der Schweizer Sammler* (Bern), Jahrg. XV, no. 9–10 (Oct. 26, 1941), p. 115.

SHERLOCK, T. P. "The Chemical Work of Paracelsus," *Ambix: The Journal of the Society for the Study of Alchemy and Early Chemistry* (London), III (1948), 33–63.

SIEVERS, GERDA. *Die Naturanschauung des Paracelsus.* Würzburg: Grasser, 1937. (Doctoral dissertation.)

SIGERIST, HENRY ERNEST. "Laudanum in the Works of Paracelsus," *Bulletin of the History of Medicine* (Baltimore), IX:5 (May, 1941), 530–44.

———. "Paracelsus in the Light of Four Hundred Years." In: *The March of Medicine.* New York: Columbia University Press, 1941. (New York Academy of Medicine Lectures to the Laity, VI, pp. [28]–51.)

SILLS-FUCHS, MARTHA. *Paracelsus und wir. Studie über die Persönlichkeit des Theophrastus von Hohenheim.* Planegg: Müller, 1941.

SPANN-RHEINSCH, ERIKA. *Parazelsus und sein Jünger.* [Poem.] Eger: Böhmerland [1921].

SPUNDA, FRANZ. *Paracelsus.* Vienna: K. König [1925].

———. *Das Weltbild des Paracelsus.* Vienna: Wilh. Andermann, 1942.

STICKER, GEORG. "Ein Gespräch des Königs Ferdinand mit Paracelsus," *Nova Acta Leopoldina* (Halle), X:69 (1941), [267]–79.

——. "Paracelsus. Ein Lebensbild," ibid., X:66 (1941), [31]–122.

STILLMAN, JOHN MAXSON. *Theophrastus Bombastus von Hohenheim called Paracelsus; His Personality and Influence as Physician, Chemist and Reformer.* Chicago and London: Open Court Publishing Co., 1920.

STODDART, ANNA M. *The Life of Paracelsus Theophrastus von Hohenheim.* London: J. Murray, 1911.

STREBEL, JOSEF. "Historische Glossen zum Namen 'Hohenheim'," *Praxis; Schweizerische Rundschau für Medizin* (Bern), XL (1951):52, 1075–79.

——. "Paracelsus und die Augenheilkunde," *Klinische Monatsblätter für Augenheilkunde und für augenärztliche Fortbildung* (Stuttgart), CVII (July–Dec., 1941), 528–33.

——. *Theophrastus von Hohenheim, genannt Paracelsus.* Lucerne: E. Haag, 1941.

STRUNZ, FRANZ. "Der echte und legendarische Paracelsus," *Das literarische Echo,* Jahrg. 24 (Mar. 1, 1922), Heft 11, cols. 647–57.

——. "Theophrast von Hohenheim, genannt Paracelsus." In: *Von deutscher Art in Sprache und Dichtung,* vol. III. Stuttgart and Berlin: W. Kohlhammer, 1941. (pp. 97–146.)

——. *Theophrastus Paracelsus; Idee und Problem seiner Weltanschauung.* Salzburg: A. Pustet, 1937.

——. *Theophrastus Paracelsus, sein Leben und seine Persönlichkeit. Ein Beitrag zur Geistesgeschichte der deutschen Renaissance.* Leipzig: E. Diederichs, 1903.

SUDHOFF, KARL. *Paracelsus; ein deutsches Lebensbild aus den Tagen der Renaissance.* Leipzig: Bibliographisches Institut A. G., [1936]. (Meyers kleine Handbücher, 1.)

——. *Versuch einer Kritik der Echtheit der Paracelsischen Schriften.* Berlin: G. Reimer, 1894–99. 2 vols.

TELEPNEF, BASILIO DE. *Paracelsus; a Genius amidst a Troubled World. A short essay on the life and the main works of this great physician, scientist and philosopher.* St. Gallen: Zollikofer & Co., [1945].

TESTI, GINO. *Paracelso e l'interpretazione chimico-fisica della vita.* Rome: Casa editrice Mediterranea, 1942. (Collana di storia della chimica, 3.)

TITLEY, ARTHUR F. "Paracelsus. A résumé of some controversies," *Ambix: The Journal of the Society for the Study of Alchemy and Early Chemistry* (London), I:3 (Mar., 1938), 166–83.

TÜBINGEN. UNIVERSITÄT. PARACELSUSFEIER. *Der deutsche Arzt; Paracelsusfeier der Universität Tübingen.* Tübingen: J. C. B. Mohr, 1941. (Articles by Otto Stickl, Albert Dietrich, Alfons Stiegele, Friedrich Koch, and Robert Wetzel.)

VEIL, WOLFGANG HEINRICH. *Paracelsus. Zum 400. Todestag.* Jena: G. Fischer, 1942.

WALTARI, MIKA TOIMA. *Paracelsus Baselissa (Paracelsus in Basel). Historisches Schauspiel in 5 Akten.* Helsinki, 1943.

WEHRLI, GUSTAV ADOLF. "Paracelsus und die Schweiz," *Praxis; Schweizerische Rundschau für Medizin* (Bern), XV (1926), nos. 19 (May 11) and 21 (May 25).

WEIMANN, KARL-HEINZ. "Die deutsche medizinische Fachsprache des Paracelsus." Doctoral dissertation, Erlangen, 1951. (Typescript.)

ZELLER, EBERHARD. *Paracelsus, der Begründer eines deutschen Arzttums.* Halle, [1936].

Addenda (1969)

I. EDITIONS OF PARACELSUS

Das Bader-Büchl des Paracelsus. Edited by O. Stöber. Linz, 1958. (Schriftenreihe des Österreichischen Moorforschungsinstituts, vol. 9.)

Books of Nymphs, Sylphs, Pigmies, and Salamanders and Kindred Beings. With an introduction by M. P. Hall. Los Angeles: Philosophical Research Society, 1964.

Das Buch der Erkanntnus des Theophrast von Hohenheim gen. Paracelsus. Edited from the manuscript, with an introduction, by Kurt Goldammer. Berlin: Erich Schmidt, 1964. (Texte des späten Mittelalters und der frühen Neuzeit, Heft 18.)

Paracelsus: Die grosse Wundarznei. Selected and introduced by Kurt Adel. Graz: Stiasny, 1962. (Das österreichische Wort, Bücherei, vol. 124.)

The Hermetic and Alchemical Writings of Paracelsus . . . the Great. Edited, with a preface, by Arthur Edward Waite. London: James Elliott, 1894. 2 vols. Reprint, New Hyde Park, N.Y., 1967.

Liber de nymphis, sylphis, pygmaeis et salamandris et de caeteris spiritibus. Edited by Robert Blaser. Bern: Francke, 1960. (Altdeutsche Uebungstexte, 16.)

Oeuvres médicales. Selected, translated, and introduced by Bernard Gorceix. Paris: Presses Univérsitaires de France, 1968.

Vom Glück und Unglück. Liber de mala et bona fortuna. With six colored etchings by Max Hunziker. Zurich: Schöb, 1964.

Werke. . . . Edited and translated (into modern German) by Will-Erich Peuckert. Stuttgart and Basel: Schwabe, 1965–
5 vols. planned.

II. Biographical and Critical Works

DEBUS, ALLEN G. *The English Paracelsians.* London: Oldburne, 1965. (Oldburne History of Science Library.)

JUNG, C. G. "Paracelsus." In: *The Spirit in Man, Art, and Literature.* New York and London, 1966. (The Collected Works of C. G. Jung, translated by R.F.C. Hull, vol. 15.) (An address delivered in June 1929 in the house where Paracelsus was born, at Einsiedeln, and published in *Der Lesezirkel,* Zurich, Sept. 1929.)

———. "Paracelsus the Physician." *Ibid.* (Translated from *Paracelsica*; see above, p. 273.)

———. "Paracelsus as a Spiritual Phenomenon." In: *Alchemical Studies.* Princeton and London, 1967. (The Collected Works of C. G. Jung, translated by R.F.C. Hull, vol. 13.) (Translated from *Paracelsica*; see above, p. 273.)

PAGEL, WALTER. *Das medicinische Weltbild des Paracelsus—seine Zusammenhänge mit Neuplatonismus und Gnosis.* Wiesbaden: Franz Steiner, 1962. (Kosmosophie [series], edited by Kurt Goldammer, vol. I.)

————. *Paracelsus. An Introduction to Philosophical Medicine in the Era of Renaissance.* Basel and New York: S. W. Karger, 1958.

SUDHOFF, KARL. *Bibliographia Paracelsica* [1527-1893]. Graz: Akademische Druck und Verlagsanstalt, 1958.

WEIMANN, KARL-HEINZ. *Paracelsus Bibliographie 1932-1960. Mit einem Verzeichnis neu entdeckter Paracelsus-Handschriften (1900-1960).* Wiesbaden: Franz Steiner, 1963. (Kosmosophie [series], edited by Kurt Goldammer, vol. II.)

WHITESIDE, BEATRICE. *Paracelse: l'homme, le médecin, l'alchimiste.* Paris: La Table Ronde, 1966.

ZEKERT, OTTO. *Paracelsus.* Stuttgart: Kohlhammer, 1968.

INDEX OF PICTURE SOURCES

References are to numbers of illustrations. Artists, printers, authors, and anonymous titles are cited.

281

GENERAL INDEX

°Illustration. †Treated also in the glossary. Otherwise, only the
Paracelsian text is cited.

A

Adam: the creation of, 16°; and
Eve, 23°; driven from Paradise, 102°
adepta philosophia, 4
age, 96, 97; of illnesses, 97; of
medicines, 97; of people, 97;
of the world, 97
†alchemy, 59, 60, 84, 93, 138,
141, 143, 144; alchemical operations, stages of, 146°; al-
chemist(s), 4, 61, 144, and
physicians, 10°; alchemistic
oven, 101°, 112°; *see also*
xxxv f.
†anatomy, 36, 125
angel, 164°; captured by devil,
190°
†*anima,* 198°
†antimony, 214
Apocalypse, 232°
apothecary, 83°
†*aqua fortis,* 214; *regis,* xxxv
†arcanum, 61, 95, 148; †arcana,
6, 84, 86, 90, 96, 148, 232
†art(s) 7, 19, 36; of acting, 138;
alchemy, 138, 141, 144; astronomy, 138, 152, 153; false
art, 131; geomancy, 138;
medicine, 56, 71, 73, 97, 138;
music, 138; philosophy, 138;
physician's, 87; poetry, 138;

the seven liberal arts, 130°;
theology, 138; transformation,
143; work of, 94
†*artes incertae,* 133
†astral body, 18
Astrolabe, 45°
astrologer, 106°; astrology, 154
astronomer, 150°, 151, 155; and
celestial globe, 113°
†astronomy, 36, 59, 60, 84, 131,
138, 150, 154, 155; lesson,
151°
*aurum foliatum, musicum, pota-
bile,* xxxv f.
autopsy, 51°

B

banquet with music, 173°
baptism, 196°; force of, 197
barber(s), 4, 7; shop, 49°;
barber-surgeon at work, 54°
bathers, 89°; bathing, prescriptions for, 90°; bathkeepers,
4, 7
beggar, 177°; poor as a, 178
birth, time of, 150
blood-letting chart, 64°, 79°,
153°
†body(ies): and soul, 212, 213;
as house of soul, 199; flesh of
Adam, 156; aerial, 155; animal, 18; earthly, 195; elemen-

284